Business Knowledge for IT in Hedge Funds

A complete handbook for IT Professionals

Essvale Corporation Limited
The Forward Thinking Company

PROFESSIONAL SERIES

Essvale Corporation Limited
63 Apollo Building
1 Newton Place
London E14 3TS
www.essvale.com

This is the first edition of this publication.

Essvale Corporation Ltd is hereby identified as author
of this work in accordance with Section 77 of the
Copyright, Designs and Patents Act 1988

Requests to the authors should be addressed to:
permissions@essvale.com.

A CIP record for this book is available from the British Library

ISBN (10-digit) 0955412455
ISBN (13-digit) 978-0955412455

This publication is designed to provide accurate and authoritative
information about the subject matter. The author makes no representation,
express or implied, with regard to the accuracy of the information
contained in the publication and cannot accept any responsibility or
liability for any errors or omissions that it may contain.

Cover design by Essvale Design Team
Design and typesetting by Boldface, London EC1
Printed by Lightning Source Ltd, Milton Keynes

Preface

Over the years, IT professionals have accepted the need to regularly update their skills in the face of constant changes in technology and upgrades to software and operating systems. This is to ensure that their IT skills do not become obsolete and that they remain competitive in the job market. However, this has become a perpetual source of frustration and drain on financial resources, especially for IT contractors who have to pay for retraining out of their own pockets.

This aspect of the IT profession has been widely regarded as one of the deterrents to the take-up of IT as a profession. In addition, IT roles are regarded as boring dead-end jobs that are not client-facing and often involve sitting at the computer for hours on end.

IT industry news reporters have constantly been reporting the attitude of prospective university students towards studying technology at university; a cross-section of those interviewed believe there is no point studying IT at this level. Many are said to have realised the futility of studying computer science, with the number of students choosing IT-related degrees almost halving from 27,000 to 14,700 between 2001 and 2005. Mathematics and computer science also have the highest university dropout rate in the UK. This makes grim reading as countries like the UK have witnessed an escalating skills crisis since the IT industry is growing five to eight times faster than other sectors and needs 150,000 new entrants each year.

However, a new paradigm is looming; the lot of the IT professional will improve, provided that they increase their business alignment. According to industry watchers, by 2010 six out ten people affiliated with an IT organisation will assume a business-facing role, which implies that the percentage of IT workers who will be required to be business savvy is undoubtedly heading upwards.

Currently, in companies across many industries, teams of technology professionals are being assembled to advise the business division. They are expected not just to interpret business requirements but actually to come up with model processes and procedures that can enhance business performance.

This book is about the business knowledge that IT professionals need to forge a career in the hedge fund sector; an exciting prospect without question. There has been a lot in the press about the phenomenal rise in the fortunes of hedge fund managers as the sector is getting into the mainstream of the financial services sector. Working alongside the rising stars of the industry, who are highly regarded as some of the best brains in the business, presents an undoubted opportunity for knowledgeable IT professionals.

The relatively small size of hedge fund management companies could also be alluring to IT professionals that choose to work in this industry, as it is a widely held notion amongst hedge managers that small is better: size is the enemy of quality. The guerrilla investor will beat the large bureaucracy, just as David killed Goliath and Sir Francis Drake's nimble warship defeated the Spanish Armada.

As the convergence of IT and business advances further, the perception of IT is set for a major revamp. We predict that with the right mix of IT and business skills, IT could become the profession of choice for future generations.

Acknowledgements

Essvale Corporation Limited would like to thank all authors and publishers of all materials used in compiling this publication. Also thanks to all the respondents to the research carried out to justify writing this publication.

We would like to acknowledge Dr Mark Mobius Executive Chairman of Templeton Investments, Dermot S. L. Butler and David Blair respectively Chair man and Managing Director of Custom House Administration & Corporate Services, Evan Debarra of HumeBrophy, Kevin Sloane of LineData, Sinead Doyle, Nick Yannoulopoulos, Kristine Kennedy of Eze Castle Software, Michael Harriman of PositiveView, James Tolve and Sachin Barot of FlexTrade, Paul Watthey and Shaun Sullivan of Advent Software, Monique Richards of International Financial Risk Institute, Nick Bell of Fundsolve, Avril Adams and Brian Collins of Brady plc, Sebastien Roussotte, Nicolas Ruellet and Benedict Aguttes of Sophis, Daniel Clarke and Leanne Brown of Progress Software, Jake Freivald of iWay Software, Annie Walsh of Orc Software and Stephen Elston, Doug Martin and Michael Palmieri of Finanalytica, Victor L. Zimmermann of Curtis, Mallet-Prevost, Colt & Mosle LLP.

Our thanks also go to Mike Ross of Tabb Group, Yolanda Adams of Aexeo Technology, Luis Zea of Imagine Trading, Roy Freedman of Inductive Solutions Inc., Professor Harry M. Kat of Sir John Cass Business School, Allison Adams of Institutional Investor Inc., William Keunen of Citco, Katie Lam of Digitterre, Sandra Andrews of Egar Technology, J Henry Haggerty of Delta Hedge Systems and Jonathan W. McCloskey of Carnegie Endowment.

We would not wish to forget to acknowledge Karen Maloney of Academy Press, Pat Winfield of Bookworm Editorial Services, Barney Lodge of Lodge Consulting, Mylene Sayo and David O'Leary of CIPS, Dr Moritz Hagenmüller and Sharon Ohrndorf of BOD, Boldface Typesetters, the helpful staff of City Business Library and Idea Store Canary Wharf, the editors and support staff at Nielsen Book Data, Daniel Page and Sara Fisher of Lightning Source, Graham Morris and Vic Daniels of Hereisthecity.com, the staff of Amazon and other bookstores worldwide. Thanks for supporting Bizle Professional Series thus far.

Contents

Introduction

This is another exciting title in the Bizle Professional Series. This book aims to get the IT professional thinking like a hedge fund manager. After reading the book, IT professionals in Hedge Fund IT will notice an improvement in their working relationship with the business side of their firms as the business knowledge gap will have been significantly reduced. For those that are aspiring to work in perhaps the most lucrative industry for IT professionals, confidence will be sky high at interviews and if they gain employment, they will be able to keep up with the fast pace of hedge funds.

This book contains information laid out in the customary 12 chapters that characterise Bizle books. The first chapter provides an overview of the hedge fund industry as a background to the following 11 chapters. The subsequent chapters describe the business environment that hedge funds operate in, investment strategies that fund managers pursue, the recent trends in the hedge fund industry and the categories of hedge fund investors.

The middle chapters deal more with the operational aspects of hedge funds and how technology is shaping these operations. Systems from leading vendors are showcased, and IT projects that form the basis for deployment of these systems, especially the trading systems, are discussed. Also included are discussions on electronic and algorithmic trading in hedge funds.

The latter chapters of the book contain a list of jargon used in the hedge fund industry and a glimpse into the future of IT and business in the hedge fund industry.

In the appendix, readers will find an overview of the hedge fund skills market. This section provides a guideline to the skills that hedge fund recruiters find desirable and the salary packages that could potentially be on offer for each type of IT role described in this section.

At this point, it is worth emphasising the importance of business knowledge for IT in hedge funds.

Why is business knowledge important?
Business knowledge is important because:

- Hedge funds are very choosy about the staff they employ and would ideally want business-focused IT staff.
- Hedge funds are getting into the mainstream of the financial services industry and could become major employers in the sector in the years to come.
- Institutional investors, such as pension funds and endowments, are increasingly pouring money into hedge funds, which could increase the number and size of hedge funds in the market.
- The prime brokerage division of most bulge bracket investment banks would preferably hire IT professionals with knowledge of the hedge fund industry.
- Fund administrators, too, will favour the same approach. Given the number of acquisitions of fund administrators by banks such as HSBC and Citigroup,

it should come as no surprise that they would desire high-calibre candidates as well.

- Naturally the prestige of working alongside the high flyers in the hedge fund firms and being able to communicate freely with them should be alluring.

- Hedge funds are usually based in some of the most prestigious areas in major financial centres in the world. In London, they are mostly based in Mayfair and St James – very attractive locations. In New York , they are based in an area dubbed "Hedgistan" – which includes the swathe of mid-town Manhattan bordered to the east by Park Avenue, to the north by Central Park South, to the west by Avenue of the Americas and to the south by somewhere around 34th Street.

It is advisable for readers to read this book in tandem with other books in series, especially "Business Knowledge for IT in Investment Banking" and "Business Knowledge for IT in Investment Management", given the correlation of these two industry sectors with the hedge fund industry.

Overview of Hedge Funds

This chapter introduces the concepts of hedge funds and fund of hedge funds, the history of hedge funds, the global market and the source of investments.

Introduction

Hedge funds are investment vehicles that take big bets on a wide range of assets and specialise in sophisticated investment techniques. Some of these funds have made huge amounts of money for their investors in recent years. They are meant to perform well in falling as well as rising markets.

Hedge funds are defined by their structure rather than any specific investment method. They are set up as limited partnerships in which the manager acts as the general partner while the investor acts as the limited partner. Strangely, the term "hedge fund" is a misnomer as not all hedge funds are hedged. Hedge funds invest in any number of strategies regardless of the common term that attempts to encompass them. These strategies include investing in asset classes such as stocks, in commodities, and in currency mechanisms that boost return such as derivatives, leverage and arbitrage.

Hedge funds are involved in a wide range of activities that are only limited by the prevailing contractual obligations of the particular fund. As a consequence, they use a wide range of complex and specialist investment strategies. The most commonly used is that of going long or short on a share.

The conventional method that private investors adopt is to go long on a share, in the hope that by buying the share they will make a profit when the price rises. However, in the situation where an investor goes short, they expect the equity to fall in value. Hedge funds take two principal approaches to achieve this. In the first instance, the fund manager "shorts" the stock, where the investor "borrows" a stock to sell it, hoping that it will decrease in value so that they can buy it back at lower price and profit from the difference.

To illustrate this, if an investor borrows 1000 shares of a company called Biz Water at £10 each, they would sell those for £10,000. If the price falls to, say, £8 per share, the investor would buy the shares back for £8,000, return them to the original owner and make a profit of £2,000.

Another approach to exploiting falling share prices is that of dealing in "contracts for difference" (CFD).[1] This provides an opportunity for the investor to make money on share price movements without actually buying the shares.

Hedge funds have a reputation of secrecy given that in most countries they are prohibited from being marketed to non-accredited investors, unlike regulated retail investment funds such as mutual funds and pension funds. As hedge funds are essentially private pools of managed assets, and as their public access is commonly restricted by governments in most countries, they have little or no incentive to release their private information to the public.

A lot of hedge funds are run by former investment bankers and traditional fund managers who set up their own funds. As a result of their risky profiles and the lack of regulations for hedge funds, they only accept investment from

---

1   A CFD on a company's shares specifies the price of the shares when the contract was started. The contract is an agreement to pay out the cash on the difference between the starting share price and the price when the contract is closed

wealthy, sophisticated investors and hence charge them very high fees. The fees are typically a 2% management fee as well as 20% of the profits, making the hedge fund managers a lot of money.

Hedge funds are classed as alternative investments, which are increasingly being viewed as comparatively safe methods of diversification.

Definition of Hedge Funds

Many descriptions have been used to define a hedge fund, despite the difficulty of finding a generic term that can be used loosely to cover a variety of trading strategies. Nevertheless, the following are some explicit definitions of hedge funds:

- A hedge fund is a fund that can take both long and short positions, use arbitrage, buy and sell undervalued securities, trade options or bonds, and invest in almost any opportunity in any market where it foresees impressive gains at reduced risk.
- Hedge funds are private, pooled, investment limited partnerships, which fall outside many of the rules and regulations for mutual funds. Hedge funds can therefore invest in a variety of securities on a leveraged basis. Nowadays, the term hedge fund refers not so much to the hedging technique hedge funds may employ as it does to their status as private investment partnerships. (IFSL)
- A hedge fund is an aggressively managed portfolio of investments that uses advanced investment strategies such as leverage, long, short and derivative positions in both domestic and international markets with the goal of generating high returns (either in an absolute sense or over a specified market benchmark). (Investopedia)
- A hedge fund is a term commonly used to describe any fund that isn't a conventional investment fund – that is, any fund using a strategy or set of strategies other than investing long in bonds, equities (mutual funds) and money markets (money market funds).

Key Characteristics of Hedge Funds

- Hedge funds utilise a variety of financial instruments to reduce risk, enhance returns and minimise the correlation with equity and bond markets. Many hedge funds are flexible in their investment options (can use short selling, leverage, derivatives such as puts, calls, options, futures, etc.).
- Hedge funds vary enormously in terms of investment returns, volatility and risk. Many, but not all, hedge fund strategies tend to hedge against downturns in the markets being traded.
- Many hedge funds have the ability to deliver non-market correlated returns.
- Many hedge funds have as an objective consistency of returns and capital preservation rather than magnitude of returns.

- Most hedge funds are managed by experienced investment professionals who are generally disciplined and diligent.
- Hedge funds represent a distinctive investment style and objective. Their strategies differ greatly from traditional funds.
- Hedge fund management companies are usually small organisations controlled by one or two key investment professionals.
- The money manager–client relationship in hedge funds is a radical departure from the traditional relationship in that the client does not merely hire the manager. Instead the client has input into the investment process like a partner, co-investing in the situations that the manager finds attractive.
- Hedge funds utilise unique "structures" to deliver their strategies to their investors. These structures could take the form of a limited partnership, a commodity pool, an offshore fund, or a specialised kind of separate account.
- Pension funds, endowments, insurance companies, private banks and high net-worth individuals and families invest in hedge funds to minimise overall portfolio volatility and enhance returns.
- Most hedge fund managers are highly specialised and trade only within their area of expertise and competitive advantage.
- Hedge funds benefit by heavily weighting hedge fund managers' remuneration towards performance incentives, thus attracting the best brains in the investment business. In addition, hedge fund managers usually have their own money invested in their fund.
- Hedge funds are exempt from many investment protection and disclosure requirements as the majority of hedge funds are domiciled offshore or subject to limited regulations by onshore regulators.

Hedge Fund Facts

- Hedge funds are not new. Despite the perception that they are a new market innovation, hedge funds have been in existence since the late 1940s.
- Estimated to be a $1 trillion industry and growing at about 20% per year with approximately 8,350 active hedge funds.
- Majority of hedge funds are domiciled offshore.
- Include a variety of investment strategies, some of which use leverage and derivatives while others are more conservative and employ little or no leverage. Many hedge fund strategies seek to reduce market risk specifically by shorting equities or through the use of derivatives.
- Most hedge funds are highly specialised, relying on the specific expertise of the manager or management team.
- Performance of many hedge fund strategies, particularly relative value strategies, is not dependent on the direction of the bond or equity markets – unlike conventional equity or mutual funds (unit trusts), which are generally 100% exposed to market risk.
- Many hedge fund strategies, particularly arbitrage strategies, are limited as to how much capital they can successfully employ before returns diminish.

As a result, many successful hedge fund managers limit the amount of capital they will accept.

▓ Hedge fund managers are generally highly professional, disciplined and diligent.

▓ Their returns over a sustained period of time have outperformed standard equity and bond indexes with less volatility and less risk of loss than equities.

▓ Beyond the average, there are some truly outstanding performers.

▓ Investing in hedge funds tends to be favoured by more sophisticated investors, including many Swiss and other private banks that have lived through, and understand the consequences of, major stock market corrections.

▓ An increasing number of endowments and pension funds allocate assets to hedge funds.

Reasons for Investing in Hedge Funds

There are different reasons for investors deciding to invest in hedge funds. Some of these are:

▓ **To increase the return on the portfolio** – the fact that hedge funds have done well, irrespective of the aggregate for a given industry, is a compelling reason for investors to turn to them. Hedge fund performance is comparetimely better than traditional investments.

▓ **To diversify the returns of assets within a portfolio** – another major read-son investors are drawn to hedge funds is diversification, which involves correlation.[2] Investors clearly appreciate the benefits of diversification as they are aware that stocks don't always move together and a portfolio can be less risky than its constituent stocks.

▓ **To reduce risk** – individual and institutional investors also invest in hedge funds to reduce the risk of their overall portfolio. Despite the role that diversification plays in risk reduction, without the obvious benefits, a lot of hedge funds have lower risk than traditional assets. One of the characteristics of hedge funds that investors are aware of is a measure of risk called volatility.[3] Even without the benefits of diversification, hedge funds can lower the return volatility of a portfolio without lowering the expected return of the portfolio.

2   Statistical measure of how two securities move in relation to each other.
3   A statistical measure of the dispersion of returns for a given security or market index. Volatility can be measured by using either the standard deviation or the variance between returns from that same security or market index.

Benefits and Costs of Hedge Funds

Investors are willing to pay the costs in order to benefit from hedge fund investment. However, they are faced with the archetypal investment issue, i.e. whether the benefits are worth the costs. Conventional wisdom suggests that good performance of the standard investment markets, i.e. stock and bond markets, would lead investors to conclude that the benefits are not worth the costs. However, when these conventional markets are less bullish, investors will gravitate towards hedge funds.

The table below outlines the benefits and costs of hedge fund investment.

How Does a Hedge Fund "Hedge" against Risk?

A number of hedge funds that are called hedge funds don't actually hedge against risk. Since the term is applicable to a wide range of alternative funds, it also includes funds that may use high-risk strategies without hedging against risk of loss. For example, a global macro strategy (see Chapter 3) may speculate on changes in countries' economic policies that impact interest rates, which impact all financial instruments, while using lots of leverage. The returns can be high, but so can the losses, as the leveraged directional investments (which are not hedged) tend to make the largest impact on performance.

Most hedge funds, however, do seek to hedge against risk in one way or another, making consistency and stability of return rather than magnitude their key priority. (In fact, less than 5 per cent of hedge funds are global macro funds.)

A true hedge fund, then, is an investment vehicle whose key priority is to minimise investment risk in an attempt to deliver profits under all circumstances.

	Benefits	Costs
Objective	Absolute return objective	May underperform in up markets
Strategies	Managers have total freedom	There is a high degree of manager-specific risk
Cultural style	Small organisations can respond quickly to changes	Results are highly dependent on one or two key people
Fees	Performance fee creates incentive to emphasise performance over asset growth	Performance fee may create incentive to take risk
Liquidity	Money manager does not have to cope with daily cash flows	Some investors prefer daily access to capital

History of Hedge Funds

The history of hedge funds began in 1949 when Alfred Winslow Jones launched the first hedge fund, A. W. Jones & Co. It was while working for Fortune magazine in the late 1940s that he wrote an article about current investment trends, giving him an insight into the workings of the financial markets and encouraging his attempt at managing money. He raised $100,000 (including $40,000 of his own money) and began minimising the risk in holding long-term stock positions by short-selling other stocks. This groundbreaking investment technique gave rise to what is known today as the classic long/short equities model. At the time, Mr Jones also sought to enhance his returns by utilising leverage.[4]

By 1952, Alfred Jones had decided to change the structure of his investment vehicle by converting it from a general partnership to a limited partnership and adding a 20% incentive fee as compensation from the managing partner. The adoption of a combination of short selling, leverage, joint risk through a partnership with other investors and a performance-related compensation mechanism placed Alfred Jones in the annals of investing as the originator of the hedge fund concept.

A. W. Jones & Co. kept going until the 1970s, compiling an impressive long-term record. Naturally the success of this fund attracted imitators and, according to experts, by 1970 there were about 150 hedge funds with total assets of around $1 billion. Early participants in the hedge fund business included Warren Buffet[5] who started Buffet Partnership Ltd in the mid-1950s and gathered an impressive record that lasted through most of the 1960s. Other early participants included George Soros and Michael Steinhardt. Soros launched a fund in 1969 called Bleinchroeder & Co, while Steinhardt and his partners founded Steinhardt, Fine & Berkowitz in 1967.

The bear market of 1973–4 led to the closure of a lot of hedge funds and a lull in activities in the industry until the mid-1980s when the stellar performance of Julian Robertson's[6] Tiger fund grabbed the headlines. This gave rise to a reawakening of interest and investors flocked in droves to the hedge fund industry which had now become more sophisticated and had an array of exotic strategies such as derivatives and currency trading on offer.

Investors were not alone in being attracted to the industry; high-profile money (fund) managers deserted the mutual fund industry in large numbers in the 1990s to grab a slice of the fortune that was on offer as well as become famous for doing so. Sadly, history repeated itself in the late 1990s and into the

---

4   Use of various financial instruments or borrowed capital, such as margin, to increase the potential return of an investment.

5   A renowned American investor and business person and among Time magazine's 100 Most Influential People in the World.

6   Founder of the investment/hedge fund firm, Tiger Management Group, famous for the best hedge fund record throughout the 1980s and 1990s.

2000s as a number of high-profile hedge funds, Tiger funds, failed spectacularly. Tiger funds' success was extraordinary and lasted a long time, only for the technology bubble to burst in 2000 and put an end to it.

Another high-profile hedge fund collapse was that of Long Term Capital Management (LTCM). In September 1998, after a succession of turbulent events in the financial markets, LTCM's equity tumbled from $2.3 billion to $600 million. The Federal Reserve Bank of New York intervened, organising LTCM's bailout of $3.625 billion by major creditors to avoid a collapse of the financial markets.

Common Myths about Hedge Funds

In recent times, there has been a lot of negative press about the hedge fund industry due in part to the huge sums of money paid to hedge fund managers. Hedge fund managers are notoriously secretive about their operations, a fact which has created the perception of them as being risk-crazy, greedy and untrustworthy. The success of the hedge fund industry has also transformed the social geography of the major hedge fund centres, New York and London. Untold wealth has been created on a scale and in a timeframe that has not been witnessed for 100 years, if ever before.

The boom of the hedge fund industry has been compared by many to the dotcom boom and it is believed that it presents an opportunity to those who missed out on the dotcom boom. Ironically, it appears that the collapse of the dotcom boom gave the industry a boost, ensuring that the pioneers made colossal sums of money that the internet entrepreneurs could only dream of. The boom has also created employment for thousands of people and supports tens of thousands of others in the City of London and Wall Street in New York, not least in the investment banks, for whom the hedge fund industry has become one of the biggest sources of fees.

So why the negative perception? Or the myriad of untruths about this industry? The answer lies in the simple misrepresentation of fact, myopia, oversimplification, or on the premise of anecdotal evidence. Nevertheless the following are popular myths about the Hedge Fund Industry.

Myth 1: Investing in hedge funds is unethical
The root of this myth is the "speculative" nature of some hedge fund strategies. Because their success depends upon the inexact science of exploiting market inefficiencies, all hedge funds have been tarnished and are viewed as risky, some what reckless investments.

There is no truth in this; in fact this is the essence of alternative investments like hedge funds. In the context of a portfolio, risk is dampened by reducing a portfolio's share of volatile assets or introducing assets with low or negative correlation to the core of the portfolio. When risk to single hedge funds is diversified, large losses hardly ever occur, especially when compared with traditional investments that are essentially long on the asset class.

Myth 2: Hedge funds are risky

It is conventional wisdom that most investors do not hold single-stock port-folios. Everybody understands the concept of not putting your eggs in one bas-ket. In view of this, hedge managers are trained to create diversified portfolios with a variety of stocks, bonds and cash. In fact, hedge funds create an attrac-tive opportunity to diversify an investor's portfolio of stocks and bonds.

A diversified hedge is risky but not more so that technology stocks, energy trading or airline stocks.

Myth 3: Hedge funds are speculative

This misunderstanding is based on the assumption that an investor using spec-ulative instruments must routinely be running speculative portfolios. Many hedge funds use speculative financial instruments or techniques to manage conventional portfolios.

Popular belief is that an investor using, for example, leveraged default deriv-atives (a financial instrument combining the three most unfortunate words in finance) must be a speculator. This is a misconception because the speculative instrument is generally used as an offsetting position. The reason for employing such an instrument is to reduce portfolio risk, not to increase it.

Myth 4: The lesson of LTCM is not to invest in hedge funds

When LTCM went bust in 1998, the public called for more regulatory supervi-sion. The more ardent campaigners advocated limiting access to such invest-ment vehicles and some proposed banning them outright.

The truth is that LTCM was not a typical hedge fund. In reality, LTCM's trad-ing strategies were more aligned to those of a capital market intermediary to the extent that LTCM viewed its main competitors as the trading desks at large Wall Street firms rather than traditional hedge funds. For this reason, using LTCM as a basis for generalisations about the hedge fund industry isn't appro-priate.

Myth 5: Hedge funds cause worldwide financial panics

Empirical evidence suggests that suggesting such culpability is injudicious. It would be ill-advised to point the finger of blame at hedge funds for, say, the 1992 European Rate Mechanism crisis, the 1994 Mexican peso crisis, or the 1997 Asian currency crisis caused by the devaluation of the Thai baht.

It is well documented that capital reacts quickly to new information. Wrong-doing on the part of governments to, say inflate their money leads to capital flight. If this is significant, it could spell disaster for a country's economy. However, the alternative to free flows of capital is not good either; it could even be worse. If investors fear they will be unable to retrieve capital, investments will simply never happen in the first place.

A significant event in the history of hedge funds was when the Monetary Authority of Singapore, in January 1999, announced its intention to attract hedge funds. This was based on the premise that the proprietary trading desks of banks trade speculatively in a more damaging fashion than hedge funds. This represented a shock reversal of the customary defamation of hedge funds as the architects of global market catastrophe.

The acknowledgment of the parallel between proprietary trading desks and hedge funds by regulators is viewed by both investors and hedge fund managers in a positive light. This recognition will likely reduce the risk that random and erratic laws will be passed to confine the activities of hedge funds.

Functions in Hedge Funds

As hedge fund management companies are relatively small, their business functions are not clearly defined as in mainstream financial services firms like banks and insurance companies. However, the activities of the different functions are worth mentioning briefly. They are as follows:

- **Sales and Marketing** – this is the business function responsible for meeting with investors to help sell the strength of the fund.
- **Analysis** – this is made up of a team of people who analyse the companies, markets and securities that the fund invests in.
- **Trading** – the trading function executes the investment strategy, buying and selling financial products according to the analysis team's recommendations.
- **Risk Management and Back Office** – this function is responsible for settling trades, working out risk exposure and making sure everything flows smoothly. Many small funds outsource these tasks to prime brokerage divisions of investment banks.

Comparison of Hedge Funds to Mutual Funds

Mutual funds, on the face of it, appear to be similar to hedge funds as they are both pooled investments. In general, the procedure for the calculation of Net Asset Value in hedge funds is similar to that of mutual funds, even though use of leverage in hedge funds has an effect on the calculation. The largest amount of money in both types of fund is invested in publicly listed common stock. The returns are also similar for many types of funds when adjusted for difference in leverage, but investors in general tolerate the nature of hedge funds over mutual funds because they generate higher returns compared to mutual funds.

However, there are five key distinctions:

1   Mutual funds are measured on relative performance – that is, their performance is compared to a relevant index such as the S&P 500 Index or to other mutual funds in their sector. Hedge funds are expected to deliver absolute returns – they attempt to make profits under all circumstances, even when the relative indices are down.
2   Mutual funds are highly regulated, restricting the use of short selling and derivatives. These regulations serve as handcuffs, making it more difficult to

outperform the market or to protect the assets of the fund in a downturn. Hedge funds, on the other hand, are unregulated and therefore unrestricted – they allow for short selling and other strategies designed to accelerate performance or reduce volatility. However, an informal restriction is generally imposed on all hedge fund managers by professional investors who understand the different strategies and typically invest in a particular fund because of the manager's expertise in a particular investment strategy. These investors require and expect the hedge fund to stay within its area of specialisation and competence. Hence, one of the defining characteristics of hedge funds is that they tend to be specialised, operating within a given niche, specialty or industry that requires a particular expertise.

3   Mutual funds generally remunerate management based on a percentage of assets under management. Hedge funds always remunerate managers with performance-related incentive fees as well as a fixed fee. Investing for absolute returns is more demanding than simply seeking relative returns and requires greater skill, knowledge and talent. Not surprisingly, the incentive-based performance fees tend to attract the most talented investment managers to the hedge fund industry.

4   Mutual funds are not able to effectively protect portfolios against declining markets other than by going into cash or by shorting a limited amount of stock index futures. Hedge funds, on the other hand, are often able to protect against declining markets by utilising various hedging strategies. The strategies used, of course, vary tremendously depending on the investment style and type of hedge fund. But as a result of these hedging strategies, certain types of hedge funds are able to generate positive returns even in declining markets.

5   The future performance of mutual funds is dependent on the direction of the equity markets. It can be compared to putting a cork on the surface of the ocean – the cork will go up and down with the waves. The future performance of many hedge fund strategies tends to be highly predictable and not dependent on the direction of the equity markets. It can be compared to a submarine travelling in an almost straight line below the surface, not impacted by the effect of the waves.

Comparison of Hedge Funds to Private Equity Funds

Hedge funds and private equity funds have a number of characteristics in common. Both are organised as limited partnerships or limited liability companies and are lightly regulated, private pools of capital that invest in securities and compensate their managers with a share of the fund's profit. Private equity funds have a fee structure fairly similar to hedge funds, even though much of the performance fee may be postponed until investments are sold. Most hedge funds invest in relatively liquid assets, and allow investors to enter or leave the fund, in most cases on the provision that they give a few months' notice. Private

11

equity fund investors may have little or no ability to withdraw capital from the fund until the manager liquidates, which means that they are "locked in" for the entire term of the fund. Hedge funds often invest in private equity companies' acquisition funds.

The table below provides a snapshot of the differences between the attributes of hedge funds and private equity funds.

Fee Structure

The fee structure of hedge funds is such that the fees are significantly higher and considerably more complicated that those of registered investment companies.

The following are types of fees charged by hedge funds.

Management Fee

Hedge funds, like other investment funds, charge a management fee. This fee is assessed based on the assets under management. The fee is usually at an annual rate between 1% and 2% of the net asset value (NAV) of the fund. However, since investors are allowed to enter and exit the funds at any time of the year, the fees are generally assessed monthly and in some cases more frequently.

Performance Fee

Performance fees provide an avenue for hedge fund managers to share in the positive returns of a fund. This is one of the major characteristics of hedge funds. Performance fees are typically 20% of gross returns and exist as an incentive for the fund manager to perform well.

The rationale behind performance fees is to better align the interest of manager and investor in comparison to flat fees that are paid to the manager even if performance is poor.

	Hedge funds	Private Equity funds
Term	Unlimited	Usually 10–12 years
Type of investment	Fairly liquid	Illiquid
Investor liquidity	Open-ended fund, periodic withdrawals possible	Closed-end funds
Capital contributions	100% contribution at subscription date	Based on capital commitment
Management fee	Based on net asset value	Based on capital commitment
Performance-based compensation	Incentive fee taken annually on realised and unrealised gains	Carried interest on realised investments

Surrender Fee

Hedge funds charge a surrender fee which is a percentage of the redemption amount for investors that wish to leave the fund. In some cases, this fee is paid back into the fund as compensation to the remaining investors for the transaction costs associated with the liquidation of assets for the redemption. This fee, when paid to the management company, acts as a deterrent to other investors who may be considering leaving the fund, and also generates additional revenue for the fund.

Hurdle Fee

Some funds specify a hurdle rate, which is a variant of the performance fee, whereby the fund will not charge a performance fee until its annualised performance exceeds a benchmark rate, such as Treasury bills or fixed percentage, over some period. This links performance fees to the ability of the manager to do better than the investor would have done if they had put the money in a bank account.

It should be noted that this practice has diminished as demand for hedge funds have outstripped supply and hurdle rates are now rare.

High-water Mark

Although performance fees are normally not refunded following a loss, the investors are usually protected so that the hedge fund manager earns no fee for making back a loss. In a typical structure, returns are determined by the Net Asset Value of a unit of participation in a fund. Each time the NAV reaches a new high level, the performance fee is calculated. When the NAV reduces in the event of a loss, no performance fee is calculated until the NAV exceeds the highest NAV used for performance fee assessment. Some funds maintain high-water marks for each individual investor and may trace multiple high-water marks on individuals if they add to their investments after a loss.

Lookback Fee

Although not a classic fee structure, some management companies refund a performance fee if an ensuing loss wipes out a gain not long after the performance fee is paid, when losses are incurred within three months of the high-water mark.

Miscellaneous Fee

The management company charges a variety of fees at their discretion if they are adequately disclosed to the investors. The fund can be charged a ticket charge for purchases and sales handled by the management company. A financing fee is sometimes charged for handling leveraged long and short financing transactions for leverage positions.

Remuneration of Hedge Fund Managers

Hedge fund managers are some of the highest paid professionals in the financial services industry as assets continue to flow into hedge funds. Their earnings are usually made up of 100% of the capital gains on the manager's own equity stake in the fund plus 20% to 50% (depending on policy) of the gains on the other investors' capital.

According to an industry publication, Alpha Magazine, the average pay for the top 25 hedge fund managers rose by 57 % to $570 million in 2006 from 2005. The pay scale findings were based on fund performance, fees and ownership structure and the increase was due mainly to rising global equity markets and adroit investment strategies.

The following is the complete top-ten list of hedge fund earners according to Reuters:

1 James Simon, Renaissance Technologies, $1.7 billion
2 Ken Griffin, Citadel Investment, $1.4 billion
3 Edward Lampert, ESL Investment, $1.3 billion
4 George Soros, Soros Fund Management, $950 million
5 Steve Cohen, SAC Capital, $900 million
6 Bruce Kovner, Caxton Associates, $715 million
7 Paul Tudor Jones, Tudor Investment, $690 million
8 Tim Barakett, Atticus Capital, $675 million
9 David Tepper, Appaloosa Management, $670 million
10 Carl Ichan, Ichan Partners, $600 million

The hefty sums of money earned by hedge fund executives highlight a disparity in pay within the ranks of executives all over the world. In the USA, for example, in 2006 the highest paid CEO of a publicly held company earned in the region of $71m. By comparison, during the same period, the president and CEO of a hedge fund management company earned $1.5 billion which breaks down to almost $29,000 a week or $200 a second.

Global Hedge Fund Industry

Hedge funds have grown rapidly in recent years and while the market is show - ing signs of maturing, institutional portfolio allocations into hedge funds have helped the rise in the number and assets of these funds. The key driver behind this growth was the ability of hedge funds – once the preserve of high net worth individuals – to deliver absolute returns in falling markets. This was a major draw to institutional investors.

The wider availability of "fund of hedge funds" products is as a result of changes to national regulations and EU-wide Undertakings for Collective Investment in Transferable Securities (UCITS III).

It is difficult to determine the exact size of the hedge fund industry as estimates vary due to restrictions imposed on advertising and reporting of performance by hedge funds. However, according to International Financial Services, London:

"Assets under management of the global hedge fund industry totalled around $1,500bn at the end of 2006." This figure represents a 33% increase on corresponding figures for 2005 and nearly 50% for 2003. Hedge funds usually use leverage and, as a result, take positions in financial markets that are larger than their assets under management.

In terms of net assets, a record $126bn of new money flowed into the global hedge fund industry in 2006, which is about a 200% increase on the amount of money raised in 2005. This follows a gradual decline in inflow between 2002 and 2005. In Europe, new hedge fund launches raised a record $38bn in 2006, up a third on 2005.

Figure 1.1 Global Hedge Funds

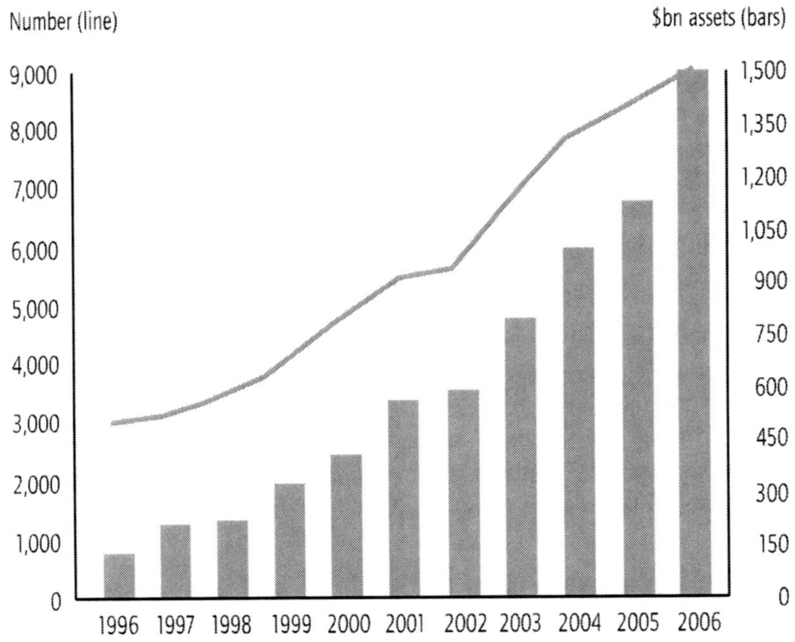

Source: IFSL estimates based on various sources

The following facts give further interesting information about the global hedge fund industry:

- Hedge funds can be registered in onshore and offshore locations; the most popular locations being the Cayman Islands followed by British Virgin Islands and Bermuda.

- In 2006, the USA was the most popular onshore location (with funds mostly registered in Delaware), which accounted for 48% of the number of onshore funds, followed by Ireland with 7%.
- New York is the world's leading location for hedge fund managers and is home to half of the domiciled hedge fund managers. It is estimated that 36% of global hedge funds assets were managed in New York in 2006.
- London is the second largest global centre for hedge fund managers with a 21% share of the global hedge fund industry.
- At the end of 2006, around 80% of European hedge fund investments, totalling $460bn, were managed out of the UK, the vast majority from London.
- There were around 1,400 European-based hedge funds in 2006, of which 66% were located in London. Other locations for hedge funds in Europe include Spain, France and Switzerland.
- Asia, especially China, is gaining importance in the global hedge fund industry. Australia was the main centre for the management of Asia-Pacific hedge funds in 2006.
- Australia-based hedge fund managers accounted for around 25% of the $140bn in Asia-Pacific hedge funds' assets in 2006.

Other important locations for Asian hedge fund management include Japan and Hong Kong.

Source of Investments

In recent years there has been a marked increase in investments from institutional investors into hedge funds. These include pension funds, universities, endowments and charitable organisations. This is in contrast to the 1990s when most hedge fund investments came from high net worth individuals.

Institutional investors accounted for 37% of the stock of single hedge fund manager investments at the end of 2006, a 12% increase when compared to 1997. Also, in 2005 around 2% of global institutional portfolio assets were invested in hedge funds. Although high net worth individuals increased their allocation to hedge funds between 1996 and 2006, their share of the total declined from 61% in 1997 to 40% in 2006 as a result of the rise in institutional capital.

Institutional investors from the USA accounted for 41% of global institutional hedge fund investment in 2005, with European and Japanese investors accounting for 44%. Most institutional investors invest in hedge funds through a fund of hedge funds and more recently through multi-strategy managers. A Greenwich Associates survey shows that, in 2006, 13% of the UK pension funds invested in hedge funds. As a result, 1.1% of UK pension funds' assets are invested in hedge funds, with 24% of pension funds planning to increase their exposure to hedge funds by 2008. UK institutional investors invest less into their alternative investments than some other European countries.

The Biggest Hedge Funds

The hedge funds industry has become increasingly concentrated at the top end in recent times. The largest 100 hedge funds accounted for 65% of total industry assets in 2005, up from 58% in 2004 and 54% in 2003.

The two largest hedge funds in terms of assets under management in the world by the end of 2006 were JPMorgan Asset Management and Goldman Sachs Asset Management. The former managed $34bn worth of assets while the latter managed $32bn. Among European-based hedge funds, Man Investment Limited was the largest with $19bn under management.

The following table shows the value of assets managed by the top ten hedge funds in the world.

Hedge Fund	Asset Management ($bn)
JPMorgan Asset Management	34.0
Goldman Sachs Asset Management	32.5
Bridgewater Associates	30.5
D.E Shaw Group	26.3
Farallon Capital Management	26.2
Renaissance Technologies Corp.	24.0
Och-Ziff Capital Management	21.0
Cerberus Capital Management	19.2
Barclays Global Investors	18.9
Man Investments Limited	18.8

List of Other Notable Hedge Funds

- Amarnath Advisors
- Aragon Global Management
- Auriel Capital Management
- Blue Bay
- BluMonth Capital
- BlueCrest
- Brevan Howard
- Capital Z Investment Partners
- Carlyle Blue Wave
- Caxton Associates
- Cheyne
- Children's Investment Fund
- Citadel Investment Group
- EIM
- Epic Capital Management
- Financial Risk Management
- Marshall Wallace

17

Figure 1.2 Global Hedge Funds by Source of Funds

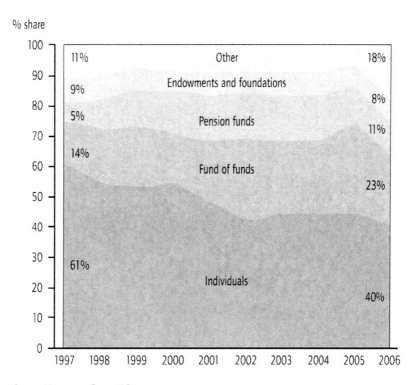

Source: Hennessee Group LLC

- Grosvenor Capital Management
- GLC Partners
- HRJ Capital
- Lansdowne
- Park Place Capital Limited
- Sloane Robinson
- Soros Fund Management

Fund of Hedge Funds

Fund of hedge funds is a rapidly growing segment of the hedge fund industry, and is often the first port of call for institutional investors.

What is a Fund of Hedge Funds?

A fund of hedge funds is a closed-end registered investment company that invests in private hedge funds and other pooled investment vehicles. Its assets consist of shares in hedge funds and private equity funds.

Figure 1.3 Institutional Hedge Fund Assets by Country/Region

% share, 2005

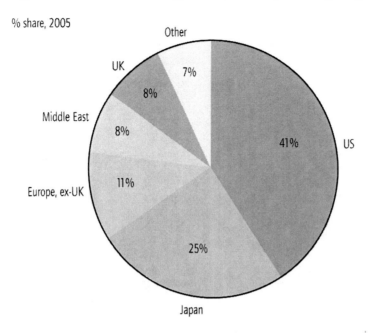

Total: $361bn

Source: The Bank of New York and Casey, Quirk & Associates analysis

Characteristics of Fund of Hedge Funds
- A diversified portfolio of generally uncorrelated hedge funds.
- May be widely diversified, or sector or geographically focused.
- Seeks to deliver more consistent returns than stock portfolios, mutual funds, unit trusts or individual hedge funds.
- Preferred investment of choice for many pension funds, endowments, insurance companies, private banks and high net worth families and individuals.
- Provides access to a broad range of investment styles, strategies and hedge fund managers for one easy-to-administer investment.
- Provides more predictable returns than traditional investment funds.
- Provides effective diversification for investment portfolios.

Benefits of Fund of Hedge Funds
- Provides an investment portfolio with lower levels of risk and can deliver returns uncorrelated with the performance of the stock market.
- Delivers more stable returns under most market conditions due to the fund-of-funds manager's ability and understanding of the various hedge strategies.
- Significantly reduces individual fund and manager risk.

19

Figure 1.4 Diagrammatic Representation of Fund of Hedge Funds

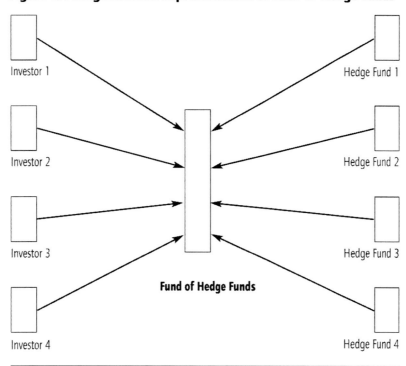

- Eliminates the need for time-consuming due diligence otherwise required for making hedge fund investment decisions.
- Allows for easier administration of widely diversified investments across a large variety of hedge funds.
- Allows access to a broader spectrum of leading hedge funds that might otherwise be unavailable owing to high minimum investment requirements.
- Provides an ideal way to gain access to a wide variety of hedge fund strategies, managed by many of the world's premier investment professionals, for a relatively modest investment.

Comparison of Fund of Hedge Funds to Multi-Strategy Hedge funds
Industry experts have opined on the superior performance that multi-strategy hedge funds deliver in comparison with fund of hedge funds. This can be attributed to the lower aggregate fees paid. In support of this, the following table compares and contrasts the benefits of multi-strategy hedge funds compared to fund of hedge funds.

Global Fund of Hedge Funds Market
The evolution of fund of hedge funds has created a lively industry for thousands of products. Fund of hedge funds is a rapidly growing segment of the investment landscape, accounting for around a third of hedge fund investments.

Benefits of MSHFs	Benefits of FoHF
Single level of fees	Outsourcing of critical diligence and monitoring functions
Returns to scale in certain strategies	Broad investment opportunity set
Absence of "netting risk" on incentive fees	Great diversification for a smaller investment
Dynamic allocation of capital and leverage	Superior liquid characteristics
Ability to attract high-quality talent	Access to closed funds Client service focus Reduced single-business risk

However about half of all institutional investments into hedge funds are via fund of hedge funds.

Assets under management of fund of hedge funds increased in value by 400% between 2001 and 2006 to reach $547bn (Figure1.5). Around 33% of fund of hedge funds are located in the USA, 25% in the UK and 15% in Switzerland. US fund of funds are usually smaller than European ones and manage about 50% of global fund of funds' assets.

According to research carried out by ABN Amro, London overtook Zurich in 2006 as the location of choice for listing fund of hedge funds. London accounted for more than £3bn in listed fund of hedge funds in 2006, more than twice the size of the Zurich market.

Largest Global Fund of Hedge Funds

Fund of Hedge Fund	Assets Under Management ($bn)
UBS Global Asset Management	45.0
Man Investments	35.6
Oaktree Capital Management	35.6
Union Bancaire Privee	20.8
HSBC Private Bank	20.2

Figure 1.5 Global Fund of Hedge Funds

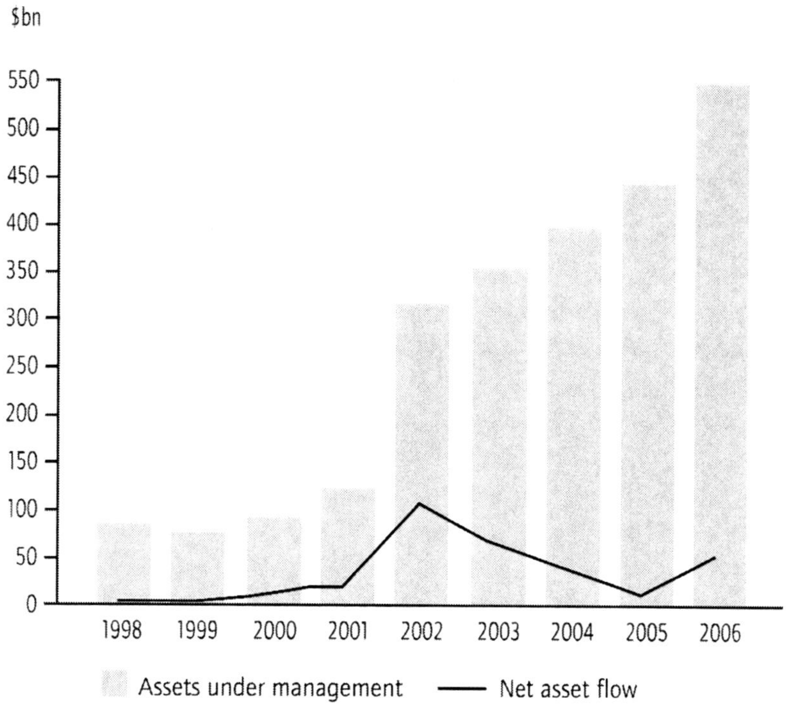

$bn

Source: Hedge Fund Research, IFSL estimates

The Business Environment

This chapter gives an overview of the business environment in which hedge funds operate, which includes a profile of the major players and allied organisations such as regulators, exchanges and service providers.

Introduction

The business environment in which hedge funds operate is characterised by the traditional economic factors, i.e. interest rates, exchange rates; the competitors, service providers and information providers amongst others, that are common to most sectors of the financial services industry. However, what sets the hedge fund industry apart is the nature of the regulation or lack of it in some regions.

Given the uniqueness of the regulatory environment in which hedge funds operate, it will be discussed in more detail than other factors in the following section.

Environmental Factors

Regulation

There are three levels on which domestic regulation takes place: the fund, the fund manager and the distribution of the fund. From a domiciliary standpoint, hedge funds can be classified according to their locations as either offshore or onshore. The regulatory environment for onshore or domestic locations will therefore be discussed as well as that for the offshore locations.

Onshore or domestic hedge funds

These are investment companies registered in an onshore location. Hedge funds registered onshore constitute around 45% of hedge funds worldwide and are mainly domiciled in the UK and Ireland.

Overviews of the US and the European regulatory environment are as follows:

Europe – European Union domiciled hedge funds have increased in number in recent times as a result of growing interest from retail and institutional investors in regulated diversified products. The Markets in Financial Instruments Directive (MiFID) which will replace the Investment Services Directive (ISD) is one of the most important regulatory reforms. It will regulate the authorisation and conduct of securities firms and markets. Changes that MiFID, which has an intended implementation date of 1 November 2007, will probably bring to the European hedge fund industry include: more formality to the organisation of hedge fund managers, more detailed rules on risk management and compliance, and management of conflicts. Conventional fund managers are generally allowed to manage hedge fund products in Europe although domestic regulation varies across the continent, and both hedge fund and conventional fund managers operate under the same regulatory regime.

In the UK, the most popular location in Europe for managers of hedge funds, the regime for hedge funds is similar to that which applies to other invest ment managers and UK managers offer consulting services such as advice on investment strategy, which is regulated by the Financial Services Authority[7] (FSA). Regulations such as the ISD provide an opportunity for hedge fund managers to offer investment services to clients in other countries in the European Economic Area[8] (EEA).

Hedge fund products cannot be marketed to the general public but UK investors can deal directly with offshore funds as the FSA specifies restrictions on sales and marketing of these products.

USA – In the past, hedge fund managers in the USA were not subject to the usual SEC (Securities and Exchange Commission) oversight. However, in February 2006, the SEC introduced a new rule requiring hedge fund advisers to register under the Investment Advisers Act. This rule was overturned by the US Court of Appeals in June 2006. In spite of this, hedge funds embraced the registration directive as it brings advantages, such as credibility to institutional investors. Only 10% of the hedge funds that signed up with SEC withdrew for this reason.

Offshore Hedge Funds

Offshore hedge funds are popular with investors as they are registered in tax-neutral jurisdictions, allowing for minimisation of the tax liabilities of investors. The corporate structure of offshore hedge funds is usually a corporational though they can be structured as limited partnerships. In general, there are no restrictions to the number of investors in these types of funds. Offshore hedge funds are often set up by onshore hedge funds to complement them in a bid to attract extra capital without exceeding the limit on the number of investors. Figure 2.1 shows the location of most offshore hedge funds.

In general, and as with any market participant, hedge funds are subject to company law and takeover panel reporting rules when they acquire stakes in companies.

Exchange Rates

This is the rate between two currencies and specifies how much one currency is worth in terms of the other. A market-based exchange rate will change whenever the values of either of the two component currencies change. A currency will tend to become more valuable whenever demand for it is greater than the available supply. It will become less valuable whenever demand is less than the available supply (this does not mean people no longer want money, it just means they prefer holding their wealth in some other form, possibly another currency).

Increased demand for a currency is due to either an increased transaction demand for money, or an increased speculative demand for money. The transaction demand for money is highly correlated to the country's level of business activity, gross domestic product (GDP) and employment levels.

---

7   More on FSA on page 32.
8   The European Economic Area (EEA) came into being on 1 January 1994 following an agreement between three members of the European Free Trade Association (EFTA), the European Community (EC), and all member states of the European Union (EU). It allows these EFTA countries to participate in the European Single Market without joining the EU.

Figure 2.1 Global hedge funds by domicile

% share, January 2006

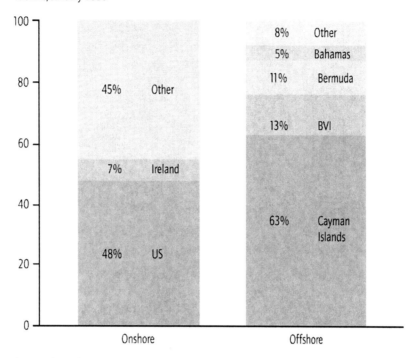

Source: Alternative Asset Center

Impact: The impact of movements in exchange rates for any convertible currency will result in losses or gains for hedge funds given the emergence of currency as an asset class and the proliferation of foreign exchange hedge funds. Also, movements in the values of currencies may also affect the value of an investor's holdings. Furthermore, the value of stocks may be adversely affected by fluctuations in the exchange rate between the investor's reference currency and the base currency of the fund.

To a lesser degree, exchange rate movements will impact on fees paid to offshore asset servicing companies.

Interest Rates

This environmental factor deserves more detailed discussion in the wake of the subprime credit crunch. First of all, it is worth mentioning that there is a strong correlation between interest rates, exchange rates, inflation rates and money supply. Secondly, the background to the credit crunch has to be discussed.

Subprime mortgage defaults in recent times have sent shockwaves around the global financial system and triggered crises that have spiralled in different directions.

What is a subprime mortgage?
This is a type of mortgage that is normally given to borrowers with lower credit ratings. As a result of the borrower's lowered credit rating, a conventional mortgage is not offered because the lender views the borrower as having a larger than average risk of defaulting on the loan. Lending institutions often charge interest on subprime mortgages at a higher rate than for a conventional mortgage in order to be compensated for carrying more risk. (Investopodia.com)

Why would financial institutions lend to people with poor credit histories?
Financial institutions have a tendency to relax lending criteria during a property boom. The longer it goes on, the more lax the rules for lending become, as has happened during past property booms. Property seemed like a sure bet and therefore lenders could charge poor credit risk customers more interest and fees in securing the mortgages. Whereas if the borrower failed to pay the loan then the lender could foreclose and sell the property at a profit and thus there was little perceived risk in the marketplace

What was the source of funds?

Low Interest Rates – The world was, and still is to some extent, awash with cheap money due to historically low interest rates; this enabled lenders to borrow at low interest rates and loan out at much higher interest rates.

Fractional Reserve Banking and the Money Supply – Basically, the governments of the world borrowed from their central banks, especially in the USA. This is, in fact, printing money. The commercial banks were able, through the fractional reserve banking system, to lend out many times more than the amount they had on deposit with the central banks, and thus created money from 10 to 20 times the original amount borrowed by governments. This flowed into many assets including being loaned out to those of a subprime risk.

The Yen Carry Trade – This is an example of the Japanese government printing money to keep their currency artificially low so as to enable Japan to export goods, mainly to the USA, through the use of very low interest rates. This enabled financial institutions to borrow in Yen at low interest rates of say 1% and lend to those of a subprime risk and charge them say 5%, and enabled Japanese investors to invest their capital abroad.

Path to crisis
The current state of the markets is a by-product of the market of six years ago. Back in 2001, fear of global terror attacks after 11 September disturbed an already struggling economy that had just begun to come out of the recession induced by the tech bubble of the late 1990s. In response, during 2001, the US Federal Reserve began subsequent cuts in interest rates until the federal funds rate arrived at 1% in 2003, which in central banking jargon is essentially zero.

27

The goal of a low federal funds rate is to expand the money supply and encourage borrowing, which should spur spending and investing. As a consequence, the economy began to steadily expand and in 2002 the US housing market was roaring ahead. As with any bubble, people saw a unique opportunity to gain access into just about the cheapest source of equity available and got carried away in terms of debt taken on and expectation of future capital appreciation.

In 2005 and 2006, which were effectively the last two years of the property boom, lenders were falling over themselves to lend money to even poorer risk borrowers so as to benefit from the extra return. However the subprime borrowers were saddling themselves with debt that even at low interest rates they would have some difficulty in servicing.

Unluckily for these borrowers, interest rates began to rise not only in the USA but in other global economies such as the UK and the rest of Europe.

Reason behind rise in interest rates

The resultant increase in consumer spending led to excessive growth in the money supply between 2005 and 2007, which in turn led to inflation. At the same time, production in China was on the up and this led to a surge in both production and speculative demand for commodities that were now selling at record high prices given that the stockpiles had been depleted. Another reason for the inflationary prices of commodities was the relatively little investment in mining capacity during the preceding 20-year commodities bear market. Gold prices were also rocketing to a new high.

Furthermore, an end had come to the deflationary effect of cheap Chinese goods due to inflationary pressures within China. This is an ongoing process that will continue for years to come and have an upward push on world inflation compared to the previous deflationary effect.

With the rise in inflation came interest rate rises in the western economies. For example, interest rates in the USA rose from 1% in early 2004 to the current 5.25% in 2007. In the UK interest rates have risen from 3.5% in October 2003 to 5.75% in October 2007. In Europe, interest rates rose from 2% in November 2005 to the current 4% in October 2007.

Loss of homes in the USA

With the onset of the credit crunch, people with poor credit were, in increasing numbers, unable to meet the higher debt repayments due to rising interest rates and were being foreclosed. As foreclosures escalated, the housing bubble burst in the USA. This started in early 2006 and continued to worsen throughout 2006 and into 2007.

Impact on hedge funds: As mentioned in previous chapters, hedge funds deploy leverage to enhance their exposure to markets, giving rise to phenomenal profits when things are moving in the right direction. This encourages hedge fund managers to take bigger bets in the hope of more substantial returns. However, when things go in a different direction to that which was anticipated, the result can be catastrophic. This is what happened with two notable hedge funds, which placed highly leveraged bets on packages of subprime mortgage derivative products. When the value and credit-worthiness of these bond packages, called collateralised debt obligation (CDO), were cut due to subprime defaults, the total value of the funds that had previously been rated as low risk was wiped out. These CDOs, most of them mezzanine[9] CDOs, could previously acquire an 'AAA' credit rating, making them attractive to hedge funds.

The root cause of this problem was that the CDOs should not have been rated as low risk. The mislabelling of the CDOs as good risks in effect resulted in the mix of good risk with bad in one product. Hedge funds therefore enjoyed a higher rate of return on what seemed like a relatively low-risk CDO package that was priced in the market as low-risk debt which they could leverage to the hilt.

The impact of the hedge fund failures has sent a financial shock to the global system, resulting in a re-rating of risk across the board as financial institutions that have previously overloaded themselves with CDO exposures look to offload them to reduce exposure.

Stock market

This is the market for equities and one of the most vital areas of a market economy as it provides companies with access to capital and investors with a slice of ownership in a company and the potential of gains based on the company's future performance.

Impact: Hedge funds are affected by long-term return expectations for stock markets. Movements in the prices of stocks in a hedge fund's portfolio have a direct impact on revenue generated from performance fees. Also, investing in hedge funds offers investors superior absolute returns, superior risk-adjusted returns and low correlation with stock market returns.

Use of technology

Technology is increasingly shaping the hedge fund industry as the industry moves into the mainstream and is more regulated. As hedge fund management companies get bigger, they tend to favour customisation of off-the-shelf packages using in-house technologists as opposed to outsourcing their IT requirements. Furthermore, developments in trade technology such as algorithmic trading and Direct Market Access (DMA) are allowing investment professionals to speed up the trading process.

Technology has also been an enabler for the exponential growth of electronic market data, which is also a boon to hedge fund managers. There are currently over 12 major databases including Altvest, CISDM and Barclay's Global Hedge Source available commercially either coupled with or downloadable into analytical packages.

Impact: Use of technology is becoming a source of sustainable competitive advantage for the larger hedge funds. This has also provided unprecedented access to information on funds in the alternative investment universe. This information is easily manipulated and analysed using analytic platforms, allowing

9   Mezzanine is the degree of credit risk that is medium risk/medium yield.

hedge funds to construct marketing materials with complex styles and peer analysis and helping to attract and keep investor allocations.

Major Players[10]

According to industry estimates, the world's hedge funds together hold about $1.5 trillion in assets. But it is difficult to establish what these secretive, diversified investment firms are up to. Nevertheless, the following is a profile of some of the major players in the hedge fund industry according to Foreign Policy.

JPMorgan Asset Management
Assets: $33 billion *
Based in: New York
What it's into: Pretty much everything. For instance, the fund manages a range of statistical arbitrage products; in other words, it exploits various inconsistencies in the market. It's into real estate, with investments in India and China as well as developed countries. Recently, it has also invested in infrastructure, including a road toll in Texas. JPMAM is continuing to move into the Asian market, where it has just secured a licence to operate in South Korea.
Strategy: Diversify, diversify, and diversify. JPMorgan Asset Management employs multiple managers using multiple strategies, with 680 specialists working within its structure. The fund insists that it maintains a balance between qualitative and quantitative financial tools to assess risks and returns. But its autonomous Highbridge division, the hedge fund in which it bought a controlling stake in 2004, utilises highly quantitative methods and manages nearly half of the $33 billion that the overall hedge fund manages. JPMAM is also enthusiastic about behavioural finance investment strategies that bet against what its statistical models perceive as irrational movements in the market. JPMAM is now also openly focusing on "absolute return investing", which means it's going for market neutrality – meeting targets in spite of what the market's doing. How? By using long-short investing techniques. This involves borrowing and then selling stocks that they believe will decrease in price in the short term, and then buying them back to return them when the price goes down, pocketing the difference. At the same time, the fund uses the extra cash from the short sale to buy other better-performing stocks that they bet will go up in the future.

Goldman Sachs Asset Management
Assets: $32.5 billion *
Based in: New York
What it's into: A lot, but like most hedge funds, the firm is pretty secretive. GSAM invests in equity – buying stocks in businesses in the United States and

---

10 © Foreign Policy. www.foreignpolicy.com(2007). Reproduced with permission. All rights reserved.

around the world, especially when it believes their prices are undervalued. It's also into currency, fixed income, private equity, real estate, and alternative assets like venture capital and infrastructure that have longer time horizons. **Strategy:** GSAM is a multistrategy fund that tends to work on under-researched markets and capitalise on arbitrage opportunities. For better or worse, the fund makes extensive use of quantitative strategies that rely on computer modelling of markets. GSAM's long-short Global Equity Opportunities fund and its Global Alpha fund both lost around 30% of their value this year as a result of their inability to predict the subprime fallout. Goldman Sachs ultimately intervened with $3 billion ($2 billion of it the firm's own money) in what many believed was a bailout. In the same way that the returns of purely quant[11] funds can be remarkable, their losses can also be magnified.

Bridgewater Associates
Assets: $30.2 billion *
Based in: Westport, Connecticut
What it's into: Currency, global fixed income, bonds, emerging markets, commodities and, most recently, equity investments.
Strategy: It's all about alpha – and a bit of beta too. In other words, it's heavily quantitative. In the early 1990s, Bridgewater essentially pioneered the separation of alpha (the gains experienced by stocks independent of general market movements) and beta (the gains in stocks that can be explained by market movements). Bridgewater is focused almost exclusively now on delivering alpha to its clients, which are primarily institutions such as foreign governments, central banks, university endowments, pension funds and charities. Reports suggest that Bridgewater is trying to convert all its clients to using alpha-generating strategies, which theoretically deliver higher returns, but can be elusive to identify. Bridgewater also uses currency overlays, which help pension funds manage the risk of currency fluctuations. To diversify, Bridgewater ensures it spreads its investments across markets and instruments that don't necessarily move together.

D.E. Shaw Group
Assets: $27.3 billion *
Based in: New York
What it's into: Buyouts of existing companies, especially ones on the verge of bankruptcy; financing and developing new companies; venture capital; distressed debt; energy and power; commodities; emerging markets; currencies; and real estate. Of late, it's been dabbling in private equity and direct lending as well. D.E. Shaw also owns two toy companies – FAO Schwarz and eToys – that it bought after they sought Chapter 11 bankruptcy protection.

---

11   A term concerned with risk management and derivatives pricing. Also used to describe those individuals involved in almost any application of mathematics in finance.

Strategy: Hire the whiz kids. For all the fund's secrecy, it is widely known that only one in 500 D.E. Shaw applicants makes the cut, and that it is staffed with numerous former Rhodes, Marshall, and Fulbright scholars as well as winners of prestigious math competitions. D.E. Shaw was one of the pioneers of quantitative investing using complex mathematical and computer techniques to figure out profitable investment strategies. Trading almost 24 hours a day, the fund seeks to profit from arbitrage. Advanced technology is one of D.E. Shaw's main strengths − in fact, it even describes itself as a "global investment and technology development firm". However, as with other quantitative funds, it has also been hit hard by the subprime mortgage fallout. It's now seeking to acquire entire companies on a long-term basis in an effort to diversify.

Farallon Capital Management

Assets: $26.2 billion *
Based in: San Francisco
What it's into: Debt and equity securities, mergers, restructurings and recapitalisations, venture capitalism, real estate and emerging markets, including India.
Strategy: Plenty of arbitrage − for instance, in risk and mergers. Farallon's clients include institutions, especially university endowments, and super-rich individuals. The fund is highly event-driven, always on the lookout for companies undergoing major changes that will result in increased value. Spotting these, Farallon invests, usually hedging on short positions in other financial instruments to help offset potential losses. For instance, Farallon may have recently cashed in on bargains resulting from the housing market's troubles. In March, it partnered with Simon Property Group to acquire another real-estate investment trust, Mills Corp., and also injected a $230 million loan into Accredited Home Lenders Holding Co., helping stave off its subprime pressures. In April, it bought Affordable Residential Communities, a manufactured-home community business.

Regulators

The hedge fund industry is characteristically a lightly regulated industry. How - ever, in recent times there have been calls for more regulation. The following area number of organisations that regulate the industry.

FSA

The main regulator for the hedge fund industry in the UK is the Financial Services Authority (FSA), which is an independent, non-departmental public body and quasi-judicial body that regulates the financial services industry in the

* Figures for these hedge funds are taken from Alpha Magazine's 2007 Hedge Fund 100 rankings, a widely respected source of data for the hedge fund industry. Figures are likely to have changed since the time of the rankings.

United Kingdom. The headquarters of the organisation are in Canary Wharf, London.

The FSA regulates the hedge fund industry in the UK. Hedge fund managers authorised by the FSA manage investment portfolios worth about $300 billion,[12] representing over three quarters of hedge fund assets managed by European-based firms, and around 20% of global hedge fund assets. It plays a pivotal role in ensuring that the UK remains an attractive and well-regulated jurisdiction for hedge fund managers, given the portable resources and technology at the disposal of the hedge fund industry.

SEC

The United States Securities and Exchange Commission (commonly known as the SEC) is a United States government agency having primary responsibility for enforcing the federal securities laws and regulating the securities industry/ stock market. Headquartered in Washington, D.C., the SEC consists of five Commissioners appointed by the President of the United States with the advice and consent of the United States Senate.

In the USA, hedge funds are not required to register with the SEC. According to the SEC website (www.sec.gov): *"Hedge funds typically issue securities in 'private offerings' that are not registered with the SEC under the Securities Act of 1933. In addition, hedge funds are not required to make periodic reports under the Securities Exchange Act of 1934. But hedge funds are subject to the same prohibitions against fraud as are other market participants, and their manager shave the same fiduciary duties as other investment advisers."*

Alternative Investment Management Association

AIMA was founded in 1990 as a not-for-profit trade association dedicated to representing the world's alternative investment community. The association provides a centre of knowledge for professional investment practitioners for addressing the real issues affecting the industry's development.

AIMA's corporate members span 47 countries on five continents, enabling the association to create global tools for the benefit of its members, institutional investors and regulators.

The objectives of the association include increasing investor education, transparency and promoting due diligence and related best practices, and working closely with regulators and interested parties in order to promote the responsible use of alternative investments.

The structure of the Association allows members the opportunity to shape the industry. This includes the council, democratically elected every two years, that governs the strategy; specialist committees, renewed each year, comprising members from around the world; and members in 47 countries on five continents that work together on national issues – such as regulation.

12 Source: EuroHedge, March 2006, and other market data.

Stock Exchanges

London Stock Exchange

The London Stock Exchange is an international stock exchange with 350 companies from over 50 countries admitted to trading on its markets. It is the premier source of equity market liquidity, benchmark prices and market data in the European time zone and is linked by partnerships to international exchanges in Asia and Africa. The business has four core areas: equity markets, trading services, market information and derivatives.

AIM is the London Stock Exchange's international market for smaller growing companies. Since its launch in 1995, over 2,500 companies have joined AIM – raising more than £34bn in the process, both through initial public offerings (IPOs) and further capital raisings.[13]

According to Reuters, the London Stock Exchange plans to launch a new market, the Specialist Fund Market (SFM), in the latter part of 2007 with lighter rules aimed at attracting hedge funds after a number of such funds have listed in rival locations such as Amsterdam.

New York Stock Exchange

NYSE Euronext operates the world's largest and most liquid exchange group and offers the most diverse array of financial products and services. NYSE Euronext, the holding company created by the combination of NYSE Group, Inc. and Euronext N.V., was launched on April 4, 2007. NYSE Euronext pulls together six cash equities exchanges in five countries and six derivatives exchanges. Service offerings of NYSE Euronext include listings, trading in cash equities, equity and interest rate derivatives, bonds and the distribution of market data.

A number of leading European hedge funds are cashing in on investor appetite for alternative investments in the USA by floating on the NYSE.

Central Securities Depositories

Clearstream International SA

Clearstream, headquartered in Luxembourg, is an international settlement and custody organisation offering services covering both domestic and internationally traded bonds and equities.

More than 2,500 customers in 94 countries are connected to Clearstream's global network. The value of assets held on deposit amounted to EUR 6.9 trillion as at 31 December 2002.[14]

13 Source: www.londonstockexchange.com/en-gb/products/companyservices/ourmarkets/aim_new/About+AIM/
14 Source: www.ecsda.com/portal/what_is_ecsda_/members/clearstream_international_sa/

Clearstream has developed innovative services in investment fund processing including Vestima, an STP solution for investment fund processing. It enables fund distributors to process orders rapidly, efficiently and safely.

Clearstream's latest post-trade solution, the Central Facility for Funds, was developed to provide a central settlement system that can plug into any order routing system, including Clearstream's own product Vestima+. The platform basically offers one single set of settlement and payment instructions for all eligible funds, including hedge funds, so that as well as reducing risk, the whole settlement process will be speeded up and simplified.[15]

Euroclear Bank SA

Euroclear Bank SA/NV, a Belgian credit institution headquartered in Brussels, acts as the International Central Securities Depository of the Euroclear group. Euroclear Bank offers a single access point to securities services in more than 25 equity markets and over 30 bond markets worldwide.

Euroclear Bank provides a range of core and value-added services including fund transaction processing through FundSettle,[16] and securities lending and borrowing facilities.

Euroclear Bank's services cover over 210,000 international and global securities from over 30 markets: debt securities, equities and investment funds.

Whilst central securities depositories such as Euroclear and Clearstream can offer funds processing services for hedge funds through their respective platforms, it should be noted that the processing of hedge fund distribution is extremely manual. It entails a lot of risks and errors and the cost of processing hedge fund transactions still remains extremely high. Furthermore, the administrators in charge of the shareholder register or fund accounting are often in the "offshore" locations where technological capacities may be more limited than in traditional locations such as Europe and the USA.

Credit Rating Agencies

Standard & Poor's

Standard & Poor's operates as a financial services company that publishes financial research and analysis on stocks and bonds. It is a division of McGraw-Hill and one of the top three companies in this business, along with Moody's and Fitch Ratings.

Standard & Poor's as a credit rating agency issues credit ratings for the debt of companies. It issues both short-term and long-term credit ratings.

15 Source: www.globalcustody.net/default/efm-european-fund-manager_feature/
16 FundSettle is a fully integrated platform for the straight-through processing of fund transactions.

Long-term credit ratings

S&P rates companies on a scale from AAA to D. Intermediate ratings are offered at each level between AA and CCC (i.e. BBB+, BBB and BBB-). For some companies, S&P may also offer guidance (termed a "credit watch") as to whether they are likely to be upgraded (positive), downgraded (negative) or uncertain (neutral).

Investment grade

Rating	Description
AAA	The best quality companies, reliable and stable
AA	Quality companies, a bit higher risk than AAA
A	Economic situation can affect finance
BBB	Medium-class companies, which are satisfactory at the moment

Non-investment grade (also known as junk bonds)

Rating	Description
BB	More prone to changes in the economy
B	Financial situation varies noticeably
CCC	Currently vulnerable and dependent on favourable economic conditions to meet its commitments
CC	Highly vulnerable, very speculative bonds
C	Highly vulnerable, perhaps in bankruptcy or in arrears but still continuing to pay out on obligations
CI	Past due on interest
R	Under regulatory supervision due to its financial situation
SD	Has selectively defaulted on some obligations
D	Has defaulted on obligations and S&P believes that it will generally default on most or all obligations
NR	Not rated

Short-term issue credit ratings

S&P rates specific issues on a scale from A-1 to D. Within the A-1 category it can be designated with a plus sign (+). This indicates that the issuer's commitment to meet its obligation is extremely strong. Country risk and currency of repayment of the obligor to meet the issue obligation are factored into the credit analysis and reflected in the issue rating.

Rating	Description
A-1	Obligor's capacity to meet its financial commitment on the obligation is strong
A-2	Is susceptible to adverse economic conditions, however the obligor's capacity to meet its financial commitment on the obligation is satisfactory
A-3	Adverse economic conditions are likely to weaken the obligor's capacity to meet its financial commitment on the obligation
B	Has a significant speculative characteristic. The obligor currently has the capacity to meet its financial obligation but faces major ongoing uncertainties that could impact its financial commitment on the obligation
C	Currently vulnerable to non-payment and is dependent upon favourable business, financial and economic conditions for the obligor to meet its financial commitment on the obligation
D	Is in payment default. Obligation not made on due date and grace period may not have expired. The rating is also used upon the filing of a bankruptcy petition.

Moody's

Founded in 1909, Moody's Corporation is the holding company for Moody's Investors Service which performs financial research and analysis on commercial and government entities. The company also ranks the credit-worthiness of borrowers using a standardised ratings scale. The company has a 40% share in the world credit rating market.

Long-term obligation ratings

Moody's long-term obligation ratings are opinions of the relative credit risk of fixed-income obligations with an original maturity of one year or more. They address the possibility that a financial obligation will not be honoured as promised. Such ratings reflect both the likelihood of default and the probability of a financial loss suffered in the event of default.

Investment grade

Rating	Description
Aaa	Obligations rated Aaa are judged to be of the highest quality, with minimal credit risk.
Aa1, Aa2, Aa3	Obligations rated Aa are judged to be of high quality and are subject to very low credit risk.
A1, A2, A3	Obligations rated A are considered upper-medium grade and are subject to low credit risk.
Baa1, Baa2, Baa3	Obligations rated Baa are subject to moderate credit risk. They are considered medium-grade and as such may possess certain speculative characteristics.

Speculative grade

Rating	Description
Ba1, Ba2, Ba3	Obligations rated Ba are judged to have speculative elements and are subject to substantial credit risk
B1, B2, B3	Obligations rated B are considered speculative and are subject to high credit risk.
Caa1, Caa2, Caa3	Obligations rated Caa are judged to be of poor standing and are subject to very high credit risk.
Ca	Obligations rated Ca are highly speculative and are likely in, or very near, default, with some prospect of recovery of principal and interest.
C	Obligations rated C are the lowest rated class of bonds and are typically in default, with little prospect for recovery of principal or interest.

Special

Rating	Description
WR	Withdrawn rating
NR	Not rated
P	Provisional

Short-term taxable ratings

Rating	Description
P-1	Issuers (or supporting institutions) rated Prime-1 have a superior ability to repay short-term debt obligations.
P-2	Issuers (or supporting institutions) rated Prime-2 have a strong ability to repay short-term debt obligations.
P-3	Issuers (or supporting institutions) rated Prime-3 have an acceptable ability to repay short-term obligations.
NP	Issuers (or supporting institutions) rated Not Prime do not fall within any of the Prime rating categories.

Note: Canadian issuers rated P-1 or P-2 have their short-term ratings enhanced by the highest long-term rating of the issuer, its guarantor or support-provider.

Fitch

Fitch Ratings is a global rating agency with headquarters located in both London and New York City. It was founded as the Fitch Publishing Company on 24 December 1913 by John Knowles Fitch in New York City. Fitch Ratings is now a majority-owned subsidiary of Fimalac, S.A., an international business support services group headquartered in Paris, France.

Long-term credit ratings

Fitch's long-term credit ratings are set up along a scale from 'AAA' to 'D', first introduced in 1924 and later adopted by S&P. Moody's also uses a similar scale, but names the categories differently. Like S&P, Fitch also uses intermediate modifiers for each category between AA and CCC (i.e. AA+, AA, AA-, A+, A, A-, BBB+, BBB, BBB- etc.).[17]

Investment grade

Rating	Description
AAA	The best quality companies, reliable and stable
AA	Quality companies, a bit higher risk than AAA
A	Economic situation can affect finance
BBB	Medium-class companies, which are satisfactory at the moment

Non-investment grade (also known as junk bonds)

Rating	Description
BB	More prone to changes in the economy
B	Financial situation varies noticeably
CCC	Currently vulnerable and dependent on favourable economic conditions to meet its commitments
CC	Highly vulnerable, very speculative bonds
C	Highly vulnerable, perhaps in bankruptcy or in arrears but still continuing to pay out on obligations
D	Has defaulted on obligations and Fitch believes that it will generally default on most or all obligations
NR	Not publicly rated

Short-term credit ratings

Rating	Description
F1+	Best quality grade, indicating exceptionally strong capacity of obligor to meet its financial commitment
F1	Best quality grade, indicating strong capacity of obligor to meet its financial commitment
F2	Good quality grade with satisfactory capacity of obligor to meet its financial commitment

17 Source: www.fitchratings.com/corporate/fitchResources.cfm?detail=1

F3	Fair quality grade with adequate capacity of obligor to meet its financial commitment but near-term adverse conditions could impact the obligor's commitments
B	Of speculative nature and obligor has minimal capacity to meet its commitments and is vulnerable to short-term adverse changes in financial and economic conditions
C	Possibility of default is high and the financial commitments of the obligor are dependent upon sustained, favourable business and economic conditions
D	The obligor is in default as it has failed on its financial commitments

Credit rating agencies have had bad publicity for the role they played in the sub-prime credit crunch. Credit rating agencies such as Fitch rated most CDOs with the highest ratings, AAA or Aaa, without giving any indication as to their debt package and hence their level of risk. Defaults on the underlying securities caused the value of the CDOs to drop, resulting in total losses of $125 million by the end of 2006.[18]

Service Providers

Hedge funds use service providers who provide a range of services tailored to their requirements. These service providers include prime brokers and fund administrators.

Prime Brokers

Prime brokers offer a special group of services (prime brokerage) to hedge funds. The services provided under prime brokering are securities lending, leveraged trade executions and cash management, among other things. Hedge funds were what started the prime brokerage option. Hedge funds place large trades and need special attention from brokerages.

Prime brokerage is a major growth area for global investment banks that are the dominant players in this service sector. The following is a list of some of the major players:

- Morgan Stanley
- Goldman Sachs
- Credit Suisse
- Deutsche Bank
- Lehman Brothers
- Bearn Stearns
- Fimat International Banque SA (Société Générale)

18 Source: www.iht.com/bin/print.php?id=5946004 as accessed on 14/10/2007.

Figure 2.2 Structure of a Typical Hedge Fund

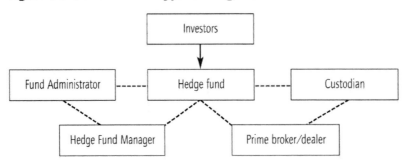

* Dashed lines indicate optional relationships
Sources: AIMA and ASSIRT Hedge Fund Booklet

Fund Administrators

Hedge fund managers usually outsource administrative functions in a variety of ways. Some choose to perform all administration in-house while others go for the option of outsourcing certain functions such as accounting, investor services or risk analysis to third-party administrators.

In general, fund administrators support hedge funds administratively and operationally, providing financial, tax and compliance reporting. This usually includes audits and tax coordination, compliance services such as anti-money laundering and know-your-client procedures, and middle-office services.

Offshore hedge funds usually rely on offshore administrators for various types of services and operational support. They also enlist their support for setting up the offshore funds as well as for providing, say, accounting and reporting services; offering advice on an ongoing basis to ensure compliance with applicable laws; or pricing of a fund's portfolio.

Notable among fund administrators that service hedge funds are:

- JPMorgan Tranaut
- BNY Mellon Asset Servicing
- International Fund Services
- Bank of Bermuda (a subsidiary of HSBC)
- Citi Fund Services (formerly Bisys Group)
- Fortis Prime Funds

Other service providers include:

- **Custodians** – these have custody of hedge fund assets including cash in the fund as well as actual securities.
- **Auditors** – while it is not a requirement for most hedge funds to have their financial statements audited given the way they are set up, some undergo internal audit in fulfilment of their contractual obligations to their investors.

41

News Agencies and Data Providers

Financial Times

The *Financial Times* (FT) is a British international business newspaper. In the UK, it is a daily morning newspaper published in London that has had a strong influence on the financial policies of the British government. It is known as one of the UK's superior daily newspapers. The periodical is printed in 23 cities. The European edition is distributed in Continental Europe, the Middle East, Africa and Asia.

Founded in 1888 by James Sheridan and his brother, the *Financial Times* competed for many years with four other finance-oriented newspapers, finally in 1945 absorbing the last of these, the *Financial News* (founded in 1884). The FT has specialised in reporting business and financial news while maintaining an independent editorial outlook. In 1995, the Financial Times group launched FT.com, now one of the few UK news sites successfully operating a subscription model for content.

The *Financial Times* has a sizable network of international reporters – about 110 of its 475 journalists are based outside the UK. The FT is usually in two sections; the first section covers national and international news, while the second section covers company and markets news.

FTfm, a weekly review of the fund management industry, is a supplement to the *Financial Times* that reports on the hedge fund industry.

Hedge Funds Review

In September 2000, Hedge Funds Review was launched to meet the growing demand for quality hedge fund information. As an information source, Hedge Funds Review provides hedge fund managers, investors and service providers with news and analysis on the trends and developments that will affect their day-to-day business and investment decisions.

Hedge Funds Review provides the following to the alternative investment industry:

- The industry's news and comment;
- Strategies dissected and re-assembled;
- Interviews with the new talent and most revered luminaries;
- Trading tips from top brokers;
- Incisive features framed in a global economic perspective;
- Practical advice from experts in their fields;
- Hedge fund investment mandates;
- Fund closure lists;
- Performance data from Eurekahedge;
- Special reports and supplements covering strategies, hedge fund centres and industry issues.

Institutional Investor

Institutional Investor is an international business-to-business publisher, focused primarily on international finance. It publishes magazines, newsletters and journals as well as research, directories, books and maps. It also runs conferences, seminars and training courses and is a provider of electronic business information through its capital market databases and emerging markets information service.

Institutional Investor runs a portal (Institutionalinvestor.com) for Institutional Investor products, conferences and events. The site provides free samples of both free and subscription products, as well as a complete calendar of their conferences, awards and events.

Institutionalinvestor.com has focused news channels covering the hedge fund industry.

HedgeFund Intelligence

HedgeFund Intelligence (www.hedgefundintelligence.com) is one of the biggest providers of hedge fund news and data in the world, with the largest and most knowledgeable editorial and research teams of any hedge fund information and news provider. They supply information on more than 7,500 funds and comprehensive news and insight from across the globe.

Since 1998 it has built up a loyal readership to its newsletters and hedge fund data products.

HedgeFund Intelligence services targetted at the hedge fund industry include:

■ **News and Analysis** – their publications AsiaHedge, EuroHedge, Absolute Return and South AfricaHedge give global coverage of the single manager hedge fund industry. AsiaHedge, EuroHedge and South AfricaHedge look closely at Asian, European and South African fund performance and report on fund news in their respective regions.
■ **Data** – data provided by the newsletters is backed up with a comprehensive hedge fund database with research, quantative and qualitative information in the same place. News and data together facilitate searches for individual funds and managers – track their performance history and relevant news reports from their archives. Independent analysis of performance and strategy is also offered.

Hedge Fund Association

The Hedge Fund Association is an international not-for-profit association of hedge fund managers, service providers, and investors formed to unite the hedge fund industry and add to the increasing awareness of the advantages and opportunities in hedge funds.

As hedge funds still suffer from misconceptions about high risk and volatility (fuelled largely by the media focus on sharp moves made by global macro hedge funds), the HFA aims to educate the investing public and legislators around the world on the true benefits as well as potential risks associated with investing in the different hedge fund strategies.

The Hedge Fund Association provides members with information on events in the hedge fund industry such as conferences and summits, and the latest news on issues affecting hedge funds.

43

MorningStar

Morningstar, Inc. is a leading provider of independent investment research in the United States and in major international markets. Morningstar is a trusted source for insightful information on the hedge fund industry.

MorningStar's products include data and proprietary analytical tools such as Morningstar Rating™, which brings both performance and risk together into one evaluation, and Morningstar Style Box™, which provides a visual summary of a fund's underlying investment style.

The company was founded in 1984 to provide individual investors with mutual fund analysis and commentary. Morningstar now serves more than 5.2 million individual investors, 210,000 financial advisers, and 1,700 institutional clients around the world.

Lipper HedgeWorld

HedgeWorld, is an information portal for the global hedge fund community that offers its members access to content in print and electronic formats, including industry news, research and events. HedgeWorld's community spans the globe, with more than 55,000 registered members in 125 countries.

HedgeWorld's TASS Database is intended for clients who are interested in researching hedge funds for allocation purposes, investment decisions or general due diligence on hedge funds. It includes over 350 fields of data on approximately 3,900 hedge funds managed by more than 1,300 fund managers.

The database is available in the following modules:

- Funds Only
- Commodity Trading Advisor (CTA) Module Only
- Funds & CTA Module
- Funds Graveyard Only
- CTA Graveyard Only
- Graveyard Combined (Funds + CTA)

In total, the database houses information on over 7,000 hedge funds. Lipper HedgeWorld is the exclusive internet distributor of TASS via TASS online.

EDHEC Risk

EDHEC Business School in France set up the Risk and Asset Management Research Centre to conduct academic research and highlight its applications to the industry. The centre's team of researchers carries out industry-sponsored programmes focusing on asset allocation and risk management in the alternative investment universe.

The Risk and Asset Management Research Centre maintains a website devoted to asset management research for the industry, circulates a monthly newsletter to over 75,000 practitioners, and conducts regular industry surveys and consultations in order to optimise exchanges between the academic and business worlds and for the benefit of institutional investors and asset managers.

Eurekahedge

Eurekahedge is one of the largest independent hedge fund research companies. Dedicated to the collation, development and continuous improvement of alternative investment data, the company publishes their research in hard-copy directories and disseminates it through a variety of data products.

The company maintains files on over 15,000 alternative funds globally in collaboration with fund managers, and the managers enjoy complimentary permissioning for the data products to which they contribute.

Eurekahedge maintains a data bank from which it generates and builds its suite of products for the hedge fund industry. These include:

- Global Hedge Fund Directory and Database
- North American Hedge Fund Directory and Database
- European Hedge Fund Directory and Database
- Asia and Japan Hedge Fund Directory and Database
- Latin American Hedge Fund Directory and Database
- Global Fund of Funds Directory and Database
- Global Emerging Markets Database

Hedge Fund Research

Hedge Fund Research specialises in the aggregation, distribution and analysis of alternative investment information. The company produces HFR Database, a widely used commercial database of hedge fund performance as well as HFR Industry Reports, a quarterly offering of hedge fund industry statistics and graphs. HFR also produces and distributes the HFRX Indices and HFRI Monthly Indices – industry standard benchmarks of hedge fund performance. In addition, Hedge Fund Research, Inc. offers HFR FOF Directory that contains analytical reports providing investors quantitative data and analysis on fund of funds from its database.

Hedge Fund Indices

The list of hedge fund indices never seems to stop growing. This is in contrast to the earliest days of the hedge fund industry, when there was only a limited number of hedge fund products and strategies, and those that were on offer were usually only on offer to a few high-net-worth individuals. However, as the hedge fund landscape and the range and diversity of its participants have expanded, investors have found it increasingly difficult to choose from the growing number of managers and strategies available to them.

The increase in the number of hedge fund indices is partly due to a desire by investors and industry participants to have a benchmark, or an indication of peer group performance or the achievements of an individual hedge fund manager. Nevertheless, the following are some of the most widely used indices in the hedge fund industry.

FTSE Hedge Indices – FTSE indices are used extensively by investors worldwide for investment analysis, performance measurement, asset allocation and portfolio hedging. They are created and managed by FTSE, an independent company owned by the *Financial Times* and the London Stock Exchange.

FTSE Hedge Indices are investable indices that allow investors to gain exposure to the investable opportunity for hedge funds at a low cost.

Another index, FTSE Hedge Momentum Index, is an investment strategy index designed to outperform the underlying FTSE Hedge Index by over or underweighting constituent funds according to whether or not they demonstrate persistent positive returns.

MSCI Hedge Fund Indices – these indices are created by MSCI[19] Inc. The MSCI Hedge Fund Indices are a family of hedge fund indices based on a comprehensive classification system and growing fund database. These indices, launched in 2002, feature more than 190 indices calculated monthly. The MSCI Hedge Fund Indices & Database were developed after consultation with hedge fund managers, fund-of-hedge-fund portfolio managers, and institutional investors globally.

Hennessee Hedge Fund Indices – these indices are used as a peer group assess ment tool for hedge fund managers to benchmark their performance against other managers with the same money management style. Over 1,000 hedge funds report their performance numbers to Hennessee Group LLC, the creators of the indices.

CSFB/Tremont[20] Indices – the Credit Suisse/Tremont Hedge Fund Indices are asset-weighted benchmarks of hedge fund performance. They are derived from the Credit Suisse/Tremont database. The analytical models used to calibrate the indices provide a set of accurate and sophisticated tools for asset class bench marking, peer group analysis, and industry-wide research. The Credit Suisse/Tremont Hedge Fund Indices are the hedge fund industry's first asset - weighted hedge fund indices.

HFRI Monthly Indices – the HFRI Monthly Performance Indices are equally weighted hedge fund performance indices broken down into 37 different categories by strategy, including the HFRI Fund Weighted Composite Index, a bench mark comprising over 2,000 funds from the internal HFRI Database.

Index Values
The following table typifies hedge Index Net Asset Values (NAVs) for instance on a daily basis.

---

19 MSCI acquired Barra in 2004 to form MSCI Barra.
20 Credit Suisse Tremont Index LLC is a joint venture between Credit Suisse, a global investment banking company and Tremont Capital Management, Inc., a full-service hedge fund of funds investment management firm.

The value for a fictional set of indices, BizHedge, can be represented on08/10/2007 thus:

Index Name	Number of Fund Constituents	Index Value	Daily Performance
BizHedge Index USD Daily Indicative NAV	45	5619.76	−0.113368
BizHedge Index Sterling Daily Indicative NAV	45	5824.08	−0.111055
BizHedge Index Euro Daily Indicative NAV	45	5404.32	−0.118043
BizHedge Directional Index Daily Indicative NAV	25	3390.35	-0.201117
BizHedge Global Macro Index Daily Indicative NAV	6	1850.70	-0.473687
BizHedge Equity Arbitrage Index Daily Indicative NAV	4	2203.71	-0.023616

Security Identifier Types

Security identifier[21] types are the various methods by which a security product or issue is identified. They are each managed and distributed by different organisations. Each country has a National Numbering Agency (NNA) which is the organisation responsible for the assignment of security identifiers to corporate security issues within its national jurisdiction. In some emerging markets, where no recognised NNA exists, a substitute agency has authority to issue numbers. Usually, central securities deposits, stock exchanges or financial publishing companies will be responsible for the maintenance of security codes. The following table illustrates the countries with their most commonly used national numbering scheme.

---

21 The security identifiers discussed above should not be confused with a Security Identifier (commonly abbreviated SID), which is a unique name (an alphanumeric character string) that is assigned by a Windows Domain controller during the log-on process and used to identify an object, such as a user or a group of users in a network of NT/2000 systems.

Country	Identifier	Character Type	Number of characters
UK	SEDOL	Numeric	7
USA	CUSIP	Alphanumeric	9
Japan	Quick Code	Numeric	5
Germany	WKN	Numeric	6
France	Euroclear France	Numeric	6
Switzerland	Valor	Numeric	9

CUSIP

The acronym CUSIP stands for Committee on Uniform Securities Identification Procedures and the 9-character alphanumeric security identifiers that they distribute for all North American securities for the purposes of facilitating clearing and settlement of trades. The CUSIP distribution system is owned by the American Bankers Association and is operated by Standard & Poor's. The CUSIP Services Bureau acts as the NNA for North America, and the CUSIP serves as the National Securities Identification Number for products issued from both the United States and Canada.

The CUSIP number acts as a sort of DNA for the security – uniquely identifying the company or issuer and the type of security. The first six characters are known as the "base" (or "CUSIP-6"), and uniquely identify the issuer. Issuer codes are assigned alphabetically from a series that includes deliberate built-in "gaps" for future expansion. The last two characters of the issuer code can be letters, in order to provide more room for expansion. The numbers from 990000 up are reserved, as are xxx990 and up within each group of 1000 (i.e. 100990 to 1009ZZ).

An example of a CUSIP number is 594918104, which is allocated to Microsoft.

ISIN

ISO 6166, the ISO standard that the International Organisation for Standardisation required to bring uniform structure to international securities identification while preserving the sovereignty of local numbering agencies to manage assets within their markets, created the rules for the International Securities Number (ISIN). The ISIN is the all-encompassing standard that combines the code assigned by a local National Numbering Agency with the ISO country code of the security issuer's domicile. A check digit is added to the standard to ensure data integrity.

An example of an ISIN number is US4592001014 derived thus:

/Country code of issuer: **US**/ + /CUSIP: **459200101**/+/
check digit calculated from algorithm: **4**/

SEDOL

SEDOL, which stands for Stock Exchange Daily Official List, is an identification code, consisting of seven alphanumeric characters, that is assigned to all securities trading on the London Stock Exchange and on other smaller exchanges in the UK. The numbers are assigned by the London Stock Exchange, on request by the security issuer. SEDOLs serve as the National Securities Identifying Number (NSIN) for all securities issued in the United Kingdom and are therefore part of the security's ISIN as well.

ISINs were to be used to replace SEDOL. However, since a single ISIN is used to identify the shares of a company regardless of the exchange it is being traded on, it was impossible to specify a trade on a particular exchange or currency. This was identified as a problem and this, amongst other issues, forced a reversal of this decision. A solution to this problem is being sought by way of expansion of the ISIN standard.

SEDOL is also used to identify foreign stocks, especially those that aren't actively traded in the USA and don't have a CUSIP number.

RIC

RIC stands for Reuters Instrument Code, a ticker-like code used by Reuters to identify financial instruments and indices. The RIC is made up primarily of the security's ticker symbol, optionally followed by a period and exchange code based on the name of the stock exchange which uses that ticker. For instance, DGE.N is a valid RIC, referring to DIAGEO being traded on the New York Stock Exchange. DGE.L refers to the same stock trading on the London Stock Exchange.

ISIN vs SEDOL and RIC

Issue	Siemens ORDs			
ISIN	DE0007236101			
Register	DE			FRI
Market	Frankfurt	Zurich	Tradepoint	Paris
RIC	SIEGn.F	SIEGn.S	SIEGn.TP	SIEG.P
SEDOL	5727973	5735233	5727973	571615
CCY	EUR	CHF	EUR	EUR

Source: Financial Information Service Division of the Software and Information Industry Association

Brief History of ANNA

The Association of National Numbering Agencies (ANNA) was created in 1992 with the task of promoting the adoption of the ISIN standard. ANNA's 61 members include numbering agencies from more than 60 countries. In November 2002, ANNA signed an agreement with two of its members – Standard & Poor's and Telekurs – to develop and manage a new entity called the ANNA Service Bureau (ASB). The purpose of the ASB is to provide a means for national numbering agencies to accomplish timely, accurate and equitable distribution of ISIN data. National agencies are to assign codes to new issues, add basic descriptive information and submit new records to the ASB.

Types of Hedge Fund Strategy

This chapter describes the strategies used by hedge funds and some of the ratios and models.

Introduction

Hedge funds differ in the amount of investment risk they are willing to undertake in order to generate attractive returns for their investors. The fundamental risk factors – stock returns, interest rates, credit spreads and volatility – impact on the choice of strategies that hedge fund managers adopt. Hedge funds are usually categorised into broad styles to provide an understanding of the risks inherent with a particular fund so they can focus on funds most suitable for introduction into their portfolios.

Hedge fund investment strategies vary a lot; some use leverage and derivatives while others are more conservative and employ little or no leverage. Strategies may be designed to be directional (which try to anticipate market movements) or market-neutral (which have low correlation to overall market movement). Owing to an increase in institutional demand, some hedge funds restrict their investments to long positions in stocks like ordinary mutual funds. Generally, the more a fund is "directional", the more volatile it is and the higher is the potential return or loss.

There are many ways to classify the investment strategies of hedge fund managers. In addition some managers combine several strategies in what are often referred to as "multi-strategy funds". The four major categories and sub-categories of investment strategies are listed in Figure3.1.

Figure3.1 Hedge Fund Strategies

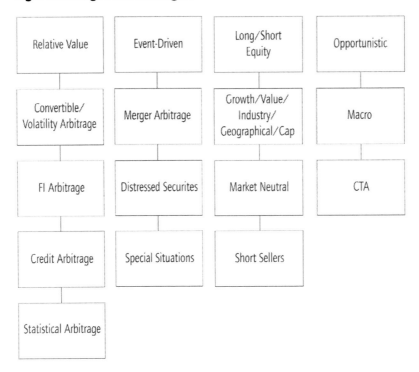

Relative Value

Convertible Arbitrage

Convertible arbitrage entails purchasing a portfolio of convertible securities while simultaneously hedging a portion of the equity risk by selling short the underlying common stock. Some managers may also seek to hedge interest rate exposure under some circumstances. The strategy generally benefits from three different sources: interest earned on the cash resulting from the short sales of equities, coupon offered by the bond component of the convertible and the so called "gamma effect".[22]

As with most successful arbitrage strategies, convertible arbitrage has attracted a large number of market participants, creating intense competition and reducing the effectiveness of the strategy.

Some of the well-known hedge fund firms such as CooperNeff (a subsidiary of BNP Paribas) and Highbridge Capital Management are listed as Convertible Arbitrage Hedge Fund Managers.

Fixed Income Arbitrage

This strategy seeks to profit from exploiting the pricing inefficiencies between related fixed-income securities while often neutralising exposure to interest rate risk. This strategy is often leveraged in order to enhance returns. Most arbitrageurs who employ this strategy trade globally as they need to seek opportunities around the world, given that more established markets have become too efficient to provide fair returns.

Fixed income arbitrage funds have lower risk than other hedge fund strategies. Unsurprisingly, they have the lowest return. This general strategy type includes basis (e.g. cash vs futures), yield-curve and credit spread trading, as well as volatility arbitrage and has the highest leverage of all major hedge fund strategies.

Fixed income arbitrage could be misused resulting in substantial losses. For example, Long-Term Capital Management (LTCM) lost US$4.6 billion in fixed income arbitrage in September 1998. LTCM had attempted to make money on the price difference between different bonds. For example, it would buy US Treasury securities and sell Italian bond futures. The concept was that because Italian bond futures had a less liquid market, in the short term Italian bond futures would have a higher return than US bonds, but in the long term, the prices would converge. Because the difference was small, a large amount of money had to be borrowed to make the buying and selling profitable.

Some of the notable hedge fund firms that currently employ this strategy include Cheyne Capital Management and Bear Stearns Asset Management.

22 Gamma is a metric used when trying to gauge the price of an option relative to the amount it is in or out of the money.

Credit Arbitrage

Credit arbitrage seeks to take advantage of pricing inefficiencies between the credit-sensitive securities of different issuers. It entails the active trading of a variety of predominantly credit-based instruments including Collateralised Debt Obligations (CDOs) and Credit Default Swaps (CDSs). A CDO is an investment vehicle that raises capital through the issuance of shares and debt and uses the proceeds to purchase financial assets, such as leveraged loans, bonds and other debt instruments. CDOs are designed to reallocate the credit risk of the underlying asset portfolio among different tranches, passing the risk of the portfolio on a tiered basis through to investors. The CDO portfolio, comprising perhaps hundreds of individual securities, is well diversified with respect to issuer, industry, and sector.

The strategy may invest anywhere across a company's capital structure and employs a fundamental value investing approach to create a diverse portfolio of situations. Positions in the portfolio may include: (1) long senior, secured investments with attractive yields, (2) relative value investments and event-driven capital structure arbitrage positions, (3) outright long or short credit positions, and (4) special situations such as stressed and distressed credits as well as post-reorganised equity. Instruments used may include, in addition to CDSs, loans and bonds. A variety of hedging techniques may be employed to reduce certain risks, including interest rate.

KBC Alternative Investment Managers is one of the global hedge fund firms that have a credit arbitrage fund.

Statistical Arbitrage

Statistical arbitrage is also called relative value arbitrage or quantitative arbitrage. Managers using this strategy seek to profit from pricing inefficiencies identified using mathematical models. Statistical arbitrage strategies are based on the premise that prices will return to their historic norms. These strategies are often leveraged in order to enhance returns.

As a trading strategy, statistical arbitrage is a heavily quantitative and computational approach to equity trading. It involves data mining and statistical methods, as well as automated trading systems.

Historically statistical arbitrage evolved out of the simpler pairs trade strategy, in which stocks are put into pairs by fundamental or market-based similarities. When one stock in a pair outperforms the other, the poorer performing stock is bought long with the expectation that it will climb towards its outperforming partner: the other is sold short. This hedges risk from whole-market movements.

Well-known quantitative statistical arbitrage fund managers include Barclays Global Investors and Renaissance Technologies.

Event-driven

Merger Arbitrage

Also known as risk arbitrage, this strategy invests in merger situations. Two principal types of merger are possible. (1) In a cash merger, an acquirer proposes to purchase the shares of the target for a certain price in cash. Until the acquisition is completed, the stock of the target typically trades below the purchase price. An arbitrageur buys the stock of the target and makes a gain if the acquirer ultimately buys the stock. (2) In a stock for stock merger, the acquirer proposes to buy the target by exchanging its own stock for the stock of the target. An arbitrageur may then short sell the acquirer and buy the stock of the target. This process is called "setting a spread". After the merger is completed, the target's stock will be converted into stock of the acquirer based on the exchange ratio determined by the merger agreement. The arbitrageur delivers the converted stock into his/her short position to complete the arbitrage.

Industry experts are of the opinion that merger arbitrage is not true arbitrage as the name implies since the success of a particular trade is dependent on the completion of the announced deal. Obstacles to completion of the deal may include either party's inability to satisfy the conditions of the merger, failure to obtain the requisite shareholder approval, failure to receive antitrust and other regulatory clearances, or some other event which may change the target's or the acquirer's willingness to consummate the transaction. Given the dicey elements of the trade, it is difficult to hedge the risk, hence the name risk arbitrage.

Distressed Securities

Distressed securities are securities of companies that are either already in default, under bankruptcy protection, or in distress and heading toward such a condition. The prices of these securities fall in anticipation of the financial distress when their holders choose to sell rather than remain invested in a financially troubled company. These sellers may be reacting emotionally to the stigma of current or potential bankruptcy, causing them to overlook or ignore the company's true worth.

The distressed securities hedge fund manager buys stocks or bonds of these types of companies, sold at deep discounts to the face value or earlier price levels. A distressed securities strategy is based on the premise that the manager is able to buy securities with enough profit potential to offset the obvious risk of loss.

Hedge funds are some of the largest buyers of distressed securities and often hold on to the securities for years. This kind of investment, being illiquid, makes the distressed securities strategy susceptible to liquidity pressures if the style should fall out of favour with investors. For this reason, funds usually enforce a longer commitment from investors.

Citadel Investment Group and Oaktree Capital Management are notable hedge fund firms in the distressed securities space.

Special Situations

Also known as corporate lifecycle, this strategy focuses on opportunities created by significant transactional events, such as division spin-offs, mergers, acquisitions, bankruptcies, reorganisations, share buybacks, and management
changes.

Hedge fund managers can capitalise on opportunities created by special-
situations fixed-income investing that provide higher returns without depend-
ence on equity investments, which tend to be volatile. This strategy entails investing in the fixed-income securities of "special situations" companies. Special
situations companies are ones that have undergone some kind of event or situation that has caused them to be misunderstood by the financial markets. These
may be companies with complicated pay-out structures or uncertain cash-flow
reimbursement streams. They may be new issues or spin-offs not yet followed by
the investment community, or companies in industries experiencing negative
publicity, causing them to fall out of favour with the market. Such companies
often offer bonds with high yields, not necessarily because they are a poor credit risk but rather because the facts surrounding these companies may be obscure
or difficult to understand without detailed research. The more complex the situation, the more misunderstood it is, resulting in lower purchase valuations and
potentially larger rewards for those able to correctly interpret the information.

Special-situations fixed-income investing provides a unique opportunity for
hedge funds to achieve steady returns with little market correlation. Furthermore, bond prices – as well as the prices of equities – will rise once the market
catches on to the mispricing that has occurred by a company being under-
researched, out of favour, or misunderstood. The reasoning is that the more a
special situations investment is overlooked, the greater the gap between its current price and the price that should eventually result from the recognition of the
intrinsic value. Once the investment community recognises this gap, a company
is re-rated, causing its bond yield to drop and the bond price to go up.

Long / Short Equity

Long/ Short Equity (Growth/ Value/ Industry Geographical)

This style accounts for the majority of the strategies used by hedge fund managers and the one that has assets under management that have grown rapidly
in recent times. It is a directional strategy that combines both long and short
positions in stocks. Long/short equity hedge funds have historically outperformed traditional long equity exposure with lower risk. This is the result of a
demonstrated capability by long/short managers to generate alpha via stocks
election, rotation in and out of cash opportunistically and timely shifts in market exposures (e.g. large vs small capitalisation, sector, geography etc.). Consequently, long/short managers have been inclined to generate a highly favourable characteristic: a higher correlation to equity markets in rising markets and
lower correlation in falling markets (sometimes referred to as an "asymmetrical"
risk/return profile).

55

Long/short managers generally hold a long equity portfolio offset by a portfolio of short equity holdings. The short portfolio serves as a hedge against market declines but also provides an opportunity for managers to add value by selecting stocks more likely to underperform the market. Long/short managers generally carry a net long bias – that is, the value of the long portfolio exceeds that of the short portfolio. As a result they are exposed to equity market risk.

Long/short equity funds currently have the largest share of the hedge fund industry's assets. While a portion of this growth in long/short is due to market appreciation, the demonstrated ability of the managers themselves is a key element of the increased inflow.

Market Neutral

This is a strategy that is designed to exploit inefficiencies in the equity market by trying to remove the element of systematic risk while extracting the stock - specific returns. These portfolios minimise market risk by balancing investments among carefully researched long and short positions of stock with different characteristics.

As an illustration, let's imagine that Biz-Cola, a fictional soft-drinks company, has just released a low-calorie drink that tastes like the original recipe that revellers love at a party. On the other hand, Bizle-Up, another fictional soft-drinks company and Biz-Cola's nearest rival, released its own low-calorie drink that revellers at the party found dry and tasteless. So, sensing a trend here, an investor rushes out and buys £5,000 worth of Biz-Cola's stock and sells short £5,000 of Bizle-Up. What the investor just did was to become a market-neutral investor. In this example, if the market goes up, both the Biz-Cola and Bizle-Up positions will rise in price, but Biz-Cola's should rise more provided the investor's analysis is correct and is ultimately recognised by others. Hence, the profit from the investor's Biz-Cola position will more than offset the loss from their short position in Bizle-Up. In addition, the investor will receive a rebate from their broker on the short position (usually the risk-free rate of interest).

Managers of market-neutral long/short equity hedge funds make scores of investments like this, picking stocks they believe are sufficiently balanced to keep the portfolio buffered from a severe market swing. Usually, they make sure the baskets of long and short investments are beta[23] neutral.

For added "neutrality", the hedge fund manager can buy equal dollar amounts of long and short investments, making the portfolio dollar neutral.

Finally, many hedge fund managers of market-neutral long/short equity trading balance their longs and shorts in the same sector or industry. Being sector neutral lets them avoid the risk of market swings that affect some industries or sectors differently to others, therefore they lose money when long in a stock

---

23 Beta is the measurement of a stock's volatility relative to the market. A stock with a beta of 1 moves historically in sync with the market, while a stock with a higher beta tends to be more volatile than the market and a stock with a lower beta can be expected to rise and fall more slowly than the market.

in a sector that suddenly plunges and short in a sector that stays flat or goes up.

In effect, what managers try to do by being beta neutral, dollar neutral, and sector neutral is make their portfolios more predictable by eliminating all systematic or market risk.

Some of the notable hedge fund firms that currently employ this strategy include State Street Global Advisors and Quantitative Management Associates a subsidiary of Prudential Investment Management.

Short Sellers

The short-selling approach seeks to profit from declines in the value of stocks. The strategy consists of borrowing a stock and selling it on the market with the intention of buying it back later at a lower price. By selling the stock short, the seller receives interest on the cash proceeds resulting from the sale. If the stock advances, the short seller takes a loss when buying it back to return to the lender.

The short-selling practice has made hedge funds notorious, accused of deliberately spreading negative stories to undermine a company. Hedge funds sell short. Short selling is always speculation, not investment. The growth of hedge funds thereby injects a much larger speculative element into the market. This makes the market much more dangerous for investors who are trying to finance pensions and retirements, college tuition and so on, by appreciation of their stock market investments.

Some speculation as a result of short selling is necessary and appropriate; it adds liquidity to the market and limits excessive optimism. But too much speculation turns the market from an investment vehicle into a casino. Hedge funds are most likely to affect the performance of the market by making it more volatile and limiting its upside potential (by much larger amounts of short-selling). Most commentators on the market ignore this. When the market suffers big losses on a single day, they find some small piece of bad economic news and attribute it to that. When the market gains a lot on a day, they look at the overall upward direction of the economy and attribute it to that. When the market stalls and seems to move aimlessly, they say the American economy is stagnating like that of Japan. The point is that even though the market is behaving in unfamiliar ways, it is explained as if it were behaving in traditional ways. Nowhere is the change in the players in the market recognised. The change in the means by which large players seek to profit, and the greater role of hedge funds and of speculation via short selling is ignored.

Opportunistic

Global Macro

Hedge fund managers use the global macro strategy of investing to attempt to generate hefty returns by in-depth analysis of global macro-economic trends such as interest rate trends, political changes, government policies etc. On the basis of these, they take leveraged positions on fixed income, currency, commodity and equity markets through either direct instruments or futures and other derivative products, hoping to profit from the direct influence of these trends on the prices of these financial instruments. It is this use of leverage on what are essentially directional bets, which are not hedged, that has the greatest impact on the performance of macro funds and results in the high volatility that some macro funds experience. That said, the leverage in this sector is typically between 6:1 and 10:1. This ratio is higher than for any equity hedge fund strategy and is significant considering the outright nature of the macro fund positions.

The term "global macro" derives from the manager's endeavour to apply macro-economic principles to identifying dislocations in asset prices, i.e. the macro part, while the global part implies the quest for dislocations across the globe. According to industry experts, the global macro hedge fund strategy has the widest mandate of all hedge fund strategies, whereby managers have the ability to take positions in any market or instrument. It is perhaps the most publicised of hedge fund strategies, even though only a small percentage of hedge funds are macro funds.

The publicity surrounding the macro funds stems from the high-profile, highly leveraged and high-stakes investments made by the likes of macro hedge fund managers George Soros and Julian Robertson. George Soros spectacularly bet $10 million, much of it borrowed, in 1992 on the expectation of the devaluation of the British Pound. His bet paid off and the investors in his fund made a profit of $2 billion. Soros became famous when he sold short sterling ($10 billion worth), profiting from the Bank of England's reluctance to either raise its interest rates to levels comparable to those of other European Exchange Rate Mechanism countries or to float its currency. The Bank of England was eventually forced to withdraw the currency out of the European Exchange Rate Mechanism and to devalue the pound sterling. However, not all bets by these macro managers went in the right direction. In 1994, some managers placed huge, unhedged bets that European interest rates would decline, causing the bonds to rise; the Federal Reserve raised interest rates in the USA, causing European interest rates to rise, and investors who bet that European interest rates would go down to lose money.

It is not surprising that macro investing is perceived by many to be a high-risk investment strategy, due in part to the sensationalisation by the world press of failures of well-known hedge fund managers. However, with the high risks come high returns and, in fact, global macro hedge funds have had some of the highest returns of all hedge fund strategies. They have had higher correlations to stock and bond returns than most other hedge fund strategies (because of outright long positions in stocks and bonds).Their correlations are still low enough to make them a valuable diversifier in a conventional stock/bond portfolio. Global macro funds are also added as a way of increasing the overall return on a conventional portfolio.

It is worth noting that there are probably as many approaches to identifying and capitalising on a macro trend as there are macro hedge fund managers.

But all players and their approaches have several things in common. First, macro players are willing to invest across multiple sectors and trading industries and move from opportunity to opportunity, trend to trend, and strategy to strategy – whatever kind of investment that expected shifts in economic policies, political climates or interest rates make attractive. Secondly, they all see the entire globe as the playing field and are well aware that events in these countries or regions have a domino effect across global markets.

CTA

CTA stands for Commodity Trading Advisor and is also known as a Managed Futures strategy. This strategy essentially invests in futures contracts on financial, commodity and currency markets around the world. Trading decisions are often based on proprietary quantitative models and technical analysis. These portfolios have embedded leverage through the derivative contracts employed.

A managed futures strategy traditionally works best at times of high market volatility because it arbitrages tiny price differences. The benefits of managed futures as part of an investor's overall asset portfolio include providing direct exposure to international financial and non-financial asset sectors while offering (through their ability to take both long and short investment positions) a means to gain exposure to risk and return patterns not easily accessible with investment in traditional stock and bond portfolios.

Hedge fund managers use this strategy to offer investors the potential for reduced portfolio risk and enhanced investment return as well as low return correlation with traditional stock and bond markets on a par with many hedge fund strategies. These benefits, as well as the ability to profit in different economic environments and the ease of global diversification, have been responsible for the recent growth in investor demand for managed futures products.

Man Investments and D.E. Shaw are among the notable managed futures hedge fund managers.

Others

Fund of Funds

Fund of funds provides a diversified exposure for multiple hedge fund strategies or to managers within a given strategy A fund of funds may overweight or underweight certain strategies or managers based on macroeconomic outlook or quantitative optimisation techniques. A typical fund of funds would provide exposure to 8 to 10 different investment strategies and 20 to 40 managers. Fund of funds managers usually charge a management fee and a performance-based fee in addition to the underlying manager fees. Broadly speaking, hedge fund of funds can be divided into two camps:

- Directional fund of funds: those with underlying investments in hedge funds that have positive beta to the equity markets and correlation usually broadly to the equity markets.

■ Non-directional fund of funds: those that strive for low correlation and beta to the equity markets and, in some cases, the fixed income markets.

Multi-Strategy

Multi-strategy hedge funds are those that invest across more than one hedge fund strategy. The term multi-strategy often refers to hedge funds with a broader expertise. Multi-strategy hedge funds typically invest in a broad enough number of strategies as they occur. Multi-strategy hedge funds are similar to fund of funds except that all assets are managed within the same organisation. Liquidity or lockup issues that are present in an individual hedge fund partnership may be avoided when the multi-strategy manager changes the weights on individual hedge fund strategies.

Emerging Markets

This strategy entails investing in stocks or bonds of emerging markets. These are considered very volatile because emerging markets typically have higher inflation and volatile economic conditions. Not all emerging markets allow short selling so hedging is usually not available.

The growth of the hedge fund industry has led to an increase in capital allocation into the fastest growing emerging market economies. The consequences for these countries have been rising equity markets, tightening credit spreads and the attention of global financial powerhouses and the media.

Farallon Capital management and Sloane Robinson are among the notable emerging markets hedge fund managers.

Mortgage Arbitrage

Mortgage or mortgage-backed arbitrage strategies invest in mortgage-backed securities, including government agencies, government-sponsored enterprises, private-label fixed or adjustable rate pass-through securities, fixed or adjustable rate collateralised mortgage obligations, real-estate investment conduits and stripped mortgage-backed securities. Managers seek to take advantage of security-specific mispricings.

Mortgage arbitrage is considered to be an extension of fixed income arbitrage.

Ratios and Models used for Performance Measurement

It is well known that the performance of a hedge fund manager is based on their skills and the strategy employed. The performance of the market is irrelevant as hedge funds have the ability to take long and short positions. Nevertheless, there are ratios and models that are used to measure performance with regard to risk and return.

Return

Most investors in hedge funds have a rudimentary knowledge of return (nominal return), which is an indicator of the performance of their investment in a hedge fund. Nominal return is represented by the ratio:

$$Nominal\ Return = Gain/Investment$$

Industry watchers assert that investors should be wary of returns that hedge fund operators claim as they believe hedge funds are not designed to serve the best interests of investors. They are designed to serve the best interests of hedge fund operators. The main reason for this is that it is widely opined that hedge fund operators expect investors to be satisfied with rate of return data and, perhaps, some accompanying commentary. But, by itself, hedge fund performance data is meaningless. Rate of return data has meaning only if investors understand how it was arrived at.

Claims by some hedge fund operators of having generated returns of more than 40% annually for 3 consecutive years should not be taken at face value, given that an informed judgement cannot be made solely based on a nominal rate of return. The use of leverage, the holding of hard-to-value securities, investment in speculative securities or exposure to derivative contracts should be taken into account when returns are evaluated.

A case in point is Long-Term Capital Management that posted annual returns of more than 40% from 1994 when it was formed until 1998 when it collapsed. According to the Financial Times, the fund employed leverage that exceeded, at times, 30 times equity. With that much leverage, it should come as no surprise that $3.6bn of equity capital was wiped out in just five weeks.

Furthermore, hedge funds lack accountability. Because the industry is unregulated or perhaps lightly regulated, the information published by hedge fund firms should be viewed with a degree of circumspection. Without sufficient regulatory scrutiny and without disclosure about how returns are generated, investors will forever be doubtful.

That said, it would be reasonable to identify the potential sources of return from a particular hedge fund strategy and from a manager's particular application of that strategy. There are four identifiable sources of returns from hedge fund strategies: static return, market exposure return, gross exposure return and manager alpha and are defined thus:

- Static return – this is defined as the return of the portfolio without any change in price of the underlying prices. For a traditional equity portfolio, it is the dividend yield and for a bond portfolio it is the coupon.
- Market exposure return – exposure to directional market moves is a source of returns in some but not all strategies. Supposing a manager was 120% long and 50% short, the 70% stock market exposure should expose the fund to 70% stock market movement. If the equity markets generate 10% long term, including 3% from dividends, then general price movements could add 4.9% annually to the hedge fund manager's long-term returns.

61

▓ Gross exposure – defined as the total of all long and short investment positions, gross exposure indicates the real level of leverage in a portfolio. This means that altering gross exposure is a powerful hedge fund management tool. It also provides insight into a manager's ability to provide equity-like returns, even when overall market exposure (to general market moves) has been reduced.

▓ Manager alpha – widely embraced as a significant component of a hedge fund manager's returns manifesting, in the case of long only investing, the value added by a manager's security selection skills.

For example, if a hedge fund adopts an equity market neutral (equal long and shorts) strategy with a zero alpha, it would earn the risk-free rate net of dividends on borrowed stock. The manager's long and shorts would wipe out any stock market impact. The manager in question will have the ability to generate 10% per annum benefits from the additional power of two sources of alpha and, possibly, from gross exposure in excess of 100%.

P/E Ratio (Equities)

One of the reasons that stock prices rise is due to supply and demand of the market. If a company is growing rapidly and earning more money each year or quarter, the stock price should increase due to the overall value of the company increasing. As the company's value increases, the stock price increases as well. When a company does poorly and does not grow or make a profit, the value of the company lessens and the stocks' worth starts to decrease because it is not in demand. The value of the company's stocks is always up to the market forces. There are no set rules on why stocks increase or decrease.

One of the many tools that hedge fund managers use when analysing whether a stock is worth its price is the P/E. P/E stands for price to earnings ratio. The P/E ratio can easily be determined by dividing the market value of a stock over the last year by the earnings per share of the last year. For instance, if a stock averages a price of £100 over the course of a year and its earnings over the last 12 months for each share were £2, the P/E ratio would equal 50. It is important to note that hedge fund managers do not base their entire analysis on a P/E. The reason that P/E isn't the best indicator is that earnings per share are the result of accounting. The P/E is only as good as its accounting methods.

The formula for calculating P/E is:

Price/Earning Ratio = Market Price per Share/Earning per Share

P/B or price book is also a good method to determine if a stock is a good buy. P/B stands for price to book ratio. The price book ratio is a way to see if the book value of a company is worth the market value at its current price. This can be a very helpful tool for many hedge fund managers. Another way to determine if a stock is a good choice is to look at the amount that it pays out in dividends. Not every stock pays dividends, but a dividend is the profits from a stock that a company gives back to its shareholders. It can be 1% of the profit or all of the profit per share that a dividend may encompass.

Dividend Yield

The dividend yield on a company stock is the company's annual dividend payments divided by its market capitalisation, or the dividend per share divided by the price per share. It is calculated thus:

$$\text{Dividend Yield} = \text{Dividend per share}/\text{Market Price per Share} * 100\%$$

Take for example a company, say BizEnergy, which paid dividends totalling £2 in the previous year and whose shares currently sell for £30. Its dividend yield would be calculated as follows:

$$\text{Dividend Yield} = 2/30 * 100 = 6.67\%$$

Dividends paid to holders of common stock are set by management, usually in relation to the company's earnings. There is no guarantee that future dividends will match past dividends or even be paid at all.

Sharpe ratio

As hedge fund investors, or any investor, would prefer a fund with a higher return to one with a lower return, and would similarly prefer a fund with lower risk than higher risk, provided that everything is equal between the two funds, there has to be a trade-off between the return and the risk the investor is exposed to in order to earn that return. The Sharpe ratio provides a measure for this trade-off between risk and return.

The Sharpe ratio, a measure of the risk-adjusted return of an investment, was developed by Nobel laureate William F. Sharpe. This measurement is very useful because although one fund can reap higher returns than its peers, it is only a good investment if those higher returns do not come with too much additional risk. The greater a portfolio's Sharpe ratio, the better its risk-adjusted performance has been. The formula for calculating the Sharpe ratio is as follows:

$$\text{Sharpe Ratio} = \text{Return}_{Actual} - \text{Return}_{Risk\text{-}free}/\text{Standard Deviation}_{Return}$$

Sortino ratio

The Sortino ratio, developed by Frank A. Sortino, is a modification of the Sharpe ratio that replaces the standard deviation in the denominator of the Sharpe ratio with downside deviation. Hence, the formula for calculating the Sortino ratio is:

$$\text{Sortino Ratio} = \text{Return}_{Actual} - \text{Return}_{Risk\text{-}free}/\text{Downside Deviation}_{Return}$$

Industry experts assert that the Sortino ratio is a more realistic measure of risk-adjusted returns than the Sharpe ratio as it penalises only those assets with returns falling below a user-specified target, or required rate of return, while the Sharpe ratio penalises both upside and downside volatility equally.

Treynor Ratio

The Treynor ratio, developed by Jack Treynor, measures the return earned in excess of that which could have been earned on a riskless investment for each unit of market risk. It is similar to the Sharpe ratio but instead of the standard deviation as a measure of risk in the denominator, this ratio uses the portfolio beta. The Treynor ratio is calculated as:

$$\text{Treynor Ratio} = \text{Return}_{Actual} - \text{Return}_{Risk\text{-}free}/\text{Beta}$$

The Treynor ratio is essentially a risk-adjusted measure of return based on systematic risk and is also known as "reward-to-volatility ratio".

Jensen's Alpha

Jensen's Alpha, also known as Jensen's Performance Index, measures the extent that performance exceeds the return expected for the amount for the risk assumed. It is used to adjust for the level of beta risk, since riskier securities are expected to have higher returns. The measure was first used in the evaluation of mutual fund managers by Michael C. Jensen in the 1970s. The formula for calculating Jensen's Alpha is:

$$\text{Jensen's Alpha} = (\text{Return}_{Portfolio} - \text{Return}_{Risk\text{-}free}) - (\text{Return}_{Market} - \text{Return}_{Risk\text{-}free}) * \text{Beta}$$

Alpha is still widely used in conjunction with the Sharpe ratio and the Treynor ratio to evaluate performance. It is also often used in hedge fund due diligence reports although irrelevant if the fund is expected to track a specified benchmark.

Models

Capital Asset Pricing Model (CAPM)

This is used in the industry to evaluate hedge fund performance. CAPM was developed by William Sharpe (of the Sharpe ratio fame) and states that the required return on a risky asset is the risk-free rate plus a risk premium which is the market risk premium times the beta of the asset. The model is symbolically expressed as:

$$r_a = r_f + [\beta(r_m - r_f)]$$

where:

r_a= expected return on the security,

r_f= risk-free rate for the expected holding period of the asset,

β = the security's beta, a measure of how risky its returns are relative to the risk on the market portfolio,

r_m = return on a diversified market portfolio,

$r_m - r_f$= the difference between the market portfolio return and the risk-free rate, i.e. the market premium.

CAPM is used by investors and hedge fund managers to determine a theoretically appropriate required rate of return (and thus the price if expected cash flows can be estimated) of an asset, if that asset is to be added to an already well-diversified portfolio, given that asset's non-diversifiable risk.

Arbitrage Pricing Theory

Arbitrage pricing theory (APT), initiated by economist Stephen Ross in 1976, is a valuation model. Compared to CAPM, it uses fewer assumptions but is harder to use. The basis of arbitrage pricing theory is the idea that the price of a security is driven by a number of factors. These can be divided into two groups: macro factors and company-specific factors. The name of the theory comes from the fact that this division, together with the no-arbitrage assumption, can be used to derive the following formula:

$$r = r_f + \beta_1 f_1 + \beta_2 f_2 + \beta_3 f_3 + ...$$

where r is the expected return on the security,

r_f is the risk-free rate,

each f is a separate factor, and

each β is a measure of the relationship between the security price and that factor.

This is a recognisably similar formula to CAPM.

The difference between CAPM and arbitrage pricing theory is that CAPM has a single non-company factor and a single beta, whereas arbitrage pricing theory separates out non-company factors into as many as proves necessary. Each of these requires a separate beta. The beta of each factor is the sensitivity of the price of the security to that factor.

Arbitrage pricing theory does not rely on measuring the performance of the market. Instead, APT directly relates the price of the security to the fundamental factors driving it. The problem with this is that the theory in itself provides

65

no indication of what these factors are, so they need to be empirically determined. Obvious factors include economic growth and interest rates. For companies in some sectors, other factors are obviously relevant as well – such as consumer spending for retailers.

The potentially large number of factors means more betas to be calculated. There is also no guarantee that all the relevant factors have been identified. This added complexity is the reason arbitrage pricing theory is far less widely used than CAPM.

Arbitrage is the practice of taking advantage of a state of imbalance between two (or possibly more) markets and thereby making a risk-free profit. APT describes the mechanism whereby arbitrage by investors will bring an asset which is mispriced, according to the APT model, back into line with its expected price. Hedge fund managers use arbitrage to enhance returns for their investors, hence this is a very important model in the hedge fund universe.

Efficient Market Hypothesis

Efficient Market Hypothesis, developed by Professor Eugene Fama in the 1960s, states that financial markets are broadly efficient, i.e. information is widely and cheaply available to investors, and that all relevant and ascertainable information is already reflected in prices of securities, i.e. bonds, stocks etc.

The efficient market hypothesis is based on the premise that it is not possible to consistently outperform the market by using any information that the market already knows, except through luck. However, Lo (2004) asserts that the emerging discipline of behavioural economics and finance contests this premise of the EMH. He argues that markets are not rational, but are driven by fear and greed instead. Other researchers have also uncovered numerous other financial market (including stock market) anomalies that seem to contradict the efficient market hypothesis. The search for anomalies is effectively the search for systems or patterns that can be used to outperform passive and/or buy-and-hold strategies. Theoretically though, once an anomaly is discovered, investors attempting to profit by exploiting the inefficiency should result in its disappearance. In fact, industry experts claim that numerous anomalies that have been documented via back-testing have subsequently disappeared or proven to be impossible to exploit because of transaction costs.

Another camp of industry experts believe that the paradox of efficient markets is that if every investor believed a market was efficient, then the market would not be efficient because no one would analyse securities. In effect, efficient markets depend on market participants who believe the market is inefficient and trade securities in an attempt to outperform the market, and that in reality markets are neither perfectly efficient nor completely inefficient. From their point of view, all markets are efficient to a certain extent, some more so than others. Rather than being an issue of black or white, market efficiency is more a matter of shades of grey. In markets with substantial impairments of efficiency, more knowledgeable investors can strive to outperform less knowledgeable ones.

Nevertheless, the efficient market debate plays an important role in the decision made by hedge fund managers between active and passive investing. Active managers argue that less efficient markets provide the opportunity for outperformance by skilful managers. However, it is as important to realise that a majority of active managers in a given market will underperform the appropriate benchmark in the long run whether markets are, or are not efficient. This is because active management is a zero-sum game in which the only way a participant can profit is for another less fortunate active participant to lose.

Types of Hedge Fund Investors

This chapter describes the different types of investors in hedge funds and their concerns about this type of investment vehicle.

Introduction

The present-day dynamics of the hedge fund investor base have been altered by the increase in the number of institutional investors. In the past, hedge fund investors were primarily high net worth individuals. According to the Hennessee Group, in 1997 individual investors made up 61%, but by 2006 they accounted for only 40% (see Figure 4.1).

Some of the elements that are enhancing the growth of the use of hedge funds by institutional investors include:

- The maturation of the industry's infrastructure;
- Recent instability in the traditional asset classes (bonds, equities etc.);
- The growing length of track records for performance and volatility;
- The growing cadre of highly talented managers;
- A wider range of strategies from which to choose than there was in the past;
- The advent of investable benchmark indices;
- The lower barriers to entry that have created numerous products from which to choose.

Figure 4.1 Global Hedge Funds by Source of Capital

% share

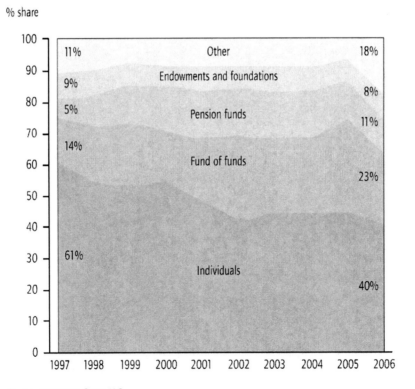

Source: Hennessee Group LLC

Until recently, alternative investments have primarily been focused on private equity and real estate, with institutional investors wary of hedge fund investment. There are a number of atypical aspects and risks associated with hedge funds that make them cumbersome investments to adopt, such as the following:

- **Lack of transparency** – as hedge funds are inherently private investment vehicles, they have been slow to meet the expectations of traditional institutional investors in terms of transparency[24] and accountability. To ensure that hedge funds are suitable for them as investment vehicles, institutional investors have, in recent times, applied enormous pressure on hedge funds to provide greater transparency. This is for the simple reason that fiduciaries[25] find it difficult to justify investment in a fund with unknown risks and exposures.
- **Insufficient diversification** – industry experts are sceptical about the ability to achieve "true" diversification through uncorrelated hedge funds.
- **Headline risk** – high-profile failures in the hedge fund industry such as Amanarath and Long-Term Capital Management have led industry experts to point out that even though an investor may get aggregate returns on a portfolio of hedge funds, a rogue fund can sometimes conspicuously weaken overall performance and generate adverse publicity.
- **Liquidity** – as hedge funds are relatively illiquid investments with "lock-up" and "liquidity" provisions, an investment cannot be redeemed during this initial period.
- **Fees** – finally, the higher fees that hedge funds charge have been a deterrent to institutional investors.

Hedge fund investors are usually classified into a small number of categories: individuals, endowments, pension funds and corporate investors. While there are significant differences between investors in each of these categories, there can be differences within the same category as well. Marketers of a particular hedge fund strategy usually exploit these differences.

Individuals

Onshore Individuals
Hedge funds have long played a role in the investment portfolios of ultra-high net worth[26] individuals, especially in Europe and North America. According to

---

24 Transparency in this sense refers to the ability of the investor to look through a hedge fund to its investment portfolio to determine compliance with the fund's investment guidelines and risk parameters.

25 Entities or people that are legally appointed and authorised to hold assets in trust for another entity or person. The fiduciary manages the assets for the benefit of the other person rather than for his or her own profit.

26 These are individuals with a net worth of at least $30 million in all assets except their "primary residence".

the World Wealth Report of 2007, there are 95,000 ultra-high net worth individuals throughout the world, with 23,200 in Europe and 38,400 in North America. The role of hedge funds in their portfolios is markedly different from that of large institutional investors (a sizable proportion of which are tax-exempt). Wealthy individuals are looking for excess return above market and their perception of risk can be viewed as the chance of losing money whereas institutions tend to focus on stable and consistent returns and take a more academic view of risk as the standard deviation of return or other statistical measures. Furthermore, institutions tend to prefer stable returns because they have to make substantial annual payouts and budget for future expenditures as opposed to wealthy individuals who can live on a small fraction of their asset base and get paid their returns in lump sums.

Individuals find the fact that most hedge funds are committed to delivering absolute returns very appealing. That is, hedge funds are not concerned with generating attractive returns relative to a benchmark; instead they try to earn high returns and avoid losses. Individual investors are also drawn to the possibility that the potential for losses in hedge funds could be justified by the potential for gains and that the losses in stock and bond indices are not used to justify losses.

It is worth pointing out that most hedge funds do not sign up non-wealthy individuals. This is mainly because of limits to the small number of investors and because their circumstances are similar to those of institutions, in that payouts are usually a significant percentage of their total asset base, but are subject to taxes.

Nevertheless, eligible individual investors are always quicker to invest in hedge funds than all other types of investors. They are typically knowledgeable investors that have the financial resources to lose their investments in hedge funds.

One category of investors, known as family offices, closely resembles individuals but they are classed as institutional investors as they make hedge fund investments as individuals while acting more like institutions. A family office is essentially a group of investors, usually close family relatives, that join together to manage their personal investments. They have become more like private hedge funds in recent years as the management of wealth has become increasingly complex. These family offices hire investment professionals to manage the investment for several members of the office. Nowadays the office operates just like a corporation, with a president, CFO, CIO, etc.

For family offices, the attraction to hedge funds mainly stems from the low correlation that allows diversification to lower risk and, of course, the desire to increase the return of their overall portfolio.

Individual investors, when assessing the suitability of hedge fund investment, factor in tax considerations. Given their opportunistic business practices, hedge funds are tax-inefficient investment vehicles and as such tend to turn over their positions before they become long-term for tax purposes. Because shorting always amounts to short-term gains or losses, irrespective of the length of time a fund holds its position, it is also tax-inefficient.

71

From a risk perspective, industry experts are of the opinion that in order to reap the true benefits of a hedge fund, an individual investor needs to target a return of at least 5% above the broad equity indices. On the assumption of a stocks return of 10% over the long term, the investor should expect 15% from their hedge fund managers.[27]

It should be noted that with the increasingly broad and sophisticated range of hedge funds available today, it is unclear whether individual investors have become discriminating in their selection of hedge funds, or whether they are, at the same time, still swayed by the dictates of financial fashion for the "philosopher's stone" of consistent, absolute outperformance.

Offshore Individuals

Offshore individuals are so called because they differ from domestic individuals with respect to the manner in which they invest in hedge funds and where the funds they invest in are domiciled.

Offshore individuals often invest in hedge funds through private banks. The hedge fund manager may not know the identity of the investors as the investment could be a single investment representing five or more individual investors. Offshore hedge fund investments can offer significant taxation benefits to an investor, depending on their country of tax residence and domicile. Other benefits include confidentiality, asset protection and diversification of investments.

Offshore funds are domiciled in "tax haven" countries like Bermuda, the Bahamas and the Cayman Islands. These offshore funds may be managed by firms that are located in Europe or the USA, but the assets of the funds are located outside these regions.

The activities of offshore individuals have been under more intense scrutiny ever since the 9/11 terrorist attacks and offshore hedge funds have been under pressure to implement "Know Your Customer" initiatives with a view to uncovering money laundering and tax evasion. As offshore funds accept assets that are already liable for taxes in the investor's home jurisdiction, there would be cases where investors will fail to pay taxes in their home jurisdictions that they ought to pay.

Institutions

Institutions belong to the category of investors known as institutional investors. The universe of institutional investors divides into taxable and tax-exempt investors. Institutional investors are not individuals but large groups of people. Almost every institution has a group of people whose responsibility includes investment activities for the institution. These are fiduciaries of the institution

27 Source: Benjamine Deschaine, Are Hedge Funds Suitable for Individual Investors, *AIMA Journal*, Winter 2005.

and their responsibilities usually reside in the board of directors, which normally forms an investment committee responsible for investment decisions. Fiduciaries are faced with a degree of complexity in their investment decisions as making decisions about personal assets is easier than having the responsibility for an institution's assets.

Figure 4.2 Institutional Hedge Assets by Country/Region 2005 (total $361 billion)

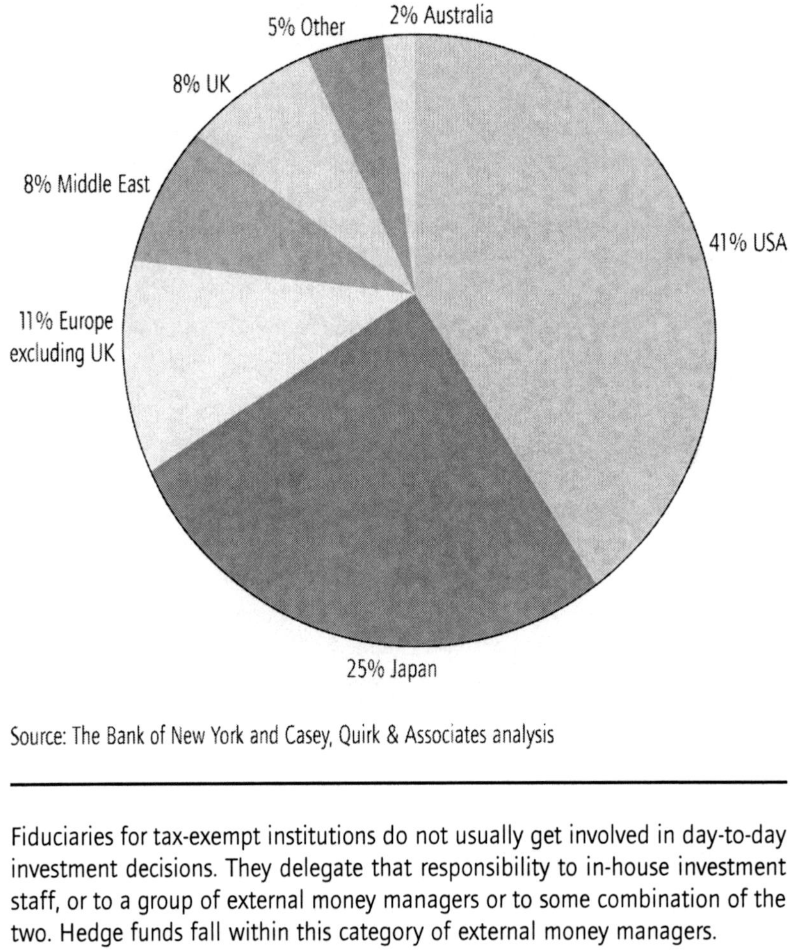

Source: The Bank of New York and Casey, Quirk & Associates analysis

Fiduciaries for tax-exempt institutions do not usually get involved in day-to-day investment decisions. They delegate that responsibility to in-house investment staff, or to a group of external money managers or to some combination of the two. Hedge funds fall within this category of external money managers.

Insurance Companies

The insurance business, especially life insurance, requires investments as an integral part of the business model. However, insurance companies have not shown a preference for hedge funds as industry data reveals a moderate investment in this asset class. Life insurance companies sell insurance and annuity products that earn a fixed income return. These products are essentially corporate debt borrowed from policyholders. Therefore, in order to profit from their investments, the returns should be higher than their fixed-rate commitments.

Insurance companies are able to allocate some money to non-standard investment strategies that have the potential to generate risk return profiles different from traditional asset classes. Hence, an investment in hedge funds results in diversification benefits, making them an interesting investment alternative for life insurance companies.

In some countries, the proportion of the asset base of life insurance companies that can be invested in hedge funds is restricted. This is because regulators perceive hedge funds as risky investments. In addition, insurance companies do not routinely mark securities positions to market. The unrealised gain or loss on a traditional asset, such as a bond or stock held as a long-term investment, can be deferred, yet hedge funds report results to investors on a monthly or quarterly basis.

Advantages of hedge fund investment, however, include:

■ Reduction of volatility of the overall asset portfolio which is especially associated with life companies with cliquet-style[28] interest rate guarantee.
■ The higher the interest rate guarantee is, the less capital an insurer holds; and the less possibilities the accounting system provides to smooth the book values of the investment portfolio, the more incentives an insurance company has to diversify its portfolio by investing in hedge funds.
■ An investment in a multi-strategy hedge fund leads to expected returns if an insurance company can tolerate a ruin probability[29] of 5%.

Other types of insurance company, such as property and reinsurance, also invest in hedge funds. Their level of investment is, however, dependent on the regulation and taxation of their jurisdictional locations.

Pension Funds

Hedge fund managers have routinely expressed concern about the relatively slow commitment of pension funds to hedge funds and the relatively small proportion of their investments compared to the total pool of pension assets.

Despite the well-documented large size of the pool of assets that pension funds control, hedge funds have yet to exploit the potential and attract pension funds. The reasons for this include a lack of understanding of hedge funds by the actuarial investment consultants that dominate trustee investment thinking. They believe the only way to maximise long-term returns is through long-only equity investments. Since they have not spent enough time trying to understand what hedge funds are capable of, they are deterred by the perception of hedge

---

28 An extended option that periodically settles and resets its strike price at the level of the underlying security during the time of settlement.

29 Ruin probability is the probability of the occurrence of ruin when negative positions in one or more of several business lines cannot be cancelled by capital transfers.

funds as high-risk, high-fee, unregulated investment vehicles that are too complex.

Trustees are often unsophisticated investors who are not risk tolerant and need to be educated to better understand the complex concepts of hedge fund investing. For this reason, many participants in a defined contribution plan would not qualify to invest directly in a hedge fund.

In most countries, occupational pension funds face future problems given the size of final salary schemes and the associated deficits. This can be attributed to inappropriate investment allocations and over-reliance on equity investment; an ideology validated by historic strong equity returns.

When returns are strong, pension fund sponsors may realise that the increase in assets exceeds the increase in pension liabilities. As a result they have been able to boost their earnings by avoiding many pension expenses as actual cash expenditures have not been needed.

However, given the negative stock returns over the last few years, many companies find that they must once more include an expense for future pension requirements. They do not welcome this additional expense at a time when corporate earnings have been under pressure for many reasons.

This presents a dilemma for pension funds as they need to boost earning for their funds and at the same time find it inconvenient to accommodate an increase in pension costs. However, with the right attitude trustees could advocate allocating more assets of their fund to hedge funds. The right balance between these two issues could result in hedge funds attracting the new money into their funds.

The challenge for hedge fund managers, especially multi-managers, is to enlighten pension fund trustees on how to use alternative investments to reduce the risk levels of their portfolios and to differentiate between hedge funds.

A sticking point is that from a cost perspective, pension funds tend to be very conscious of the level of management and performance fees, given that in traditional, unleveraged, long-only investing, there is little difference between money managers before accounting for fees, and that managers with the lowest fees tend to provide the highest net return. This is the reason why industry experts suggest that pension fund trustees may have trouble justifying the level of fees charged by hedge fund managers.

Endowments

Endowments are major tax-exempt institutional investors. They are essentially charitable gifts donated to institutions such as universities, colleges, or similar non-profit institutions, and are designed to support their activities.

Universities were among the earliest institutions to discover the benefits of hedge fund investment. A number of universities, especially in the USA, found that hedge funds were a useful source of diversification and growth for their endowments and hence committed aggressively to hedge funds.

Endowments have unique investment objectives in that they exist mainly to provide income for institutions engaged in charitable activities. They may not have significant amounts of new money coming in and have an obligation to future generations to preserve the spending power of the endowment.

Industry experts maintain that institutions have to balance spending to meet the needs of the current generation with the need to make sure they can meet the needs of future generations by a policy of purchasing power preservation.

Since endowments have longer-term horizons, they can be more tolerant of swings in the net asset value of a fund. They tend to take a long-term view of their investments and not engage in speculative activities. As a consequence they typically opt for investment strategies that involve illiquid securities such as real estate that may require a "lock-up" of funds.

Furthermore, an endowment's tolerance for risk – which impacts on their spending plans – influences their choice of investments. Endowments generally spend most of the returns from their investments; therefore minor swings, while not enough to force a change in spending plans or commitment, should not escalate into major losses that could force an endowment to cancel programmes or defer projects. This is a major source of concern for endowments.

Foundations

Foundations are tax-exempt organisations like endowments. They have made substantial investments in hedge funds, like other non-profit organisations, to improve their investment returns. Like endowments, they also favour low leverage for tax reasons.

Foundations, like endowments, are often longer-term investors, although for a shorter period than endowments. If a foundation has had good returns in hedge fund investment, it will enhance its chances of attracting more funds from donors. However if a media report says that a foundation has lost money in, say, a fraudulent financial scheme, its ability to get donations could be severely damaged.

As hedge fund performance is closely tied to the expertise and capability of the manager, so being able to evaluate and review managers to determine their capability, as well as monitor their performance once they're hired, is crucial. Selecting a manager involves not only an analysis of the manager's background and qualifications and the fund's investment strategy, it also means making sure that investing is in a manner consistent with its stated strategy and is achieving appropriate levels of return relative to its strategy and level of risk. Not all foundations have the management capability to do this, nor can they take the same risks that some can with their investments. As a result, most foundations hire an investment consultant who assists with the structuring of their asset allocation model, which could include hedge funds.

There are subtle differences between the investment profile of an endowment or foundation and the profile of a pension fund. A pension fund is not able to simply reduce the level of benefits paid to retirees should the fund experience disappointing returns. However, a foundation or endowment could alter their spending policies in line with the performance of their assets and can therefore accommodate some year-to-year reduction of the level of spending. As a result of this, endowments and foundations are usually more aggressive than pension funds in their investment activities and can afford to allocate more money into equities and illiquid alternative investments and hedge funds.

Offshore Institutions
Offshore institutions that invest in hedge funds include tax-exempt institutions such as endowments, foundations and pension funds. Many offshore funds resemble domestic funds of funds. They could be commingled[30] individual investments made directly by financial institutions.

Many non-profit organisations are taking advantage of the tax benefits of investing in offshore hedge funds. These include health-care providers, colleges and philanthropies with major endowments steering large chunks of their portfolio away from the volatile stock markets and into less traditional investments – particularly hedge funds, many of which are registered in traditional offshore locations such as the Cayman Islands and the Isle of Man.

Fund of Funds
Many individuals and institutions invest directly in hedge funds, but many individuals would prefer to diversify their hedge fund commitments into several different funds. This is because the level of fund risk can be very high if the invest or uses only one hedge fund. Depending on the investor's requirements, he or she may use three or four funds or even up to ten or more. However in order to pursue this strategy, the investor needs a sizable amount of money to invest as most funds impose a minimum requirement. For example, an individual must have a portfolio that is worth at least £20 million if they intend to invest no more than 5 per cent of their portfolio in hedge funds, and the minimum requirement is £1 million in order to comply with the asset allocation decision and satisfy the minimum requirement. If the individual were to invest in four or more funds, then they would need to have an entire portfolio worth £80 million.

The alternative is for the investor to invest in a fund of funds that contains at least ten fund investments to get substantial diversification. However, this strategy may be cumbersome if the hedge fund portfolio includes a large number of managers, as the job of monitoring and managing the portfolio can be demanding.

Specialised investment firms, a sort of "manager of managers" outfit, create a fund of funds for this sort of investor, and offer diversification and professional management for investors that are not willing or able to construct their own portfolio of hedge funds. These firms usually have research departments that

---

30 These are investments consisting of assets from several accounts that are blended together. Investors in commingled fund investments benefit from economies of scale, which allow for lower trading costs per unit currency of investment, diversification and professional money management.

conduct a thorough due diligence review of all potential investments and tend to informally share information about individual managers, reducing the likelihood that they will invest in inappropriate or fraudulent funds.

The benefits of these types of arrangement for smaller investors include the diversification which larger investors can achieve by investing directly in hedge funds. For less sophisticated investors, the benefits are more obvious in the portfolio management performed by the fund of fund managers.

Requirements for Institutional Success

To appeal to institutional investors, hedge fund management companies should possess some key attributes. The attributes are listed below on the assumptions that hedge fund success is as a result of the fund manager's ability to deliver returns in line with clients' expectations and that managers are of equal skills and are appropriately aligned to financial interests.

1 Business management

The advent of the growing "institutionalisation" of hedge funds requires greater resources and higher professional standards in order for them to succeed. Organisation of these resources and the inculcation of professionalism require a degree of deftness in business management. Strong business acumen is also essential in the larger and more complex hedge fund firms.

2 Culture of integrity

The integrity of a hedge fund firm that is reflected in the high standards for professional conduct throughout the entire firm is high on the list of demands of institutional investors. They require assurance that their advisers are acting in the best interests of their clients at all times.

Hedge fund managers must encourage all members of their staff to maintain impeccably high standards, leaving little room for infringement. Adequate resources must be dedicated to compliance.

3 Operational excellence

Institutions are placing greater importance on hedge firms' business infrastructure, requesting evidence of operational and infrastructure excellence as well as outstanding risk management. They require clarification of hedge fund firms' policies on:

- third-party verification of pricing;
- documented policies and procedures;
- well-designed trading infrastructure that links trade order management, portfolio accounting, and risk management;
- robust disaster recovery;
- outsourcing;
- professional operational leadership, independent of the investment team.

4 Disciplined investment process

It is widely accepted among institutional investors that effective investment management is a blend of art and science. However in order to appeal to institutions, hedge funds must demonstrate how they make clear investment decisions. Hedge funds must ensure that their investment processes are understandable, consistent, risk-aware and perceived to be repeatable. In addition, a clearly defined investment process establishes credibility among buyers and intermediaries. It establishes confidence in the consistent delivery of performance within the agreed-upon risk parameters.

To appeal to institutional investors, it is imperative for hedge funds to articulate the competitive edge they possess in regard to their delivery of alpha in clear and concise manner that is unique and convincing.

5 Investment strategy innovation

Institutions expect hedge fund firms to dedicate resources to constantly evaluate the effectiveness of their investment process, given that hedge fund investment strategies face cyclical and secular trends that impact on their effectiveness. Successful hedge funds will need to enhance their core competence by augmenting their investment capabilities, either through the continual development of new quantitative models or by hiring a new trading desk.

6 Comprehensive risk oversight

Hedge fund managers are expected to have effective risk control in place. Institutions expect them to have a strong handle on all market risk factors to which a portfolio (not just an individual security) is exposed. Proprietary tools are encouraged, while thoughtful application of third-party packages is also satisfactory.

7 Sophisticated client interface

To be successful in the institutional market segment, hedge fund firms will require a broader set of distribution skills in contrast to the historical product-driven approach, whereby clients were only focused on after products had been created and were ready for sale. These skills include:

- dedicated client service;
- quality communications;
- solution resources;
- willingness to provide transparency.

Sophisticated client interaction will provide avenues for raising future funds as well as generate a more stable capital base for existing products.

Investors' Concerns

As investors often regard hedge funds as "Black Boxes", that are risky in nature but offer high potential returns, first-time investors tend to opt primarily for long/short equity strategies whose investment style is similar to that of traditional investment funds.

The chart below shows the distribution of primary concerns about investing in hedge funds.

Figure 4.3 Primary Concerns about investing in Hedge Funds

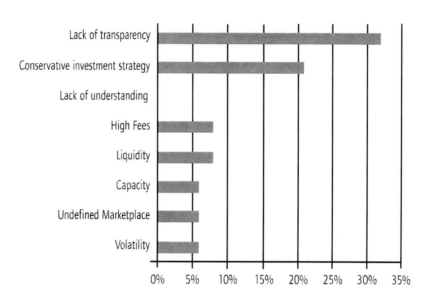

Source: *Barra Strategic Consulting Group – Fund of Hedge Funds market Survey*[31]

Although investors are naturally bound to have concerns about hedge funds, it is researchers that are calling for a more serious look at hedge funds. It has become clear to researchers that hedge funds are more complicated than traditional assets such as common stocks and bonds, and may not be as extraordinarily attractive as hedge fund managers and marketers would like investors to believe. According to Kat (2003), 10 things investors should know about hedge funds are:

- The available data on hedge funds is far from perfect.
- Funds following the same type of strategy may still behave differently.
- Similar indices from different index providers may behave differently.
- The true risk of hedge funds tends to be seriously underestimated.
- Sharpe ratio and alpha of hedge funds can be misleading.
- There are no shortcuts in hedge fund selection.
- Hedge fund diversification is not a free lunch.
- Hedge funds do not combine well with equity.
- Modern portfolio theory is too simplistic to deal with hedge funds.
- At least a 20% investment in hedge funds is required to make a difference.

31 Includes both investors currently investing in hedge funds and those who do not.

In conclusion, it would appear that hedge fund investing requires a much more intricate approach than that which most stock and bond investors are used to. An instinctive decision-making process, as is normally used for stock and bond investing, may lead to nasty surprises.

Trends in the Hedge Fund Industry

This chapter introduces the trends that are shaping the hedge fund industry and its service providers: prime brokers and fund administrators.

Introduction

In the face of changes in the hedge fund industry such as the increase in regulatory demands and the number of industry players, hedge funds, prime brokers and fund administrators have to adapt radically to cope with changes. Furthermore, the industry is growing in leaps and bounds and the growth is underpinned by key trends in the industry.

The following are recent trends that are shaping the hedge fund industry.

UCITS III Regulations[32]

Background
The original UCITS directive (Undertakings for Collective Investment in Transferable Securities) was enacted by the European Union in 1985. Its objective was to enable uniform regulation of retail investment funds across Member States and allow cross-border marketing and distribution of funds throughout the EU.

However, the original UCITS did not fully achieve this goal as constraints in the definition of eligible investments restricted the market potential of UCITS funds. In addition, each Member State created individual rules which created obstacles to cross-border marketing.

A revised set of directives, UCITS III, were enacted in January 2002 and implemented throughout 2007 in two parts.

Management directive
This enabled a "European passport" for investment managers to operate through out the EU and widened the activities which they were allowed to undertake by defining control mechanisms for the protection of retail investors. These included the requirement for a simplified prospectus to be provided to investors.

Product directive
This widened the scope of investment objectives for an UCITS fund, enabling investments in money market instruments, derivatives, index-tracking funds and funds of funds, and allowing asset classes to be mixed in one fund.

Eligible Assets
After a lengthy consultation process, the EC Eligible Assets Directive was agreed in January 2007, based on CESR (Committee of European Securities Regulators) advice. CESR published guidelines concerning the eligible assets allowed for investment by UCITS in March 2007. These were designed to ensure a uniform interpretation of the UCITS directive and include:

32 Contributed by Michael Harimman of Positive View Ltd.

- Article 2   Transferable securities (incl. embedded derivatives)
- Articles 3–7   Money market instruments
- Article 8   Financial derivative instruments
- Article 9   Financial indices
- Article 10   Securities which embed derivatives
- Article 11   Efficient portfolio management
- Article 12   Index replicating UCITS

Derivatives

A significant impact of UCITS III is the ability to use derivatives for investment purposes, i.e. to increase the investment return and enable innovative products, rather than purely for the purpose of hedging, reducing risk and/or costs. This enables UCITS managers to adopt many of the investment characteristics of higher risk, higher return hedge funds including a wider use of over the counter (OTC) and credit derivative instruments.

Credit derivatives are derivatives which transfer the credit risk of an underlying instrument from one party to another without transferring the instrument itself, e.g. credit default swaps.

UCITS III requires that exposure to derivative instruments does not exceed 100% of the net asset value of the overall fund. The interpretation of exposure varies between the regulatory authorities of each Member State. However, the principle of the directive is that a formal risk management process is required which is proportionate to the complexity and the sophistication of derivatives within the fund.

Commitment approach

For a "non-sophisticated" UCITS fund, the derivative exposure can be measured through a "commitment approach", whereby the exposure is calculated from the nominal value of the underlying instrument(s).

Value at risk

A "sophisticated" UCITS fund generally requires Value at Risk (VaR) monitoring supplemented by stress testing and scenario analysis. VaR measures the historical volatility and covariance of a fund's assets and calculates the maximum loss that could be expected in a given period with a given level of confidence (e.g.99%).

EU guidelines do not clearly define a "sophisticated" UCITS, which leads to differences of interpretation between Member States. The general principle implies that more sophisticated investment strategies require sophisticated risk management procedures (i.e. VaR).

Principles-based Regulation

In the UK, UCITS III has been implemented by the FSA within the New Collective Investment Schemes sourcebook (COLL) and all UCITS funds were required to convert to UCITS III by 28 February 2007.

The FSA has pressed for the eligibility of assets within UCITS III funds to be judged on a principles basis as part of its overall drive towards "Principles-based Regulation". The balance of the FSA Handbook and the FSA approach to supervision will rely increasingly on principles and outcome-focused rules rather than detailed rules prescribing how outcomes must be achieved.

This increases the flexibility and the scope for UCITS managers to innovate; however the impact of such regulation is to:

- increase focus on the quality of the investment management decisions;
- impose fewer restrictions on investment instruments, with less prescriptive rules but increased monitoring, fiduciary control and risk management requirements;
- extend the range of instruments and new fund products requiring flexibility of systems and processes to enable timely introduction of new instruments;
- intensify the need for quality and depth of data, which creates pressure on firms to focus on data management;
- expand the number of regulatory guidelines, which will require firms to adapt their business processes and controls.

Implications of UCITS III on Information Technology

Investment firms face an increasing pressure from the culture of compliance across the enterprise and an increased demand for transparency in the investment process to conform to the principles-based regulatory environment introduced with UCITS III.

There are impacts on IT systems across the enterprise including: front office, trading, data management, portfolio valuation, risk management, client reporting, performance measurement and compliance.

Key provisions include the following.

Full instrument coverage

While the focus of automation has traditionally been on purpose-built front-office systems, the increased use of OTC derivatives has initiated a shift in focus towards the automation of alternative assets in the middle and back office.

Valuation and reconciliation

Portfolio accounting systems must be able to ensure a reliable and timely valuation on a daily basis. Processes must be in place to calculate derivative exposure and enable reconciliation of OTC positions.

Investment compliance and risk monitoring

The increasing innovations in the development of new derivative and structured products and the interest of traditional fund managers in these new products and in new strategies such as overwriting strategies and long/short (130/30) funds all contribute to creating a greater investment monitoring compliance challenge.

In respect of derivatives alone, there is a range of monitoring that needs to be performed, including total exposure, global exposure and leverage monitor-

85

ing, look through to the underlying security of a derivative, counterparty exposure, netting and collateralisation monitoring.

The increasing innovations in the development of new derivative and structured products for "sophisticated" UCITS III funds require sophisticated risk processes and controls including VaR monitoring tools with stress testing and scenario analysis support.

For many managers, full demonstration of compliance will only be achievable using advanced investment compliance monitoring systems that can disagregate baskets, indices and structured products and provide exception-based reporting.

Comprehensive data management support

IT systems must have the capability of recording, processing and controlling an expanding range of asset classes with variable data attributes, contractual obligations and processing requirements.

It should be possible to decompose structured products, including asset-backed securities, credit-linked notes and collateralised debt obligations (CDOs), to their constituent components and underlying instruments.

Document management

A direct consequence of the move towards principles-based regulation is the weight regulators place on the fund documentation and internal controls rather than conformance with a prescriptive regulator rule set. Electronic document management solutions reduce operational costs and reduce human error, assisting investment firms to achieve this goal.

Compliance monitoring and incident resolution workflow

Of critical importance in monitoring UCITS III funds is the ability of pre-trade and post-trade compliance monitoring tools to adapt to new asset classes and the variable rules required for principles-based regulation. Integration with a variety of IT solutions is critical. Incident resolution management is required to enable transparency of the monitoring process and regulatory review.

Flexible solutions

The primary challenge facing information technology in supporting UCITS III funds and the new principles-based regulatory environment is the ability to adapt.

The overriding requirement is flexibility in the design and configuration of systems and procedures to adapt to new regulations, guidelines and interpretations.

Potential Product Opportunities for Hedge Funds

While hedge fund managers find the investment restrictions in UCITS III difficult to grapple with, they are continually on the look for potential product opportunities offered by UCITS III. Their success in devising a UCITS III fund depends on the type of investment strategy they adopt and their target investor base.

Given the disintermediation of product creation and ultimate distribution, hedge funds can sell their products to various European banks or institutions who can then potentially distribute them to their retail investors.

With respect to the investment strategy that can be adopted, the fund manager must obey the regulations which lay down investment and borrowing restrictions as well as comply with restrictions regarding investment of no more than 10% of the Net Asset Value in any single security. Since UCITS III, unlike its predecessor UCITS I, permits a broader range of derivatives to leverage the UCITS III fund by up to 100% and for investment purposes, hedge fund managers will be interested in exploiting these benefits.

Introduction of MiFID

What is MiFID?

MiFID is the Markets in Financial Instruments Directive of the European Union.It contains 73 articles, applies to all investment firms in the EU and impacts on all asset classes except currency. MiFID is a directive that will replace the existing Investment Services Directive (ISD), the most significant European Union legislation for investment intermediaries and financial markets since 1995. MiFID is an integral part of the creation of a wider European market with liquidity to compete with the USA.

The introduction of MiFID will promote market transparency and change the shape of sales distribution networks. Investment management firms will have to look at their cost base through a different lens than the one used today.

Stated Aims of the European Union

The main objective of MiFID is to help issuers and investors by opening up markets and cutting the costs of securities trading. For example, investment management firms doing cross-border business will be affected by MiFID as it will simplify and streamline the passporting regime, increasing competition and enabling greater EU financial integration. These effects may act as catalysts for improved market efficiency.

The so-called concentration rule, which allows member states to give preference to regulated markets as distinct from other venues for the execution of securities transactions, will also be abolished in accordance with MiFID. Other aims of MiFID include setting a pan-European best execution obligation, which should enhance investor protection and price formulation, and allowing investment managers to realise the economic value of their trade data.

Impacts on Investment Management Firms

MiFID will impact on the following aspects of the investment management function:

- Order handling and best execution
- Transaction recording and record keeping

- Investor protection
- Pre- and post-trade transparency
- Conflicts of interest
- Outsourcing management
- Risk management
- Compliance
- Data management
- Investor administration
- Client communication

Impacts on Hedge Funds

Hedge fund management firms need to make changes in order to comply with MiFID. Although not intended to affect the organisation or distribution rules for hedge funds, the principal regulator's implementation process in the respective member states will determine the full implication of MiFID. In the case of UK-based hedge fund managers, it is mostly likely to be that of the FSA. It is estimated that managers authorised in the UK manage 15–20% of global hedge fund assets with much of the balance managed in the USA, where estimates are that hedge fund managers based there manage 70% of global hedge fund assets.[33] It is currently unclear whether implementation of MiFID, given its aspiration to build European capital markets, will influence these shares of the market.

It should be noted that most hedge funds are domiciled offshore and usually use service providers such as administrators in other locations. For example, UK-based hedge funds usually use Ireland-based administrators, but this structure will not necessarily be affected by MiFID as it contains rules regarding outsourcing. However, in the structure described above, rather than being a delegate of the UK-based hedge fund manager, the Ireland-based administrator will be a service provider to the Cayman-domiciled hedge funds and hence would be unaffected by these requirements.

Key Changes

The required changes for compliance are both internal and external. Internal changes will be centred on organisational changes while external changes will essentially be in client-facing processes such as client categorisation, client agreements, execution and client order handling.

Internal

One of the foremost internal changes required by hedge fund managers is an independent risk management function, an internal audit function as well as a compliance function which is dependent on the nature, size and complexity of their business. Even where the absence of a separate risk management function is justifiable, MiFID will require the establishment, implementation and maintenance of adequate risk management policies and procedures to identify and manage risks.

33 Source: TASS and FSA.

External

MiFID will introduce a client classification system which divides clients into the following categories: retail professional and eligible counterparty. This will require hedge fund managers to examine their clients against the MiFID criteria and compare them against existing rules. In the UK they compare them with current classifications of "private", "intermediate" and "market counterparties" though definitions may vary significantly. Although not a strict compliance requirement, all clients will have to be informed of their post-MiFID classification.

Sarbanes-Oxley Act of 2002

The Sarbanes-Oxley Act of 2002 (known as SOX) was sponsored by US Senator Paul Sarbanes and US Representative Michael Oxley and it signifies the biggest change to federal securities laws in a long time. Large accounting scandals involving companies such as Enron, WorldCom, and Arthur Andersen, which resulted in billions of dollars of corporate and investor losses, instigated the changes to restore investor trust in the financial markets.

Since 2006, all public companies have been required to submit an annual assessment of the effectiveness of their internal financial auditing controls to the Securities and Exchange Commission (SEC). The types of companies affected include publicly traded companies in the United States, including all wholly owned subsidiaries, and all publicly traded non-US companies doing business in the USA. Also included are private companies that are gearing up for an Initial Price Offering (IPO), which have to comply with certain aspects of the regulations.

There are 11 sections of the Sarbanes-Oxley Act, including sections 302, 401, 404 and 802. Section 404 – management of internal control – requires that financial reports must include an Internal Control Report stating that management is responsible for an "adequate" internal control structure. This is the most difficult section of the Act to comply with.

Non-compliance and submission of inaccurate certification could lead to a fine of $1 million and 10 years' imprisonment, even if committed in error.

Impact on Hedge Funds

In a lightly regulated environment, SOX is shining more of a spotlight on the hedge fund industry than has been the case in the past as it significantly increases the responsibility of managers of hedge fund firms for attesting to the integrity of their company's financial statements. This will increase the internal transparency within their organisation.

Hedge Funds in Emerging Markets[34]

Hedge funds are alive and well in emerging markets and this is good news for all fund managers. Hedge funds have helped emerging markets in a number of

89

ways. First, emerging markets generally benefit from the higher market liquidity created by hedge funds. Also, their ability to make concentrated investments without the diversification requirements of mutual funds and the ability to hedge risky investments emboldens them to enter emerging markets at the early stages. They then drive up liquidity in those markets and attract other investors, thus expanding the overall trading environment and stimulating new company investment research. Fund managers have noticed this in a number of emerging or "frontier" markets. Hedge funds are particularly suited for illiquid, small and volatile emerging markets since they are able to take both long and short positions, can use arbitrage, trade options or bonds, and generally are free to invest in any market or security. More importantly, their high fees provide a nice benchmark for other fund managers. So when a client says fees are too high, these other fund managers can point to those deliciously high hedge fund fees which make their fees cheap in comparison! With those generous fees, it is no surprise that the number of hedge funds has been booming with the latest count being over 8,500. Hedge fund assets under management (AUM) are estimated to be in excess of US$1,000 billion and are growing at about 20% per year.

Are hedge funds an element in emerging markets? Most decidedly yes. In 2006, one survey indicated that there were 81 US hedge funds dedicated to emerging markets and managing an estimated $89 billion. Of course that's only one per cent of all the hedge funds out there and only about 8% of the total hedge fund AUM. But that does not really reflect what is going on since hedge funds that are not dedicated to emerging markets still invest a considerable amount into emerging market stocks, bonds and currencies, not to mention the many emerging market derivatives that are increasingly available. Given the rapid rise of global capital markets buttressed by the spectacular economic growth in emerging markets, we expect that the hedge fund industry will continue to raise its overseas investments and a large part of that will go into emerging markets.

In India, for example, it is estimated that during the last few years, hedge fund flows into India's stock markets reached at least US$2 billion annually. One way to determine hedge fund activity in India is to track the trading of "participatory notes" issued by offshore brokers representing share investments in on-shore India. They tend to be used by hedge funds almost exclusively since the trading in those notes takes place offshore and thus avoids the registration process and other complications. The hedge funds are able to move in and out of stocks quickly and efficiently. One Indian brokerage house has estimated that about 40% to 50% of the overseas money flowing into the Indian market is through participatory notes with most of it coming from hedge funds. The Securities and Exchange Board of India (SEBI) has expressed concern regarding the high turnover and speculative nature of hedge fund activity in the Indian market and thus has tried to restrict the use of participatory notes but when it announced restrictions, the Indian market nose-dived and SEBI had to amend its plan.

34 Contributed by Dr Mark Mobius, Chairman of Templeton Asset Management.

All hedge funds are not created equal. There are many different hedge fund investment styles that can have varying impacts. Theoretically, the main aim of hedge funds is to reduce volatility and risk while attempting to preserve capital and deliver positive returns under all market conditions, but the blow-up of a number of hedge funds in recent years indicates that they do not all achieve those objectives. More importantly, the original meaning of "hedge" has lost its relevance in today's hedge fund world. Many hedge fund investment styles do not embody any type of hedging activity. Some analysts have identified as many as 14 distinct hedge fund investment strategies. "Macro" hedge funds take positions in stocks, bonds or currencies based on their view of global shifts in political and economic developments. "Distressed Securities" hedge funds buy the debt or equity of companies nearing or in bankruptcy. "Relative Value" hedge funds look for price differences of related investments and take advantage of price inefficiencies. In addition to those styles, there are "Aggressive Growth", "Funds of Hedge Funds", "Income", "Market Neutral", "Market Timing", "Opportunistic" and a number of other styles in addition to the specialised "Emerging Markets" hedge funds.

What impact and risks do hedge funds present to emerging markets? Certainly hedge fund activity can result in market disruptions and particular systemic risks. In emerging markets as well as other markets, many hedge funds tend to reject the "buy and hold" strategy but rather move in and out of markets quickly to take advantage of short-term opportunities. Prime brokers to hedge funds are exposed to any problems their client hedge funds may face arising not only from the frequent and large trading activity but also because of the OTC derivative trading which, done on large margin, can be risky and substantial. Banks in emerging markets can also have exposure through collateral and margin arrangements. Hedge funds can also impact the integrity of emerging markets' transactions arising from their use of price-sensitive information since their large leveraged positions can create "events".

The other area of risk is the credit derivative markets and the tendency for a significant backlog of transaction confirmations, which can pile up and clog the system. Then there is the major risk of misvaluation of complex illiquid instruments. The recent US sub-prime crisis has revealed this risk. In emerging markets, when hedge funds establish large and concentrated positions in stocks or bonds, this can result in a sudden and unexpected liquidity contraction when there are a few large players establishing positions. This can lead to significant volatility and have a paralysing impact on the markets. If a hedge fund has adopted a momentum style, the rush to take a certain position by a group of funds, the results can be self-fulfilling and can lead to significant risks when the momentum reverses. Nevertheless, a number of academic studies have not been able to conclusively show that hedge funds increase volatility significantly. Higher liquidity does not necessarily lead to higher volatility.

The 1997 Asian crisis is worth examining with regard to the role of hedge funds. That crisis was precipitated by a massive currency devaluation in Thailand. The so-called "carry trade", a strategy where hedge funds are able to build large leveraged borrowings in a low interest rate currency to then speculate on higher-yielding currencies or even bond or stock investments, has been blamed for the precipitation of that crisis. Such trade transactions can also be executed in forward currency markets by taking long positions in a higher-yielding currency and short positions in a lower-yielding currency. For a number of years prior to the crisis, the Thai central bank had successfully pegged the Thai bait to the US dollar, but on 2 July 1997 the bank was forced to allow the bait to float after foreign lenders decided to unwind their carry trades in Thailand. They sold bhat and bought dollars in the spot market, putting tremendous pressure on the Thai central bank to supply US dollars to support the bait. The bank had the option to supply the dollars on the market to enable the unwinding, thus draining its official US dollar reserves, or it could postpone that by engaging in forward dollar sales with commercial banks in the hope that the bait selling would subside. Since the commercial banks doing the forward transactions with the Thai central bank were faced with being long a lower-yielding currency (the dollar) and short the higher yielding one (the bait) and thus having a negative carry, they agreed with hedge funds to engage in offsetting transactions. Therefore the hedge funds accumulated forward positions over a short period of time estimated at a massive $5 billion. The Thai central bank basically bet that the pressure on the bait would subside and it then would be able to close out the forward transaction. Although the hedge funds had a negative carry position, they were betting to make a profit in the event of a large bait devaluation. When it was rumoured that the central bank had sold all of its foreign reserves forward, the currency speculators made massive bets against the bait by selling that currency aggressively. Finally the central bank could not continue the defence and the institutions holding the forward positions realised large profits.

This put pressure on other managed Asian currencies including the Malaysian ringgit, the Indonesian rupiah, the Philippine peso and the Korean won. Those currencies all crashed and devalued by between 40% and 60% against the US dollar. Since a number of Asian corporations had massive US$ borrowings, many went bankrupt when their US$ debts exploded in local currency terms. A number of Asian government officials blamed the crisis on hedge funds and currency speculators who, they said, attacked their currencies by making massive leveraged short positions.

Did hedge funds cause the crisis? One view is that they did not since they were only able to accumulate their forward positions because the central banks were entering in forward interventions. The International Monetary Fund (IMF) studied the crisis and identified a number of potential causes of the large market disruptions. They found that a trader holding a single large position could precipitate such a crisis. "Positive feedback" trading strategies, where positions were added as the market moved in favour of the existing positions, had an impact. This was related to "herding" by traders who followed other traders in a lemming-like movement. Surprisingly, the IMF professionals concluded that hedge funds did not play a central role in causing the crisis. But that conclusion has been disputed by others.

In conclusion, hedge funds will continue to be important players in the emerging markets. Their presence will continue to be felt not only in the currency markets but also in fixed-income and equity markets. As regulations requiring greater transparency are introduced, their role will be better understood and welcomed.

Growth of Credit Derivatives Market

Investors have traditionally been fascinated by the latest inventions in the world of high finance. If there is an asset class that is rapidly increasing in size they often like to be exposed to it. Credit derivatives fall into this category. As a result of its elegant simplicity, it is highly regarded as one of the most powerful tools in modern finance. Half-yearly credit derivatives data released by ISDA says that credit derivatives volumes, as of end of June 2007, have gone beyond $45.46 trillion. This scales a growth of 32% from the $34 trillion data as of end of 2006, and nearly 75% growth over the half year of 2006.[35]

Credit derivatives were mentioned briefly elsewhere in this book, but are explained further below.

What are Credit Derivatives?
Credit derivatives, and more specifically, credit default swaps, are financial contracts that allow two or more parties to effectively "swap" default risk. A lot like insurance contracts, an investor will be paid a premium for taking the default risk of a particular company. For example, an investor might be willing to take the risk that a fictional company BizGlobal files for bankruptcy sometime over the next five years – they effectively "sell" protection to another party in exchange for periodic "premium" payments. In exchange for taking the risk of a BizGlobal default, the "seller" of default protection agrees to reimburse the "buyers" of protection for any losses should BizGlobal file for bankruptcy.

What are the benefits of Credit Derivatives?
Quite simply, credit derivatives help companies manage credit risk more effectively: whether it is traditional investors taking a view on credit or companies concerned about concentrated exposures to key customers. By making it easier to transfer risk, most industry experts believe that credit derivatives have had a beneficial effect on the integrity of the global financial system.

Credit derivatives are naturally flexible and transparent, and those that have an understanding of how to use these instruments can use them to spread risk efficiently.

Users of credit derivatives have become more diverse. The key players in the credit derivative market have been banks and brokerage firms and insurance companies. The dominance of this group, however, is in decline. Hedge funds are increasingly a major player, while traditional credit investors are increasingly utilising credit derivatives as an alternative means of risk.

35 Source: Fitch, 2007 (5 June). Hedge Funds: The Credit Market's New Paradigm. Special report on the role of hedge funds in the credit market.

In terms of products, single-name credit default swaps are the most popular product in the market, though the use of credit derivative indices is growing.

Credit derivatives have been growing at an annual rate of nearly 100% since 2003. This statistic was valid until the tremendous credit squeeze that started in the wake of the subprime crisis that are likely to affect their growth. There are several reasons for this – hedge funds who became primary players in credit derivatives in 2004 onwards are likely to stage a retreat or at least slow their activity in the near future. CDO activity in general is likely to be moribund for the foreseeable future as the market becomes increasingly risk averse.

One of the foremost ratings agencies recently came up with a special report on the role of hedge funds in the credit market. The report contains information that only those with an insight into the credit derivatives market will surely know and could be shocking to those that don't. According to the report, the credit derivatives market is not where banks meet to swap each other's risks. It is fast becoming an arena for risk-takers who take leveraged positions on credit risks. Hedge funds occupy nearly 60% of this market today.

Industry experts have also opined that apart from sheer volume of trade, the impact of hedge funds on the credit markets cannot be measured simply by trading volumes, but also must contain hedge funds' willingness to be risk takers by investing lower in the capital structure. By investing in instruments that are themselves leveraged, hedge funds are able to create a multiplier effect by combining financial leverage with so-called economic leverage. The combination of the two can be regarded as the effective leverage.

It is increasingly evident that hedge funds, in search for high returns, take subordinated positions in pools of credit. Apart from that, they are major players in the equity tranches of the indices.

The highly leveraged positions taken by hedge funds could have consequences for the credit markets similar to the highly correlated moves by several hedge funds trying to unwind their positions due to their mandates or deleverage triggers that led to sharp mark-to-market losses as a result of downgrades for Ford and MGM in May 2005. Credit assets could behave in a more correlated, synchronous fashion if one or a number of hedge funds were focused to liquidate positions following some catalyst events in the markets. Investor redemptions and/or increased margin calls from prime brokers' banks could exacerbate a larger unwind of credit assets as hedge funds are more unstable investors than buy and hold investors of relationship banks.

Besides, hedge funds are typically short-term strategy based. Many of them have short horizons within which they either perform or wind up. While hedge funds have continued to improve their risk management abilities, there is no way they can eliminate risk, and the next downturn in business cycle may really bring forth this critical situation.

Growth of Prime Brokerage[36]

Prime brokerage was once an unloved function in the investment banking world. Not so long ago, prime brokers were virtually anonymous and were barely notice able in the City and Wall Street. However in recent times, the proliferation of hedge funds and the business of servicing them have elevated the prime brokerage division of big investment banks to the upper echelons of the business divisions.

The prime broking function is now seen as a highly profitable business and increasingly as a main route to selling other services to hedge funds, which have in recent times been thrust into the mainstream of the financial services industry and have become one of the most important clients of investment banks.

Growth of the prime brokerage industry appeared to be underpinned by the rising number of "start-up" hedge funds. The hedge fund industry is full of stories of ex-traders in investment banks with few financial resources and a viable business plan managing funds in excess of $1bn less than 10 years later.

Initially these budding hedge funds were reliant on a single prime broker for all the services they required as they lacked the expertise of running a business despite their dexterity at managing money.

Prime brokers offered services including consultancy, technology and office space and subsequently acted as the agents for hedge funds, dealing with the various counterparties such as lawyers, accountants and administrators, creating in the process the concept of turn-key services.

Clearly this was advantageous to prime brokers. There are opportunities that come with getting involved in the growth phase of a hedge fund's lifecycle as rewards can be reaped when the company becomes a fully fledged multimillion pound fund. This guarantees a certain degree of loyalty amid stiff competition from other prime brokers.

Expansion of turn-key service offerings naturally followed as more hedge funds were launched. Other services offered included finding IT hardware and personnel and even more unusual services such as finding accommodation for hedge fund managers and suitable schools for their children.

However, nowadays these turn-key services are becoming uncommon as firms deviate from the "one-stop shop" model to become more of a consulting service. This is due to the fact that prime brokers are becoming discerning about the funds they service in the wake of increasing scrutiny from regulators who are increasingly apprehensive about the damage that the collapse of a big hedge fund could cause, having damaging implications for the wider financial system. According to industry experts, the US and UK regulators are keen to use the prime brokers to gain an insight into the activities of the secretive hedge funds.

The prime brokerage business was once dominated by a handful of players, notably Morgan Stanley and Goldman Sachs, but recently competition has

36 Prime brokerage is discussed further in "Business Knowledge for IT in Prime Brokerage".

Figure 5.1 Largest Global Prime Brokers

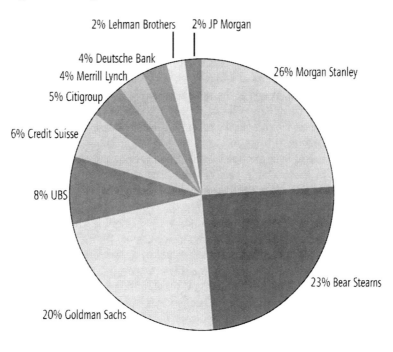

Source: Institutional Investor

intensified as new entrants have entered the market in order to grab a market share. Figure 5.1 shows the distribution of clients' assets amongst the largest global prime brokers in 2006.

Industry experts have likened the prime brokerage sector to "the financial equivalent of providing picks and shovels to those mining the world's markets for hidden gems and a scene for an ultra-competitive land war". The who's-who in the banking world, including UBS, Deutsche Bank, Citigroup, JP Morgan and Bank of America, all want a slice of the proverbial pie.

Some other experts are of the opinion that technology-induced collapses of margins for traditional institutional equity broking, where commission levels have crashed by almost 25% annually in recent times, have been one of the drivers for this trend.

Prime brokers expect to generate sizable revenue from the high margins available on lending both money and stock to hedge funds in addition to trading revenues. Celent, a Boston consulting firm, estimates prime brokerage revenue will hit $8,500bn in 2007.

Hedge Fund Cloning

Hedge fund clones are a relatively new type of investment product that is being offered in the global financial centres such as Wall Street and the City of London. The rationale behind creating these types of funds is to attempt to clone or replicate the investment strategies of hedge funds with a view to generating returns on a par with hedge funds and at the same time minimise fees and reduce "lock-up" periods for the client base. Fees, at around 1%, are well below those of traditional hedge funds, which typically collect a 2% asset-backed fee and a 20% performance-based fee.[37]

Industry experts are of the opinion that these hedge fund clones are a natural evolution in the market; a kind of index fund targeted at high net-worth individuals. Some attempt to track the indexes of hedge funds while others have more complex formulas.[38]

One of the drivers for growth of the hedge fund clones is the acknowledgment that a large part of hedge fund returns comes not from alpha, but from "alternative beta" factors – systematic exposures to a diverse array of risk premia including credit risk, volatility risk, the small company effect and so on. One of the key implications of "alternative beta" theory is that it is possible to replicate the alternative beta exposures of hedge funds

Nevertheless, the most common approach for creating hedge fund clones is the "factor model approach". This involves analysing historical hedge fund returns over a period of time based on data from hedge fund indexes. These returns are reverse-engineered using complex mathematical models with the aim of creating a portfolio of securities that delivers returns equivalent to hedge funds over the same period.

A crop of industry watchers are yet to be convinced about the claims of hedge fund-like returns made by some of the firms that have recently launched these clones. The argument is that while the factor model is based on historical hedge fund performance, hedge funds are continually adjusting their portfolios. Others believe that only a fraction of the returns delivered by hedge funds can be achieved by these clones as hedge funds are difficult to mimic given that their holdings are of unconventional, hard-to-trade securities not accessible to clones.

A host of notable financial services firms have launched hedge fund clones recently. These firms include Goldman Sachs, State Street Global, Merrill Lynch, Morgan Chase, and Deutsche Bank.

It should be noted that these recent developments mirror those which took place in the traditional fund management industry some 20 years ago when indexed tracker funds were introduced. The initial take-up was slow, but in time these mechanistic funds, with their lower fees, gained a significant market

37 Source: Hedge Fund "Clones" by Eleanor Laise. The Wall Street Journal as accessed on 19/10/2007.
38 Ibid.

Figure 5.2 Number of Funds of Hedge Funds

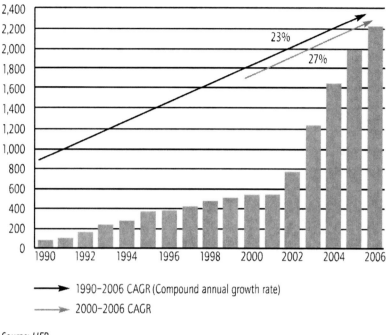

1990–2006 CAGR (Compound annual growth rate)

2000–2006 CAGR

Source: HFR.

share. The popularity of hedge fund clones is likely to soar in the near future if only for the transparency they offer, which is in direct contrast to the secretive nature of hedge funds.

Growth of Funds of Hedge Funds

The fund of hedge funds industry has grown dramatically in recent years, controlling US$624 billion in assets at the end of 2006. This growth has been driven by the sheer number and diversity of individual hedge funds, coupled with the complication of hedge fund portfolio management.

Two major trends are responsible for the growth of the fund of hedge funds industry. The first is the interest of institutional investors in hedge fund investments. The total quantity of institutional assets in hedge funds is rising, as is the number of institutions making investments. The second is the general public's tremendous interest in hedge fund investments, given its frenzied growth. This interest has led traditional asset managers to offer hedge fund products, and hedge fund managers to partner with traditional financial distribution channels to access individual assets.

Another reason for the strong demand for funds of hedge funds is that in spite of the vast number of funds in the hedge fund universe, few investors have the extensive resource capabilities to research the market, let alone the experience and expertise to determine the optimum blend of strategies and managers that will provide the best risk-return profile. While basic due diligence on long-only funds is possible from information in the public domain, this is not an option with less regulated hedge funds where information is much more difficult to obtain.

Multi-strategy funds of hedge funds are currently the most popular with investors as some multi-strategy funds of funds have vast numbers of underlying hedge funds and cover all available strategies across the hedge fund universe. These funds make allocations by strategy, then by sub-strategy and manager.

However, more sophisticated hedge fund buyers, such as private banks and family offices, are increasingly carrying out their own research and due diligence and devising their own investment processes. These investors may buy more specialist funds of hedge funds, such as arbitrage or macro funds, often from different providers, but still prefer a fund of funds approach that diversifies the risks associated with single-manager funds. As with a multi-strategy fund, the performance of a single strategy fund of hedge funds depends on blending managers with different styles and approaches.

The following are also some of the endogenous factors shaping and being shaped by the growth trend.

- **Fund size** – There has been a marked increase in the number of smaller-sized funds (<US$100 million), whose share of the total number of funds rose by 10% points to 55% as of the end of 2006. This indicates a general lowering of the size barrier, among other things, to new entrants into the market.[39]
- **Strategic mandate** – the majority of global funds of hedge funds tend to allocate to multiple hedge fund strategies with 75% of the industry assets in multi-strategy funds. Multi-strategy allocations form only about a fifth of the total fund of fund assets, while equity long/short is the most popular with over one-third of industry assets in this category.
- **Geographic mandate** – the performances of hedge funds of funds by investment region suggest superior returns and increasing asset flows towards emerging markets-focused funds. Returns in these funds have indeed steadily gone up over the period from 2001 to 2006, with 2006 returns breaching the 20% mark. Fund allocations to Europe have similarly been positively impacted by bullish emerging markets in Russia and Eastern Europe.
- **Manager location** – the USA and UK are the key centres of fund of hedge funds management activity together with Switzerland, France, offshore financial centres such as the Cayman Islands and Bermuda, accounting for 90% of industry assets in 2006.

39 Baddepudi, R. (2007). Key Trends in Hedge Fund of Funds. EurekaHedge.

Figure 5.3 Asset Management Breakdown by Manager Location

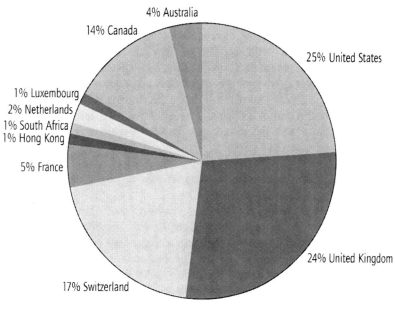

Source: EurekaHedge

The continued significance of these locations for fund of hedge funds managers can be explained by the fact that the choice of manager location is a function of both investor location as well as hedge fund location.

The outlook for the global hedge fund of funds in terms of performance and growth looks positive for the foreseeable future despite their higher cost to investors than those of hedge funds and long-only funds. The high cost base is, however, offset by the steadier risk-adjusted returns.

Evolution of Islamic Hedge Funds

A growing number of hedge funds are looking to attract the excess liquidity in the Middle East banking system as Islamic investors are looking for alternative means to make their money work for them. The market for Islamic finance is already worth about US$230 billion and is expected to grow consistently at the rate of 10–15% over a 10–15 year period in the near future.[40] The poor equities market performance coupled with the repatriation of funds from post 9/11 has led to an explosion in the demand for Islamic fund products. With Islamic

40 Source: www.islamica-me.com

equity investments growing at an unprecedented level, the days of Islamic hedge funds, according to industry experts, are not far off.

While the market for Islamic hedge funds has shown promise, it is yet to reach critical mass due in part to the difficulties in putting an Islamic hedge fund together. As stated in previous chapters, the strategic aim of a hedge fund is to actively manage a portfolio of assets, mostly listed stocks. However in most cases, the goal is to adopt an absolute return strategy with a view to earning profits independent of whether the market goes up or down.

An example that can be used to illustrate this strategy, without reference to the stock market, is that of a wholesale trader of grains expecting a rise in the price of corn but a fall in the price of rice. The following are two options at their disposal to profit from this scenario:

1. Increasing their stock of corn to gain advantage by buying more and reducing their stock of rice to a minimum ("long only");
2. Buying corn and selling rice with future delivery (Islamic term: "Salam" conventional term: "short") against full payment today. The wholesaler's perspective on the market is such that they take a bearish view on rice and a bullish view on corn. Their position can be described as being market neutral with respect to the general trend of the grains market if they buy a value of corn and sell the equivalent value in rice. If the general trend goes up, they win on the corn; if the market goes down; they win on the rice but lose on corn.

This investment strategy adopted by the wholesale trader of grains is analogous to the long/short equity strategy popular with many of the hedge funds. Instead of selling grains like the trade in the example, hedge fund managers invest in the stock markets and use a technique called a short sale, which is essentially a forward contract.[41] While Shari'a Law permits a grains trader to package their investment as they do in the example, conventional hedge funds are not afforded that type of luxury. This is because of the lack of social and ethical screening criteria, the method of leveraging and the way hedge funds benefit from the downside of price development.

There are a number of Shari'a compliance issues that would, at first glance, make Islamic finance and hedge funds irreconcilable. Shari'a screening criteria include a number of industry exclusions (alcohol, pork, gambling etc.) and adherence to certain ratios to identify Riba[42] income and shun activities that could be deemed speculative, involve uncertainty or entail the payment of interest. Furthermore, the transactions must be asset backed.

Hedge fund managers can, however, overcome these obstacles when replicating some of the conventional hedge fund strategies by employing some of

41 A cash market transaction in which delivery of the commodity is deferred until after the contract has been made. Although the delivery is made in the future, the price is determined on the initial trade date.
42 Excessive and exploitative charging of interest, forbidden by the Koran.

the already accepted concepts in Islamic finance. For example, short selling could be replicated by the use of salaam contracts, short-term agreements for financial institutions to make full prepayment for an asset prior to delivery. The sale price may incorporate the time value of money but, unlike a conventional short sale in which the borrowing and the sale are two distinct transactions, there is no borrowing of the stock, which means the dividend has to be estimated and factored into one price paid upfront.

While there are methods, such as that described above, which circumvent the Shari'a laws, there is the issue of the controversial nature of hedge funds. There have been high-profile failures like the LTCM, Quantum Fund and Amaranth which went bust with losses of about $6 billion. Nevertheless, not all hedge funds have performed badly; in fact many funds reportedly outperform conventional long-only mutual funds.

Algo Al-Qayyim Fund, Swiss-Asia Mashriq Alternative Fund (Japan and Asia Focus) and Gabelli Merger Arbitrage Fund (based on Shariah Capital's platform) are some of the Islamic hedge funds that are either active or have been announced. Barclays Capital is one of the few well-known financial services companies that have recently announced the imminent launch of a hedge fund that is compliant with Islamic law.

Popularity of Energy and Environmental Hedge Funds

Energy and environmental hedge funds are gaining traction in the industry as the environment and all things "green" are getting increasingly popular with investors. Energy-related environmental investment opportunities present a number of global opportunities in areas such as emissions, carbon finance, clean technology and renewable energy. The sustained higher and more volatile energy prices in recent years have attracted the attention of investors who have hitherto been hesitant to invest in the energy sector.

Investors are always on the lookout for superior returns and have been turning to the energy market space in droves. Whilst energy is a risky business, it is the world's largest business with over $4 trillion in annual trade, and in terms of financial maturation is only behind agriculture, the world's second largest business. Another factor in favour of energy is that commodities in general trade 6 to 20 times the physical market,[43] lending credence to the argument behind market maturation.

There are a number of strategies adopted by hedge funds for targeting energy and environmental markets. Equity long/short funds, whilst mostly undistinguished, target specific industry sectors such as utilities, exploration and production, and oilfield services to name a few. Some funds have a focus on the public-traded securities; others will invest more speculatively in pre-IPO compa-

43 Source: Fusaro, P and Vasey, G. (2005). Energy Hedge Funds: It's all about risk/reward.

nies and/or those traded on less liquid markets such as the Alternative Investment Market (AIM) in London.

According to Fusaro and Vasey (2005), in addition to the above, many hedge funds are utilising the various exchange traded funds (ETFs) available in energy for hedging purposes, including energy commodity focused ETFs. Others have taken direct exposure to energy commodities via a percentage of assets under management invested in commodity futures and options. On the energy environmental side, green equity long/short equity funds have similar differentiated strategies, targeting renewable energy, clean technology and alternative energy equities.

They also stated that the same diversity of strategies exists in the energy commodity trading fund universe. Some funds focus on natural resources, investing in a basket of broader commodities, while others are more focused on a particular energy commodity or geographic market – for example electric power in the mature NoodPool power market in Scandinavia where around 10 or so hedge funds exist.

In recent times, the number of energy hedge funds has exceeded 500 or around 5% of the entire hedge fund universe. This is about a 400% increase given that there were only about 100 in 2003, which goes to show that energy as an investment opportunity is incredible. In addition, there has been extraordinary growth in energy-specific funds, i.e. those funds that focus exclusively on energy, and the most recent activity seems to be in Europe, especially in the UK and France.[44]

It is evident that the number of energy funds will increase at a rapid rate. Even with energy prices and activity levels remaining high, it is unquestionable that the growth rate will continue. However, what seem questionable are the consequences of a sharp fall in price.

130/30 Strategies in Hedge Funds

The demand for 130/30 funds in the hedge fund industry is set to grow in the coming years as hedge funds try to get into this space. Current estimates put the industry in the $50 billion–$60 billion region and expectations of significant growth are high. The increasing popularity of these investment strategies and the threat they pose to hedge funds have led industry experts to dub them "hedge fund lite" or a natural extension of the hedge fund strategies. These funds provide general exposure to hedge-fund-like investing strategies but with lower fees and often under the umbrella of large, well-known financial services companies. They are being touted as the optimal investment solution that is grounded in efficiency without increasing risk.

103

Figure 5.4 An example of equity long-short strategy with 30% short position

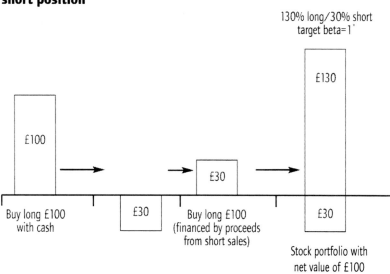

* Beta=1 products have primary risk coming from market exposure not from active risk or the stock selection around the benchmark

What is a 130/30 Fund?

A 130/30 fund is considered a long-short equity[45] fund, meaning it goes both long and short at the same time. The "130" portion stands for 130% exposure to its long portfolio and the "30" portion stands for 30% exposure to its short portfolio. Although leveraged, the strategy for these funds' net market exposure – the value of the longs less the value of the shorts – closely approximates the initial investment. For example, a strategy that allows 30% short positions would hold about £130 of stock long and £30 of stock short for each £100 invested. See Figure 5.4.

130/30 funds have been compared and contrasted with long-only funds. Industry experts see similarities between the two to the extent that they build a portfolio as normal, allocating 100% net asset value to long positions. They attribute differences to the extent that they then sell securities to the value of 30% of net asset value.

Another area where 130/30 funds differ from long-only funds is the fee structure. According to industry experts, a recent Merrill Lynch report indicated

45 When a hedge fund buys long, it means it is betting on stocks that it expects to appreciate or go up in price (this is a typical investment). When it shorts stocks, it means it is betting on stocks it expects to decline (this is done by borrowing stocks now and buying them back later).

that fees charged by 130/30 funds are higher than those normally charged by long-only funds. Where a typical US long-only manager will charge 30–50 basis points management fee, a 130/30 can typically charge 60–100 basis points. However, there is no evidence to suggest, that despite the relatively higher fees charged by fundamental 130/30 managers, their performance fees can match those charged by hedge fund managers.

In Europe, it is expected there will a be continent-wide investor base since funds established under UCITS III rules are afforded the opportunity to go short thus creating an opportunity for investment managers to invent more creative products.

In general it appears that 130/30 funds are largely running quantitative strategies and industry experts estimate that as many as 80% of these assets are in quant strategies.

One other key aspect of the proliferation of 130/30 funds to be considered is the number of entities that will benefit from this development. If these products realise their potential, prime brokers and hedge fund administrators will be some of the major beneficiaries. Prime brokers are well placed to benefit with regard to the scale of the operations that will accompany growth of the market while fund administrators will be the best positioned to value these funds.

Given these characteristics of the 130/30 strategy of investing, it remains to be seen if the funds could be a substitute for hedge funds. One thing is for sure, there may be problems for hedge funds with regard to the consequent increase in demand for margins and stock borrowing, and the rising cost and shorting of stocks may encourage some hedge funds to use exchange-traded funds, rather than individual stocks, to hedge their portfolios.

Hedge Fund in Parallel with a Traditional Fund

One of the most popular trends in recent times in the traditional asset management industry is the launching of a parallel hedge fund to take advantage of the investing talent they already have and to secure higher margins on their assets. Ironically, the world's larger hedge funds are also making a push into traditional asset management to diversify their customer base. This trend toward the convergence of hedge funds and traditional asset management is tagged "Hedge Funds as Asset Management Complexes".

While the model has reaped financial rewards, running hedge funds in parallel with traditional funds presents many challenges.

The primary challenges are managing the different styles of investing required and creating a structure that does not conflict with the existing business.

From a bigger picture perspective, the convergence of traditional asset management strategies and hedge fund strategies, particularly in institutional management, is an issue that needs to be addressed when pursuing this strategy.

For example, a 130/30 strategy can be offered to investors by a big traditional asset manager like, say, a fictional firm BizStreet and by a fictional hedge fund BizPartners. This convergence implies that for some big institutional managers, managing hedge fund money is not dissimilar to what they already do.

According to the Financial Times, the term "unconstrained investing" is being used to describe true hedge funds, in part to distinguish them from more general institutional strategies. Quantitative managers, who are a relatively new crop of sophisticated investors who base their investment decisions on complex algorithms that often use derivatives and synthetics,[46] exemplify this convergence.

They adopt an underlying strategy with the intention of separating beta[47] from alpha.[48] This investment style allows for short selling of stocks and well as selling stocks long and is amenable to using a full range of financial instruments. These styles are usually associated with hedge fund investing.

However, conventional managers may have difficulty with the shift in investing mindset as their business is modelled on a single manager selecting stocks on the basis of his or her view of a company.

Whilst long-only mutual funds assume that shorting stocks will be relatively easy given that research material is already at their disposal and that they are sufficiently knowledgeable about the stocks that are likely to perform badly, industry experts dismiss their presumption as being theoretical. This is because in practice it so happens that the skills required are markedly different and a number of mutual fund managers that made the transition to long/short investing got badly burned. In addition, quantitative investing, another common hedge fund strategy increasingly used in the long-only fund world, requires a sizable investment in technology and infrastructure for it to be effective.

One other issue to be considered is remuneration conflicts for the traditional managers moving into the hedge fund space. First, institutional investors may be uncomfortable with offerings from a company using two different fee structures sometimes for strategies that do not appear that different. This is because conventional management of an equities portfolio, for instance, will cost a big investor less than 50 basis points (about 0.5% a year). This "conventional management" is increasingly making use of sophisticated strategies similar to those offered by hedge funds, yet still demands modest fees.

As mentioned in Chapter 1, hedge funds normally charge a flat fee of 2% a year and 20% performance fee. This also poses a problem for asset managers as to how they will separate the hedge fund offerings and defend the higher fee, if they move into hedge funds.

It has been noticeable in the industry, however, that some top-notch mutual funds have consistently produced returns in line with average hedge fund returns but without the risk and also with the daily liquidity that mutual funds offer and not paid the way hedge fund managers are.

---

46 A synthetic in this context means a financial instrument that is created artificially by simulating another instrument with the combined features of a collection of other assets.
47 Market returns.
48 The excess return of the fund relative to the return of the benchmark index.

According to the *Financial Times*, Franklin Resources, one of the world's biggest fund managers – which trades as Franklin Templeton – is one firm that has found a way to manage these conflicts as it plans to increase its alternative assets (that is the hedge funds, private equity and property) and set them up as a separately run, independent division to avoid the appearance of conflicts.

Unsurprisingly, hedge funds offering more constrained institutional products feel the same conflict in reverse. To the disbelief of industry watchers, one of the most successful hedge fund groups recently launched an institutional fund and charged much less than their widely published 40% performance fee.

Hedge Funds Trading in Weather Derivatives

While weather-dependent businesses and farmers are traditional users of weather derivatives, hedge funds are the biggest drivers of growth. The increased competition in the hedge fund industry and lacklustre performance seen in some of the strategies in recent times have made more and more hedge funds look for alternative strategies and sources of revenue, hence their interest in weather derivatives.

The need for energy companies to hedge the impact of much warmer or colder weather than normal is partly the reason for the birth of the weather derivatives market. According to Haglund (2006), *"In the time of the regulated energy market, the energy companies were often allowed to adjust the price towards the consumer as a result of unusual weather. When the market was deregulated, this adjustment of tariffs was no longer available and the price is now set in the open market and therefore the weather has to be hedged by other means."*

Nevertheless, hedge fund managers have been attracted to the weather derivatives market as it has many of the characteristics they are looking for. The market is far less efficient than the traditional markets, such as equities or bonds, where hedge funds are generally active. Lack of liquidity, endemic in new markets, has been an issue in the weather market but is changing rapidly. This is comparable to the market for credit derivatives which initially was relatively illiquid. The credit area is now an integrated part of many hedge fund strategies. Similarly, weather derivatives will generate arbitrage and trading opportunities from the price discrepancies in weather products for hedge funds.

The impact and correlation of weather derivatives with a number of other regularly traded assets such as retail and energy stocks, different soft commodities and a number of new products, for example trading in emission rights, is an area of special interest to hedge funds. Cross-market trading the weather risk in these products as well as intra-market trading based on e.g. the correlation, will offer plenty of very interesting trading strategies and opportunities for hedge funds in the coming years.

The following are some of the trading strategies involving weather derivatives that can be applied by hedge funds:

▦ **Directional trading** – this type of trading involves establishing a long or short position in a weather-related product based upon a meteorological model or forecast.

▦ **Correlation trading and relative value arbitrage** – A correlation trading strategy is based upon the correlation between two entities, e.g. the temperature between two weather stations in the same area.

▦ **Cross market trading** – Weather derivatives can be used as a tool to isolate weather risk impacting other markets such as commodities and equities. Hedge fund managers can structure arbitrage strategies to exploit mispricing of weather risk in a commodity relative to the weather risk reflected in the weather derivatives market.

Hedge fund managers also arbitrage temperature indexes, located at airports for instance, against prices of everything from soybeans to oil and gas. They play temperature versus commodities as weather derivatives rise and fall more slowly than commodity prices so there is an opportunity for arbitrage. For example, a hedge fund could buy (or go long) protection on an index of rainfall, and sell (or go short) a commodity at the same time.

As the market for weather derivatives grows, there will be plenty of new and interesting trading opportunities for hedge funds and with improved liquidity the number of potential strategies will increase dramatically. In addition, the characteristics of weather as an underlying asset, e.g. on an aggregated basis uncorrelated to traditional assets, mean reverting and highly volatile, are also increasing the allure of these products. The combination of traditional markets for hedge funds, such as equities and commodities, with the use of weather derivatives that can enhance performance and simultaneously lower risk, is also a compelling reason for hedge funds managers to trade in weather derivatives.

Continued Evolution of Fund Administrators

With the relentless proliferation of hedge funds and the spotlight on talented fund managers and the investors sponsoring them, fund administrators have risen to the occasion by assuming a more integral role in the investment process.

The main reason for this development is the increased focus on the integrity of the operational infrastructure of funds, resulting in a search for an added-value fund administration service that meets their needs. Fund administrators see this as the opportunity to create a service offering that is integral to a hedge fund's investment process.

The hedge fund industry has historically lacked serious interest in the fund administration side of the business. The absence of any meaningful due diligence process meant the selection of a fund administrator was based on references from associates or advisers to the fund. It was not until recently that the importance of the administrative side of the business took on significance.

In light of the more structured due diligence exercises that hedge funds perform to select a suitable fund administrator, the following are some of the considerations:

- **Alignment of administrator to hedge fund investment philosophy** – The fund administrator should have a detailed understanding of the hedge fund manager's investment philosophy. It is equally important that there is the right chemistry between participants as each hedge fund is different, and the relationship forms a critical part of the day-to-day interaction between manager and administrator.
- **Experience and knowledge** – The administrator's experience with the types of security that the fund intends to trade should be demonstrable. Client references of funds with similar strategies should be made available. The staff employed to work on a fund should be sufficiently qualified to understand the different types of structure that a fund employs and how to implement them from an accounting, corporate and investor perspective.
- **Technological edge** – Given the high expectations these days for timely reporting and transparency, the trend in the industry is leaning towards enhanced reporting capabilities. Administrators will be required to demonstrate a commitment to technological capabilities evident in integrated systems featuring real-time automated processing and reconciliations, the use of independent pricing services, and reporting capabilities with multiple features, such as multi-currency and multi-security functionality. The administrator should be able to demonstrate the use of the systems by relevant staff, together with the available output in order provide an estimate of their capabilities.
- **Location** – With regard to location, one of the most important characteristics that a fund administrator should demonstrate is local knowledge (of a domiciliary, tax or regulatory nature) and willingness to respond proactively. Another important characteristic is the ability to communicate effectively with the main players in a fund, regardless of time differences, proximity or even language differences.

Recent trends in fund administration
There are a number of trends shaping the future of the fund administrator industry and are determinants of its continued evolution. These trends also outline some the challenges that will be faced as the industry matures further.

- **The growth in the hedge fund industry** – The challenges posed by the explosive growth of the hedge fund industry and the increasing number of new entrants will undoubtedly put pressure on the infrastructure of fund administrators to cope with the additional volume of work. In addition, as hedge funds increase in size they will be looking to focus on their core competency, i.e. money management, and outsource non-core aspects of the business that are not differentiating factors or do not provide a competitive edge.

109

- **Straight-through processing** – As part of the evolutionary process for fund administrators, they now assume the role of a back office as opposed to being just a service provider. The role entails calculation of daily P&L numbers and net asset values (NAV). Where systems are built to track a hedge fund manager's activities straight through to back-end accounting systems, the administrator will learn to track the results of the fund seamlessly. Pressure for this service comes from both the managers who prefer to outsource this work and the investors who crave the information that gives them a more interactive role. The challenge to the successful implementation of these processes comes from the very nature of the hedge fund product which is still varied and unique its application.
- **Web-enabled reporting** – Advances in technology makes the internet the ideal delivery medium for critical information. Hedge fund managers and investors are receiving reports via secure-access websites with the appropriate level of security.
- **Multiple prime broker relationships** – With the single prime brokerage relationship of hedge funds becoming overstretched as the bigger funds are seeking to execute trades in multiple securities in numerous markets, many hedge funds are now settling on two or three prime brokers. In addition, the competition offered by best execution and the concept of counterparty risk lends credence to the multiple prime brokerage relationship.

Despite the primary fiduciary duties of the administrator to a fund's investors and the additional specialist knowledge that is gleaned from complex securities and structures, administrators have to differentiate themselves with value-added services by wearing many hats to survive and succeed.

How a Hedge Fund Business is Built

This chapter introduces the requirements for starting a hedge fund business including the marketing, taxation and regulatory requirements.

Introduction

The remuneration of hedge fund managers is one of the most discussed topics in recent times. On the face of it, it appears that anyone with the right mix of start-up capital, talent, entrepreneurial drive and courage can set up a hedge fund. Hence, it could be assumed that every trader in the global investment banks and every money manager in global asset management firms could potentially be at the helm of their own hedge fund, managing vast sums of money and competing toe-to-toe with the world's top traders.

That said, it is getting easier for the suitably qualified professional to join the hedge fund industry as setting up a hedge fund is becoming easier by the day. Through a network of personal and business contacts, the proprietor of a hedge fund can access brokerages, lawyers and accountants that team up to provide a one-stop-shop approach to developing and launching a hedge fund. In these days of improved communications, many information exchanges can be done on the phone, by email or by videoconferencing.

Furthermore, the impetus for starting up a hedge fund derives from the fact that in Europe, as in the USA and Asia, the hedge fund industry is in the midst of a dramatic metamorphosis from what was once viewed as a cottage industry not so long ago to a diverse, dynamic and increasingly mature business that is altering the dynamics of the global asset management landscape. Coupled with this, several hedge fund groups that have been operational for just a few years in these parts of the world, especially in the USA and Europe, have already grown into powerful financial entities in their own right that have proven their resilience in the face of testing market conditions and ensured that the structures they have built are robust and sustainable, giving the business the chance for long-term survival.

Typical Hedge Fund Business Plan

Hedge fund start-ups need to create a business plan as an effective way to organise the entrepreneurial tasks required to create a new business. In some cases, the hedge fund and management company are created together, necessitating either a business plan encompassing both entities or two separate plans. As these entities are different from manufacturing and conventional service companies, their business plans should reflect their unique requirements.

Nevertheless, the following is a checklist for the content of a hedge fund business plan. While these checklists are very important, they are not the only assessments used and therefore should not be tackled in an academic fashion. What is important here is that each of these items represents something that hedge funds principals should give careful thought to.

Feasibility

Some analysis is required to ascertain whether or not this endeavour is feasible. A consultant is usually required to assist in determining feasibility. A feasibility study should include the following:

- original seed capital;
- assets to be managed/invested;
- some investors/partners with assets;
- strategy to trade and invest for performance;
- contingency plan for at least 18 months;
- focus and commitment on the part of the promoters.

Budget

A simple comprehensive budget is required to assist in planning and executing the plan of action for starting a hedge fund. Budget items should include:

- administrative expenses like legal, accounting, consulting, and brokerage fees;
- operational costs;
- set-up/start-up costs including printing memorandums, business cards, etc.;
- website;
- reporting;
- marketing;
- office expenses.

Legal & Admin

Administrative issues can make things complicated. Professional accounting, audit, office administration, operations and consulting assistance are definitely required. Legal services to set up your offering, partnership agreement and subscription agreement are essential for creating a clean, legal, private placement. A hedge fund consultant is usually retained to provide the exact details for each of these issues.

Trading Strategies

Volumes have been written about the multitude of diverse trading strategies, each with its own pros and cons. For a hedge fund, having some system or strategy in place and a process of execution, measurement, and feedback and fine-tuning is more important than which strategy yields the highest returns. There are a number of distinct investment strategies (see Chapter 3) used by hedge funds, each offering different degrees of risk and return.

Operations

A method or plan to run daily operations should be included. Here a hedge fund consultant is invaluable because of their experience and current regulatory and market knowledge. Operations include:

- calculating the net asset value of the fund;
- apportioning of each of the partners/investors gains and losses;
- a tracking method for cash – daily/monthly etc.;
- trade and positions – daily/quarterly etc.;

- independently audited trails;
- system for billing and fees;
- account filing;
- reallocation of profits;
- trade history;
- website integration;
- updates.

While some of these are minor operational issues, some can be major systems that may well have accounted for the failure of a few funds, even with successful trading strategies.

Web Initiative

A large number of the expense items may be reduced drastically by using the web/internet for information dissemination, reporting, etc. While not essential, a web strategy for a new fund could prove to be an advantage if the fund has some experience with internet-related sites. Some of the newer hedge fund consultants can assist in setting up a site with all the basic information necessary.

Marketing

Marketing is a very delicate and risky issue, as regulators usually forbid direct advertising to the public for hedge funds. However, hedge funds are increasingly devising ways of circumventing the regulations regarding marketing and advertising.

Launch

The pilot launch requires timing of the coordination of subscriptions and contributions of partner investors and the start of trading. A hedge fund consultant usually guides the principals through all the nuances and issues to reach this stage. Part of the business plan's purpose is to reach this stage with all other structures in place.

Start-up Requirements

While it is agreed that starting up a hedge fund business is getting easier, the running of the business requires more than the trading nous of the promoters of the business. In order to ensure that the business is sustainable, the promoters have to get the right blend of the key items required to start the business successfully.

It is essential for the hedge fund promoter to get the right ingredients in order to win the faith of the investors and get to manage their money. The investors will have to be convinced of the hedge fund's clear and demonstrable trading edge and its competitive edge in an increasingly crowded market of equally talented operators.

To emphasise the need to get the start-up process right, industry statistics have shown that despite the proliferation of new funds, an increasing proportion of these new funds shut down after a few years of operating. These statistics would lead any observer of the industry to believe that many of the funds that shut down were run by novices who should not have tried to enter the business in the first place. Whilst this might be true to a certain degree, others argue that many of these funds were launched by talented and credible managers who were forced to give up in some cases due to sheer bad luck over timing or choice of partners.

Nevertheless, the following are the key items required. It should be noted that requirements vary from country to country and that these items serve as a guideline and are by no means exhaustive.

Money

The first ports of call for seed capital money are usually friends and family members of the hedge fund promoter as it is unusual for an institutional investor to want to invest in a new fund. The fund manager will have to tap into the network of close associates who may have confidence in their abilities.

As the fund grows, it could employ a variety of methods to raise capital, including in-house marketing staff, prime brokers and outside consultants. Each of these methods has its own strengths and weaknesses. If the fund utilises the services of an outside consultant, the manager essentially has another partner in their management company along with the seed investor. However, since it is paramount that a fund wishing to access the institutional market be positioned professionally from the start, the new fund may well look to utilise the services of a consultant to raise the seed capital and present it to the institutional marketplace.

Legal Services

The legal development process usually commences with a planning consultation. At this stage, important issues (e.g. depending on the country: location of the hedge fund, investment adviser registration, and reliance on safe harbours and exemptions, etc.) are addressed and resolved. During the legal consultation, depending on how well it is conducted, areas that need further planning are exposed. A soon as this is complete, the legal development process begins. The fund and management company entities are initially formed in their jurisdictions. This allows the fund manager to begin the process of opening bank and brokerage accounts and preparing for the administrative needs of the hedge fund. After the entities are formed, the legal team gathers the necessary information.

Prime Broker Services

Forming a relationship with a prime broker is the next step, once the lawyer has been engaged, the hedge fund organised and the offering documents drafted. A good prime broker will offer marketing and capital introduction services. Although hedge funds are not allowed to advertise or use other conventional forms of marketing, brokers have developed workarounds to get the fund manager the right kind of investor attention.

hedge fund start-up managers must think through thoroughly. As the hedge fund industry has evolved and a greater number of service providers has emerged, some hedge fund managers are of the opinion that the prime brokerages' product offering is becoming commoditised and, therefore, simple factors shape the prime broker selection process. In reality, there are still many elements of the prime brokerage service that are differentiating factors between firms. For that reason, a hedge fund start-up manager should ensure that they have a comprehensive understanding of their own requirements so that the prime broker they ultimately select will be an effective partner and enabler of a successful launch.

Office Space

The location of an office has become irrelevant in recent times as advances in technology have it made it convenient for professionals to work from any location where there is high-speed internet access. Also, the proliferation of information that has made investment research and trading convenient as well as efficient makes it easier to run a hedge fund in a hedge fund hotel[49] or even at home.

Increasingly, start-up managers are choosing serviced offices to avoid longer-term leases and the significant upfront expenses that go with owning premises. In the event of rapid growth that might require a move to larger premises, they will not be faced with the expensive task of breaking or assigning the lease and walking away from the initial fit-out costs. However, some hedge funds, especially those that are confident that their business will survive in the long term, choose to rent offices in prime areas in cities like New York, London and Hong Kong. In London for instance, US hedge funds choose to base their London operations in areas like Mayfair and St James. UK and European hedge funds also have offices in these locations. A village community feel has developed in these areas as funds have opted for a less formal, cosmopolitan environment that provides smaller space in high-quality buildings and locations.

Hedge Fund Mechanics

To get a hedge fund up and running, the budding hedge fund manager has to set up the hedge fund entity and management company. In the USA, for instance, the hedge fund is typically established as a limited partnership and in some cases a limited liability company. According to Terhune (2006), with hedge fund start-ups, the management company will also function as the hedge fund's general partner and is set up as a limited company or, in some special cases, as a corporation.

---

49 A service provided by companies such as investment banks for new hedge funds which includes office space, technical support, incubation and other services in the hope that they will become big clients.

Authorisation

Some jurisdictions around the world do not require hedge funds to be registered with the competent authority before they commence any regulated activity. Others like the UK, however, require registration with the Financial Services Authority (FSA), which is empowered by the Treasury and statute.

The FSA requires firms wishing to register to be *"authorised in accordance with Part IV of the Financial Services and Markets Act 2000"*. Fund managers must make an application to the FSA for Part IV Permission by submitting the relevant forms and supporting documentation to the corporate authorisation department. With professional assistance, a typical fund management company's application is likely to take one or two weeks to construct.

The FSA have a statutory time limit of no more than 12 months to consider an application. While this limit is defined by the Act, the FSA attempts to reach a decision on an application much more quickly. An application managed by an appropriate adviser, such as a professional compliance consultant, is more likely to be authorised within 12 weeks. The FSA encourages the use of compliance professionals as this usually results in a more complete application and rule-based approach.

Before authorisation, the FSA will require firms to provide evidence that they meet the five threshold conditions of authorisation as they apply to hedge fund management. These do not constitute a hurdle to overcome but more of a plateau to reach and maintain. Some of the conditions are quite straightforward to achieve and evidence whereas some are more subjective. Nevertheless, all five are specific to the nature and complexity of the application.

The five threshold conditions are as follows:

- Legal identity
- Location of offices
- Close links
- Adequate resources
- Suitability

In other parts of Europe, the regulatory situation for hedge funds is diverse. In Switzerland, hedge funds need to be authorised by the Federal Banking Commission but once authorised, hedge funds have few restrictions. Swiss hedge funds may be advertised and sold to investors without minimum wealth thresholds. In Ireland and Luxembourg, hedge funds and offshore investment funds are even allowed listings on the stock exchange. At the other extreme, France has greatly restricted the establishment of French hedge funds, and French authorities frown upon offshore investing (Connor and Woo, 2003).

Information Technology

Start-ups that perceive their IT infrastructure as an invaluable resource can gain a competitive edge over their rivals. It could also strengthen their pitch to investors who are increasingly reluctant to allocate capital unless there is proof

117

of integrated systems, complete with disaster recovery provisions. Regulators also require proof of a full audit trail of time-stamped data.

The success of a hedge fund start-up could be dependent on its willingness to spend money on getting its infrastructure right at the outset. In addition, it should be well placed to uncover and deal with errors that originate from manually intensive business processes, unnoticed business exposures and so on. Failure to do this effectively could potentially lead to failure of the fund at an early stage.

Hedge fund principals (promoters) may not understand enough about technology in order to grasp the importance of putting the right infrastructure in place from day one. They may underestimate the disruptive effect of future systems changes and upgrades that are inevitable as a business grows. They will need technology providers that can plan their future requirements and advise them accordingly about the capital outlay needed to fulfil these requirements. If the capital outlay is out of their reach, some technology providers offer alternative payment plans.

The role of technology in hedge funds cannot be overstated. Traditionally, most managers have recognised that technology allows them to access and process relevant information at least as quickly and accurately as the rest of the market, giving them a potentially superior performance to their rivals. This means they need – at the very least – a data feed, a fast broadband internet connection, email and basic Microsoft® Office to generate revenue. However, in order to maximise revenue, the manager ought to be able to distinguish between investment decisions that generate revenue and those that do not, including all of the ancillary costs that are implicit in any investment decision ,i.e. transaction fees, financing fees, ticket fees etc. Many of these costs can be directly reduced by the use of technology – for example, trading electronically can significantly cut commission paid. What appears to be crucial is the use of technology with a view to gaining an understanding of it. The compulsory use of portfolio management systems in the front office is a case in point.

There are other considerations apart from the front office for the principal of a hedge fund management company, given that net profit for the company is revenue less operating costs. Technology plays a major role in the investment process and obviously the analysis of which activities generate revenue and which do not.

The role of technology in modern-day activities that occur after an order has been fulfilled should also be discussed. In yesteryears, rooms full of people were responsible for confirming, communicating and reconciling all of the information that goes with every single trade, ensuring that the front office was using accurate data for investments. As a result, there was plenty of room for human error. These days, many of the people have been replaced by software. Orders can be placed electronically by the investment manager and automatically filed and posted to the portfolio management system, with the appropriate allocation between funds and managed accounts. From here, they can be confirmed electronically using automatic matching networks, and automatically reported and reconciled with the systems at the prime brokers and administrators. This does not imply that operations professionals are not required to oversee all these steps but it takes fewer of them than in the past, resulting in cost savings.

Hedge fund start-ups that survive the early phases usually plan the investment process alongside the rest of the workflow. Technology improves the efficiency of that workflow, just as it improves the efficiency of the investment process. The key to achieving this is to give it thorough consideration, well in advance of the launch of the hedge fund.

One other key consideration for start-up hedge funds is whether or not to outsource their IT infrastructure. This is because most hedge fund start-ups take the view that they are not IT specialists and therefore hire an IT services firm, familiar with the needs of the alternative investment manager, to help build their infrastructure to the extent that it is hosted on their own premises; which in effect is a form of outsourcing. Buying a specialist portfolio management or risk system instead of developing a proprietary one also constitutes a form of outsourcing. However, the most viable form of outsourcing is the Application Service Provider (ASP) model, which entails the use of technology provided by an ASP that is hosted off-site and accessed via a high-speed broadband connection.

Hedge fund start-ups find the idea of using ASP technology irresistible as it involves no capital expenditure and can be deployed immediately, given that there is no physical installation involved. Applications hosted by the ASP can be easily accessed via the internet, offering users superior mobility. Key benefits of the ASP model include the reduction of the burden of maintaining in-house systems, and outsourcing of disaster recovery planning.

Another trend in outsourcing that hedge funds could find compelling is the bundling of software, by providers of middle- and back-office outsourcing services, with their existing packages. This provides the business the option of taking the system in-house should the need arise.

Fund Administration

In building a hedge fund business, the importance of an administrator is a decision that is well worth researching in order to make the right choice. An administrator is usually seen as a long-term strategic partner whose service levels meet the expectations of the fund management company and, equally important, its investors.

Start-up managers usually underestimate the requirements for the day-to-day running of a hedge fund business and take for granted the support and resources that were available to them in their previous employment.

The administrator usually provides considerable assistance during the set-up phase of a hedge fund. The administrator should be able to understand complex fund structures, help with performance fees structuring, liaise with the fund's lawyer, review and comment on the prospectus and agree appropriate wording relating to the day-to-day operation of the fund.

Of late, there has been a consolidation of hedge fund services. Investment banks have acquired administration firms with a view to bundling their services

119

together. As a result, hedge funds can now source administration, custody, clearing, stock lending and financing from one of the providers in a coordinated manner. The competitive nature of the provision of hedge fund services has led to greater economies of scale. If a hedge fund is sourcing a number of higher-margin products from a bank, it is quite possible that the administration service will be offered at a low price – or even for free.

Fund administrators consider the provision of administration services a low-margin business and so tend to focus on the larger hedge funds. For the start-up hedge fund, this means that the principals should clarify the level of service they expect from the administrator by requesting answers to questions such as:

- What is the commitment of senior management to the administration business?
- What is the quality of the day-to-day service?
- What is the IT offering?
- What is the level of commitment to the start-up business?

Once hedge fund principals engage the services of a fund administrator, they expect them to play a key role in the pre-launch process. A full-service administrator should employ an in-house legal counsel team that can offer advice on the fund structure, equalisation[50] methodology and incentive fee calculations.

Figure 6.1 Interaction between Fund Administrator and other parties involved in a fund

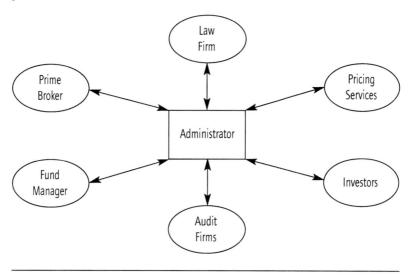

---

50 Equalisation is the accounting process whereby profit calculations are adjusted to accommodate shares bought by investors at different times with different net asset values (NAV). This concept is explained further in .Chapter 7.

The administrator's in-house counsel will also review all of the fund's legal documents and liaise with the fund's manager to ensure the fund is ready for launch. In the launch phase, the hedge fund manager will provide the administrator with the list of potential investors and they will then send out offering documents and subscription agreements to these potential investors. The administrator will also coordinate the receipt of all completed subscription documents. At the same time, the administrator will be checking the fund's escrow account. As the subscription amounts are received, they will match them up with the subscription agreements and ensure that everything is in good order. The administrator will work closely with the fund manager to ensure that they are aware of how much money will be available for investment on launch date. On launch date, they will move the funds to the prime brokerage account. Once the fund is running, the administrator carries out a number of vital functions namely:

- Shareholder services
- Net asset value (NAV) calculation
- Corporate secretariat
- Tax services

Incubator Hedge Funds

As cost is a major consideration when setting up a hedge fund, some budding hedge fund managers decide to test the waters before spending a relatively sizable amount to set up a fund. Apart from the cost considerations, some may not have a usable track record.

For budding hedge fund managers who would like to start their own fund but who are not ready to incur the associated expenses and/or do not yet have the performance history they need to attract investors, the solution lies in an incubator hedge fund.

Hedge funds that start out using the incubator method have the opportunity to break down the hedge fund development process into a cost-manageable undertaking. It is a two-step approach to starting a hedge fund. In the first step, the legal entity is created, but investors are not yet accepted. The manager trades with their personal funds and when the manager is ready for investors, the legal documents for accepting investors are drawn up and the hedge fund is fully formed.

This two-step process has a number of advantages. In addition to eliminating the prior performance problem, it makes getting started much less expensive. What makes the fund expensive to start and to run are investors. Because there are fewer documents to draw up and fewer accounting chores, an "incubator" hedge fund costs a fraction of what a fully fledged fund costs. The two-step approach also gives the manager an opportunity to fine-tune their business plan and investment strategies before preparing their offering documents.

The obvious limitation with this strategy is that the fund is not able to accept outside investors. It may be possible for family members and close friends of the manager to invest, but the manager is not allowed to accept compensation of any kind. However, these restrictions might make the two-step solution seem like no solution at all.

Typical Business Structures

This section describes the typical business structures for hedge funds. Before proceeding with the description, an often confusing aspect of hedge funds needs to be elucidated. The keywords that should be noted are shown in italics. As stated elsewhere, a hedge fund is a vehicle for holding and investing the *funds* of its investors. The fund itself is not a genuine *business*, having no *employees* and no *assets* other than its *investment portfolio* and a small amount of cash, and its *investors* are its *clients*. The portfolio is managed by the *investment manager*,[51] which has *employees* and *property* and which is the actual business. An investment manager is commonly termed a "hedge fund" (e.g. a person may be said to "work at a hedge fund") but this is not technically correct. An investment manager may have a large number of hedge funds under its management.

The specific legal structure of a hedge fund – in particular its domicile and the type of entity used – is usually determined by the tax and regulatory environments of the fund's expected investors. Since the USA has been the centre of hedge fund activity, its environment will be used here.

Corporation
A corporation is a business entity created under state law, which stands as an independent legal "person" apart from its shareholders and directors. A corporation's owners or shareholders receive the benefit of limited liability for the obligations of the corporation, and are thus ordinarily shielded from the corporation's creditors even in the event that the corporation cannot pay its obligations. There are procedural requirements imposed on corporations which may deter some businesses from opting to incorporate.

The well-known corporation in the USA is the C Corporation. The C Corporation may become a public corporation, with its shares being bought and sold either through a stock market or "over the counter". The C Corporation may ordinarily deduct the entire value of the fringe benefits offered to shareholders who also serve as employees. Unlike an S Corporation (see below), there is no limit on the number of shareholders and shares may be held by people who are neither citizens nor residents of the United States. One of the major advantages of the C Corporation is its flexibility to carry corporate losses forward to future tax years.

---

51 Note that the investment manager in this context is the hedge fund management company, the term used in most parts of this book.

There are, however, disadvantages to adopting the C Corporation business structure as in some circumstances corporate profits will be subject to "double taxation", first as corporate income and second as income to the ultimate recipient. For example, if a corporation issues dividends from its profits, it has already paid income tax on that money, but the dividends remain taxable as income to the shareholders.

In regard to taxation, a C Corporation prepares an annual tax return, deducting its business expenses from revenues in order to determine and declare its taxable income. Generally speaking, the taxable income will be the money the corporation retains at the end of the year for its future needs and operating expenses, and the amount it distributes to its shareholders as dividends.

For some business owners, the corporate tax rate will be lower than their personal marginal tax rate, and they may thus obtain a benefit from having the corporation retain profits taxed at the lower rate. However, as with the evaluation of the tax benefits of incorporating and choosing between an S Corporation or C Corporation, and because of the limits on the amount of income a corporation may retain, the assessment of any tax benefit is best made with the advice of a qualified financial professional.

Subchapter S Corporation

An "S Corporation" is a corporation which has elected to have its profits pass through to its shareholders, in the same manner as a partnership (see below). The shareholders of an S Corporation receive the benefit of limited liability, and are treated in the manner of partners for purposes of taxation.

Several limitations make the S corporation unsuitable for some companies. There can be no more than 75 shareholders (investors). And there can be only one class of stock (although differences in voting rights may be allowed). All owners must be individuals, not businesses like banks and insurance companies. Furthermore, all shareholders must be citizens or residents of the United States. Non-resident aliens may not hold shares.

In regard to taxation, under normal circumstances an S Corporation does not pay corporate income taxes. Instead, the corporate profits are passed through to the shareholders, who report the distribution on their individual tax returns.

If the promoters of the hedge fund do not feel these limitations are important, the S corporation is one of the preferred structures for a management company of a hedge fund.

Partnership

The partnership is a business entity, ordinarily comprising two or more individuals, although under some circumstances a partnership will be formed between other business entities, or between individuals and a business entity. In the USA, the partnership is not taxed as a business entity. Instead, the net income is declared in the returns of the investors. For this reason, a partnership is often described as a "flow-through entity" (McCrary, 2002).

One of the main advantages of this business structure is that investors pay tax only once on revenue generated by the partnership. Other advantages

123

include the ease with which the requirements for a partnership can be satisfied. There must be at least two investors. The partnership is at liberty to allocate income and expenses to a partner in accordance with the rule stipulated by the partners.

There are significant liability issues raised by a partnership. Ordinarily, a partner is individually liable not only for business debts and liabilities, but also for most business-related conduct of the other partners.

Limited Liability Company

A limited liability company, or LLC, is a business entity that enjoys many of the advantages of being a corporation, including limited liability, while avoiding many of the more significant burdens imposed on corporations and retaining many of the characteristics of unincorporated entities such as partnerships.

Members of a limited liability company enjoy protection from individual liability similar to that afforded to corporate shareholders. That is to say, if a business is sued or is unable to pay its debts, the creditors can ordinarily only reach the LLC's assets and cannot reach the assets of the members.

An LLC, like the S Corporation, is a flow-through tax entity. It must have at least two but may have many investors. A limited liability company is one of the two structures commonly created to assume general partner responsibility (McCrary, 2002).

It is a widely held view that the LLC will completely replace both the partnership and the S corporation.

Offshore Hedge Fund

US-based hedge fund managers who have significant potential investors outside the United States and/or US tax-exempt investors typically create offshore funds. The offshore hedge fund (Figure 6.2) is typically a corporation. The fund is located in a country that levies few or no taxes, so the penalty of double taxation is minimised (McCrary, 2002).

Figure 6.2 Offshore Hedge Fund Structure

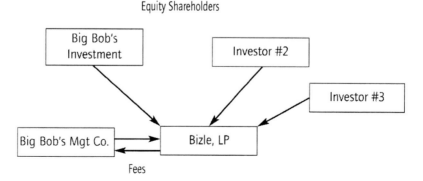

Many hedge fund managers use offshore hedge funds to provide privacy for investors. In those cases where complete investor confidentiality and privacy are necessary, an offshore fund should not accept US investors and the fund manager should not be based in the USA.

Offshore funds generally attract the investment of US tax-exempt entities, such as pension funds, charitable trusts, foundations, retirement plans and accounts, and endowments, as well as non-US residents.

US tax-exempt investors favour investments in offshore hedge funds because they may have exposure to US taxation if they invest in US-based hedge funds.

New hedge fund managers, who are small operators and for whom the extra costs are a major burden, usually launch an offshore hedge fund in the Cayman Islands or the Bahamas.

Master Feeder Hedge Fund

This structure, also known as a "hub and spoke", allows investors residing in the USA and investors residing offshore to invest, indirectly, in the same offshore corporate entity commonly known as the "master fund." The master fund is typically structured as a limited partnership. Ordinarily, US-taxable investors investing in a master feeder structure invest directly in a limited partnership organised in the United States. This limited partnership is referred to as the "domestic feeder". The domestic feeder invests its assets in the master fund. The offshore investors and US-tax-exempt organisations invest directly in an offshore corporation. This offshore corporation is referred to as the "offshore feeder". The offshore feeder also invests its assets in the master fund. The hedge fund manager then purchases and sells securities in an account held in the name of the master fund.

The master feeder structure is represented diagrammatically in Figure 6.3.

Figure 6.3 Master Feeder Structure

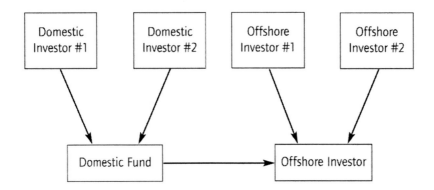

Marketing of Hedge Funds

Hedge fund start-ups are increasingly seeking the services of third-party marketers to source investors. As the demand for hedge funds continues to grow,
hedge fund marketing has evolved into an industry of its own. As a result, the
service offerings from third-party marketers (TPMs) – unaffiliated firms that
enter into agreements with managers to find investors for their hedge funds –
are becoming increasingly sophisticated. These firms also offer specialised marketing services as they face not only increasing demand for their services, but
increasing competition from new firms as well as prime brokerage departments
and internal marketing staff. These services include working with managers on
strategy and market positioning, developing market intelligence and identifying
prospective investors, arranging meetings to pre-qualify prospective investors in
terms of overall suitability, accompanying managers to investor presentations,
preparation of marketing materials, follow-up with prospective investors, and
acting as client liaison throughout the investment period. TPMs often demand
an exclusive arrangement with the manager and approximately 20% of all fees.

Hedge funds find the idea of engaging a TPM compelling despite the high
fees and the exclusivity demands. On the face of it, it would appear that they
would be better off choosing the gratuitous services of prime brokers or even
hiring internal marketing staff. However, they choose this option for a number
of reasons. First, the increasingly global nature of the hedge fund business may
require a manager to hire a specialist to access potential investors based in

**Figure 6.4 Relationship of a TPM with the Investor Base and Hedge
Fund Manager**

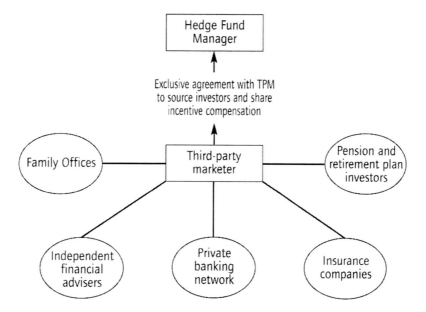

countries around the world. The efforts of the internal marketing staff and prime brokers who could provide introductions may be inadequate for some hedge funds trading in, say, the US markets, hoping to reach investors in Europe and Asia. Engaging a TPM which has an office or established relationships in Europe and Asia may be the right option for these hedge funds. In addition, a TPM may have a better understanding of investor needs in these continents and will be in a position to advise on structuring the fund to appeal to an investor's concerns in such areas as tax and reporting.

Other benefits of engaging a TPM include directing a fund to investors who it knows would have an interest in the particular strategy it focuses on and that is also employed by the fund. A TPM can also act as an independent consultant to the hedge fund manager and provide a variety of services in addition to those a prime broker may offer, which may assist a manager in attracting investors. The TPM can regularly assess the strategy, execution, risk management processes, reconciliation and reporting processes of the manager, which in the end may enhance the attractiveness of the fund to investors.

There are a number of dedicated TPMs that hedge fund start-ups can engage to fulfil their marketing requirements. These firms are based either in the UK or the USA. UK-focused marketers Altus Hedge Partners, RAB Capital and Capital Services Ltd are all in London. In the USA, Far Hills, based in New York, and Coronado Investments, based in California, are two of the three TPMs with a presence in the region.

Case Study on the Launch of a Maritime Hedge Fund

In the hedge fund universe, 12 months is considered a short time for establishing and raising money for a new hedge fund. However, it took F2I Management, a fictional hedge fund management company, 18 months to attract the initial $15m (£7.5m) it wanted to launch its Bahamas-domiciled Global Maritime Hedge Fund. The time was not just spent in raising assets but also in setting up F2I Management, implementing the necessary risk management system and testing the investment idea.

The idea for establishing the Global Maritime Hedge Fund came at a cocktail party in London where the now joint managing directors of F2I, Malcolm Biggs and Greg Burton, met in 2005. In October 2006, they launched the fund which trades the shipping freight market by investing in both futures and the physical markets. This includes buying and selling capacity on ships and arbitraging differences in prices between transporting freight in the Atlantic and the Pacific.

Both managing directors had a lot experience in the shipping industry and trading derivatives but had not previously managed a hedge fund.

Mr Burton has been a ship broker since 1986 and in 1994 established MLM, a London-based freight trading company. Mr Biggs was at Sakamoto from 1993 until joining BB Lincoln as manager of Bahamax Freight Operations in 1999.

These men identified an investment opportunity in this market, put togeth-

127

er a business plan and worked closely with institutional investors who were interested in becoming seed investors for the fund.

They were able to attract investors through referrals and word of mouth. These investors were keen on the shipping market and were interested in investing in it.

On launch day, the fund had five investors. They were two investment banks, two family offices and a shipping company. The launch was held back until the fund raised $15m because they deemed this amount as the minimum amount of money needed to get credit lines from their counterparties.

While the concept of the unconventional fund seemed to appeal to potential investors, the principals found it more difficult to get investors to invest than they would have in more conventional funds. They had to educate potential investors about the rudiments of shipping.

The press coverage of the launch in November 2006, however, seemed to shorten the time from first enquiry to investment as the keywords in the coverage, i.e. new, fund, shipping and non-correlated, sparked interest in the fund.

The performance of the fund from launch in October 2006 to April 2007 – 16 per cent return, annualised volatility of 3.7 per cent and a Sharpe ratio of 6.4 – was also a factor in the increase in investor interest.

In order to grow the fund to $40m52in assets to achieve profitability, the managing directors had to be amenable to operational due diligence of F2I by their potential investors, reference checks on the directors and security checks to ensure that they did not have any criminal records.

Some of the more fastidious investors wanted to see evidence of the veracity of their trades by asking for signed copies of some the contracts for these trades. Others interviewed their risk manager and chief financial officer individually and also examined their systems.

As the fund grows in size, the principals (directors) are looking to expand their business by recruiting marketing help for the chief financial officer and expanding their product range.

Case Study on the Launch of an Eastern European Hedge Fund

Hungary-based Forinox Fund has started relatively small – at $13 million – but as these assets are almost double its seeding capital, the fund is attracting the attention of institutions.

The formation of the Budapest-based Forinox Fund in 2004 was innovative in at least two ways: one, it was the first hedge fund to be based in Hungary; and two, it was the first Malta-domiciled hedge fund to be listed on the Irish Stock Exchange.

52 The principals believe that the 2 per cent they can charge as management fees would make
    the fund profitable and stable.

Forinox was set up in July 2005 as a management company and had its inaugural long/short global equity fund up and running by the start of September.

So far, performance has been excellent – with the fund up more than 20% in its first six months, and up 7.5% in February alone, to put it among the top five best-performing global equity strategies in the EuroHedge league tables.

Assets are still relatively small – at $13 million, predominantly from wealthy Hungarian individuals. But the size of the fund has almost doubled from its launch size of $7.5 million and London-based funds of funds and other institutional investors are starting to take an interest.

Key to the ability to get the fund up and running quickly were the pedigrees and existing client relationships of the firm's three founding partners – all of whom had previously worked at BigFund Asset Management, the asset management arm of BigFund Bank, a Dutch Bank, in Budapest.

Daniel Knight, the lead portfolio manager who is in charge of day-to-day management of the company, was formerly managing director and chairman of the board of directors of BigFund Asset Management (Hungary). Before that he was a founding partner of Pacivic Financial Markets, an independent securities firm set up in 1993 that grew to become one of the largest institutional brokerages on the Budapest Stock Exchange. He joined BigFund's asset management arm in 1999 when he sold a subsidiary that he had bought from his fellow partners, Pacivic Portfolio Management, to the Dutch bank.

Jan Pollit, who is in charge of client marketing, was also at Pacivic and at BigFund Asset Management, where he was head of the private client department. And Hana Dominik, head of operations, previously worked in similar positions at both firms.

The fourth director of the firm is Maltese lawyer Peter Busietta, who is responsible for compliance and who handled some of the operational aspects of setting up the fund, which is registered as a Maltese SICAV.[53]

The long/short equity strategy runs a concentrated and leveraged portfolio of US and European stocks – usually in the order of around 50–55% western European equities and 40% US shares, with the remainder invested in other developed equity markets around the world.

The strategy is designed to have low turnover, running no more than 15 to 20 positions. All long positions are in individual stocks, while short positions and portfolio hedging are carried out mainly through index derivatives. The fund does not short individual stocks and the portfolio may not go net short.Leverage is permitted up to five times – which is relatively high for a long/short equity strategy – but usually runs at a level of two to three times.

With a total staff of five, Knight believes the fund can handle assets under management of up to $200 million with the firm's existing resources. The up-

---

53   A SICAV is an open-ended collective investment scheme common in Western Europe, especially Luxembourg, Switzerland, Italy and France. SICAV is an acronym for Société d'investissementà capital variable which can be translated as Investment Company with variable capital.

front costs of setting up the fund – estimated at around €50,000 – have been absorbed and, with asset size growing, the running costs are no longer exercising a drag on returns.

Having decided against registering in the Caribbean, Forinox's founders looked instead for an EU-based solution. Dublin and Luxembourg were potential candidates, but Knight and his partners were impressed by the enthusiasm of the Maltese authorities, who were keen to promote the island's credentials as a financial centre.

It took three months to register the fund. The lawyers were given the go-ahead in Malta in April and the fund was registered on July 1, 2005.

Regulatory Issues

Hedge fund start-ups have to comply with regulations, however light, in their jurisdiction for their long-term survival. In the UK, for instance, the Financial Services Authority (FSA) permits the use of derivatives for investment purposes as well as short selling provided that the short position is liquid and can be cash-settled or is covered by long positions with a return profile that is highly correlated to that of the short positions. This is one of the hallmarks of hedge fund investing and presents opportunities for start-up hedge fund managers.

According to Price Waterhouse Coopers, the FSA plans to undertake increased data collection from hedge fund managers via regulatory returns and asset valuation is one of the areas for further focus. It has also set up a dedicated supervisory team to oversee the hedge fund industry in the UK and this team will play a major role in analysing any additional data that will be obtained as well in performing themed visits. The visits will focus on valuation methodologies, including the role of the hedge fund manager in valuing positions.

As stated in a KPMG report, regulation in most major hedge fund markets bars all but the wealthiest and most sophisticated private investors from buying hedge funds, although some European countries are to some extent liberalising, or consulting on liberalising, regulation prohibiting hedge funds from distributing their products to retail clients. UCITS III too, while not intended to be a mechanism for the establishment of hedge funds or funds for retail distribution, is expanding the list of allowable investments to include certain types of derivatives which could enable some hedge fund strategies to be employed in UCITS III retail funds. Overall, these changes have been welcomed worldwide, though there are concerns that the registration requirements may slow down the rate of start-ups in countries like the USA; and the recent reinterpretation of tax laws in the UK may cause a brain drain. It is also recognised that the next wave of growth in hedge funds still carries two sets of risks which no regulator can control.

The first of these is the performance risk, arising from poor returns, overcapacity and inadequate talent inflow. Pension funds are especially concerned about overcapacity. The second one is the intrinsic risk, arising from price valuation of complex instruments and copycat strategies forced by market conditions. Administrators are especially concerned about operational risk arising from valuation changes.

There is recognition that the ability to generate high and consistent returns is influenced by many factors. Some, like innovation, velocity and leverage, are controllable. Others, like style concentration, market evolution and high volatility, are not. Indeed, in today's low volatility environment, style concentration is a major concern as unexpected events can potentially cause havoc.

Taxation Issues

For hedge fund management companies just starting out, there are tax issues that should be given careful consideration to ensure that the fund, the investors, the manager and the promoters are in the best position possible.

Taxation rules vary from jurisdiction to jurisdiction and therefore the location of the fund or fund manager determines the tax implications for all parties involved in the fund. In the UK, for instance, individual investors are taxed at up to 32.5% on dividends from non-transparent overseas hedge funds. Individual investors will also be subject to tax on non-dividend income and capital gains up to 40%. As for corporations, they are subject to 30% tax on income derived from an offshore hedge fund. The return from a foreign hedge fund may be taxed on an annual mark-to-market basis for corporate investors in certain circumstances. The offshore fund rules do not apply in these circumstances. Pension fund investors are tax-exempt.

Investment in a foreign hedge fund is likely to constitute an interest in an offshore fund. This means that UK-resident investors may prefer the foreign hedge fund to obtain UK distributor status in order to safeguard the tax treatment of realised capital gains as opposed to having an income receipt of disposal.

According to Sanger and Ward (2003), in general there are four parties that are involved in tax structuring for hedge funds: the investors, the fund itself, the fund management company and the founders, i.e. the owners of the fund management company. Largely, the objective is to ensure:

- no taxation of the fund;
- no additional taxation on the investors due to investment in the fund;
- minimisation of the taxation worldwide of the fund management company (or companies); and
- maximisation of the allowances/reliefs from capital gains for the founders.

Operational Procedures

This chapter describes some of the operational procedures of hedge fund managers including the trading life cycle and performance fee equalisation.

Introduction

Operational procedures in hedge funds include trading, reconciliation and reporting, and performance fee equalisation. Hedge funds can perform some or all of these operational tasks internally or outsource them to a fund administrator or prime brokerage firm.

In recent years, operational procedures of hedge funds have come under scrutiny as institutional investors carry out operational due diligence reviews of the fund manager's organisation, fund structure, back office, valuation and independent oversight. This comes as a result of increasing inflows of capital into hedge funds and some well-publicised fraud cases which have caused losses for even some of the most sophisticated investors in the industry.

Trading

Hedge fund managers have a choice between outsourcing some or all of their trading procedures. In either case, the fund managers usually ensure that the service provider they select meets their specific requirements.

The trading lifecycle in hedge funds is described in Figure 7.1. This representation is relatively simplistic as there are other procedures involved in the trading lifecycle such as market risk, credit risk and end-of-day processing. However, since most hedge funds are small firms, it is best to make it as basic as possible as some of these procedures could be outsourced.

Figure 7.1 The Trading Lifecycle

Trade Capture

Trading usually entails the hedge fund manager placing either a buy or sell order with a broker for a security, i.e. stock, bond etc. The hedge fund manager executes a trade; the details of the trade are recorded in the firm's trading systems and also sent to its prime broker(s) and fund administrators. With the advent of electronic trading, an order management system interfacing directly with the fund manager's portfolio management system can be used to record trade details.[54] In some cases, a manual or system-generated deal ticket can be input directly into a portfolio management system.

54 Electronic trading will be discussed further in Chapter 10.

Different trading systems have different data entry requirements, i.e. the input fields on the GUI are different from system to system. Details of individual trades are also different. Nevertheless, regardless of the trade type, the following details amongst others are recorded:

- the security that is traded, e.g. IBM stock;
- the security identifier such as ISIN, RIC, CUSIP and so on;
- the trade counterparty;
- trade type, i.e. buy or sell;
- transaction type, i.e. whether it's a swap, option, ordinary transaction;
- amount of security traded, i.e. quantity of units;
- trade date;
- settlement date;
- account that the trade should be allocated to.

Depending on the operational policies of the firm, the details of the trade are communicated to the relevant prime broker and fund administrator. Some hedge funds have electronic interfaces to these service providers to facilitate the communication in order to reduce, or in some cases eliminate, administrative errors.

For regulatory and auditing purposes, hedge fund managers usually maintain records of their trades for a period of time according to their company policy and the respective local regulators.

Trade Confirmation

Hedge fund managers as a matter of routine confirm all trades, be they OTC or exchange-traded, with their counterparties. Trade confirmation is an acknowledgment by the counterparty, indicating that a trade has been completed. This includes details such as the date, price and settlement terms of the trade.

Trade confirmation also includes trade matching carried out by the hedge fund manager or an outsourcer like Merrill Middle Office Solution. In the instance where it is outsourced, the outsourcer sends daily records of any unmatched trades and the details of the appropriate action required to rectify the mismatch.

Trades that are OTC may involve a central counterparty like LCH Clearnet, in which case hedge fund managers usually need to communicate events such as novation[55] to all counterparties involved.

Trade Settlements

After trades are successfully confirmed and matched with counterparties, they are settled according to the terms of the agreements governing the trade. In some instances, hedge fund managers send out standard settlement instructions (SSIs) with a view to reducing the risk of incorrect details on payments.

55 Novation is the act of replacement one participating member of a contract with another, or the exchange of new or existing debt or obligations for older ones.

Settlement is an automated process whereby the prime broker, acting as a settlement agent, liaises directly with the counterparty to facilitate the payment process. If the trade is OTC, payments of collaterals and margin[56] are also included in the settlement process.

A trade mismatch discovered at the time of settlement is often communicated by the execution broker and records are updated accordingly. The impact on the fund's net asset value (NAV) is routinely assessed and appropriate steps are taken to rectify it.

Reconciliation

Reconciliation entails ensuring consistency between the securities holding in the trading portfolio and the underlying records maintained by the prime broker, administrator and, in some cases, the counterparty for the OTC contracts.

Regular automated exchange of information on the hedge fund manager's stock positions is used to reconcile the stock position between the hedge fund manager, the prime broker and the fund administrator.

The output from the reconciliation process, i.e. the report, shows the position breaks, i.e. the difference between the positions held by the different parties. This applies to both exchange-traded and OTC trades.

The same procedure applies to cash reconciliations.

Figure 7.2 Reconciliation of Hedge Fund Trades

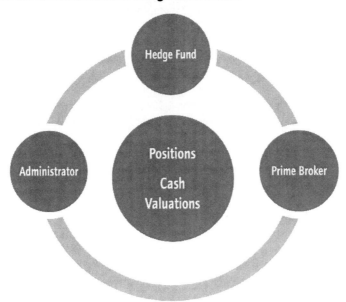

---

56 Money borrowed when buying securities.

Accounting

Accounting in hedge funds is a very critical process as both fund managers and investors can be said to be obsessed with returns. The accounting rules and conventions such as FAS 133 that hedge funds follow are pretty much the same as in other industries such as manufacturing and retailing. Trading transactions in hedge funds, given their uniqueness, require specialised accounting methods which are outside the scope of this book.

Performance Fee Equalisation

With the advent of increased investment in hedge funds from larger institutional investors, such as endowment funds and pension schemes, hedge fund managers have been under pressure to eke out every last penny from an investment.

These days it is rare to see a fund launched on the market which does not employ some method of equalisation, be it an equalisation factor, with its many variations, or a form of continuous offering with multi-series being issued within one fund class.

What is Equalisation?

In the context of hedge funds, the term "equalisation" refers to an accounting methodology designed to ensure that not only is the fund manager paid the correct incentive, performance or profit sharing fee, but also that the incentive fees are fairly allocated between each investor in the fund.

There are numerous methods of implementing equalisation, which are usually variations on a concept as the differences in the results are minimal. In order to appreciate the jargon surrounding equalisation, some terms need to be defined.

Definitions

- Gross NAV – this is the net asset value before accrual of fees.
- Net NAV – this is net asset value after accrual of fees.
- High Water Mark NAV and Loss Carry Forward – respectively, the higher of the NAV at the date of subscription and the previous highest NAV at which an incentive was paid or, if the fund lost value, in addition to no incentive fee accruing to the manager, a loss carry forward is calculated, whereby the fund must recoup prior losses before any fee can begin to accrue.
- Inequities – these are inequities that can occur when hedge fund managers charge an incentive fee on a fund, where there is no method of equalisation in place, and are twofold, i.e. "unfair clawback" and "free ride".
  - Unfair clawback: A fund will accrue an incentive fee as the fund increases in value during the performance period. Without an equalisation scheme, a new investor during the performance period would pay only the Net NAV after incentive accrual for new shares. If the fund subsequently lost value, the incentive fee accrual would reverse to the bene-

fit of all shareholders, including the new investor. This would be inequitable because all shareholders would benefit from the reversal when only the original investors suffered the cost of the original incentive fee accrual.

■ Free ride: If the fund has lost value prior to the issue of new shares, new investors will benefit from a "free ride" until the loss carry forward has been recovered at the fund level. This is inequitable because the new investors have not paid the incentive fee, even though they have personally benefited from the positive return on their individual investment. This situation arises when an investor buys into a fund during the performance period, at a NAV which is lower than the net asset value at the beginning of that period. In the absence of equalisation, a performance fee calculation would be levied on appreciation of the fund's NAV over the value at the beginning of the performance period. However, the investor who bought in during the period at a lower NAV would not be charged a performance fee on the appreciation from the lower NAV (at the time of subscription) to the NAV at the beginning of the period. This is referred to as a "free ride". Depending upon how this situation is accounted for (i.e. in the absence of equalisation), it can be to the detriment of the investment advisor, the original shareholders, or both.

Equalisation is implemented to ensure shareholder equity while still maintaining only one NAV per share, to facilitate the calculation of an incentive fee at the fund level. There are a number of different methods of implementing equalisation, and they can be tailored to the individual fund requirements. There are a small number of equalisation software providers. Most systems can be tailored to individual requirements and specifications and can also generate share registers, transaction reports, incentive fee reports, shareholders statements and loss carry forward information on a shareholder and tax-lot basis, which can be very advantageous for producing tax return information for investors.

The following section contains an illustration of the concept of Equalisation. It was extracted from the paper "Equalisation – What it is; Why it is Necessary; and How it Works" by Dermot S. L. Butler.[57]

The Free Ride
Industry experts believe "free ride" was the original reason and justification for the introduction of equalisation in the first place.The following is an illustration.

■ Mr Big Investor buys one share at £100.
■ At the end of the first quarter, gross NAV per share has risen to £110.
■ NAV per share published at £108 – (£110 – £2 incentive fee).

57 Dermot S.L. Butler and Custom House Group (2007). Reproduced with permission. All rights reserved.

- New high watermark – £110.
- At end of the following month, the NAV per share falls to £100.
- Mr Little Investor buys one share at £100.
- High watermark still £110.
- If NAV per share rises to £110 again, Mr Little Investor will have a £2 (20% of £10 profit) "Free Ride".

This example assumes that a fund starts trading at £100 per share and that there is an initial investor – Mr Big Investor – who buys one share at £100. Let us now assume that, at the end of the first quarter, the gross NAV per share has risen to £110. This will result in a NAV per share of £108, net of the incentive fee of £2 (20% of the £10 profit), which has been paid.

It could be assumed that one month later the NAV per share has fallen to £100 again and a second investor – Mr Little Investor – comes in and buys one share for £100. If the gross NAV was once again to climb back up to £110, unless one of the equalisation methods is being applied, the fund manager would not be able to charge any incentive fees on this second investor's subscription until the NAV per share had risen back up to over £110. If that happened, Mr Little Investor would get a "free ride" of £2 per share, being the incentive fee that he would not be paying on his profit of £10 per share.

Equalisation will eliminate this anomaly by charging an incentive fee to Mr Little Investor.

Rising Share Price

In some circles it is accepted that the "free ride" is the sole justification for equalisation, but this is not true. It is a fact that without some form of equalisation being applied when investors subscribe at different NAV levels, one shareholder will always be subsidising another shareholder, to some extent or another, even with consistently rising NAVs. The example below sheds light on this.

- Mr Big Investor buys one share at £100.
- NAV per share rises in the second month to £110.
- NAV per share published at £108, net of 20% incentive fee accrual.
- Mr Little Investor buys one share at £108.
- At quarter-end, the gross NAV per share has risen to £120.
- Gross profit is £32, calculated as follows:
  - Mr Big Investor invested: £100
  - Mr Little Investor invested: £108
    Total invested: £208
  - Gross NAV at end of quarter: £240
    Gross profit: £32
- Incentive fee at 20% of £32 = £6.40 gross, or £3.20 per share.
- NAV per share = (£240/2) = £120
  Minus the incentive fee of £3.20 = £116.80 per share.
  Therefore:

- Mr Big Investor effectively pays £3.20 incentive fee on a profit of £20, which equals 16.4% of the profit made by Mr Big Investor; whereas,
- Mr Little Investor effectively pays £3.20 incentive fee on a profit of £12, which equals 26.66% of the profit made by Mr Little Investor.

Like the previous example, again it is assumed that Mr Big Investor buys one share at £100 when it is launched. We again assume the market rises, but this time by the end of the second month, to £110 gross NAV per share. The NAV per share is published at £108, net of the 20% incentive fee accrual.

Mr Little Investor now buys one share at £108, being the published NAV. Let us now assume that at the quarter end, the gross NAV per share has, in fact, risen to £120. This results in gross profits of £32 based on the following calculation:

- Mr Big Investor invested £100 and Mr Little Investor invested £108, for a total sum invested of £208. The gross NAV (GNAV) of the fund at the end of the quarter was £240 (2 x shares at £120). This represents a gross profit of £32 over the total sum invested of £208.

To be equitable the profits should be allocated as £20 to Mr Big Investor, who bought at £100, and £12 to Mr Little Investor, who bought at £108. However, let us look at how the incentive fee, which will now be due, will be calculated.

The incentive fee should be 20% of the gross profit of £32, which is £6.40, or £3.20 per share. Thus, the gross NAV of £240, less the incentive fee of £6.40, results in a net NAV of £233.60, or £116.80 per share.

What does this mean?

It means that Mr Big Investor has effectively paid £3.20 incentive fee on a profit of £20, which equates to 16.4% of Mr Big Investor's profit, whereas Mr Little Investor also effectively pays £3.20 incentive fee, but does so on a profit of £12, which equates to an incentive fee of 26.66% of Mr Little Investor's profit. This is obviously inequitable.

Equalisation will eliminate this anomaly by allocating the correct incentive fee to each investor's account.

The Clawback Syndrome

Naturally, equalisation is also necessary to avoid the "clawback" syndrome defined above. This occurs where, following the initial rise to £110 shown in the two examples that have already been reviewed, the price per share falls back to, say, £96 at the end of the quarter as shown in the following illustration.

- Mr Big Investor buys one share at £100 per share at launch.
- At the end of the second month the gross NAV per share has risen to £110, i.e. £108 net of incentive fee accrual.
- Mr Little Investor now buys one share at £108.
- The NAV of the fund is now £218 excluding incentive fee accrual.
- The fund loses £26 in month three. The gross NAV falls down to £192 or £96 per share.

139

- The loss per share should be £26/2, which equals £13 per share.
- Given that the fund has lost £13 per share, the fair value of Mr Big Investor's investment should be £97 (£110 less £13) whereas the fair value for Mr Little Investor would be £95 (£108 less £13).
- The actual loss to Mr Big Investor is £14 (£110 less £96), whereas the loss to Mr Little Investor is actually £12 (£108 invested less £96).

The incentive fee accrual made at the end of the second month would now revert back to the fund. Without equalisation, that accrual would benefit all shareholders, including the new investor, whereas the original incentive fee accrual was only accrued in respect of Mr Big Investor's investment and not Mr Little Investor's investment.

Remember, the gross NAV of the fund at the end of the second month was in fact £218, even though the NAV was published at £216 (£108 per share), because the £2.00 incentive fee had only been accrued, it had not been paid out. Because in the following month the fund declined and lost £26, the NAV of the fund declined from £218 to £192. Thus, the NAV per share at the end of the quarter was £96.

However, as the fund had lost £26, the equitable allocation would have been to debit £13 to each investor's account. Thus Mr Big Investor, whose account was worth £110 at the end of the second month, before accruing the incentive fee, would have seen the value decline by £13 to £97; whereas Mr Little Investor, who only subscribed £108 at the end of the second month, should also have seen his NAV per share decline by £13 to £95. As stated above, the incentive fee accrual of £2, which was applied at the end of the second month, related to unrealised gains on Mr Big Investor's account. However, because this has been "clawed back" by the fund as a whole, it has been allocated to shareholders on a pro-rata basis. Thus, without equalisation, the value of Mr Big Investor's holding has dropped not to £97 but to £96, a loss of £14, whereas Mr Little Investor benefits from an allocation from part of Mr Big Investor's incentive fee accrual, to the value of £1, so that the NAV per share of his investment is now £96, a loss of only £12, instead of £95.

Equalisation will eliminate this anomaly by reimbursing the accrued incentive fee to Mr Big Investor, who had already "paid" it.

Equalisation Methods and how these anomalies are eliminated
One of the key advantages of implementing equalisation as an accounting methodology is that it will eliminate the problem of one investor being penalised to the advantage of another. Today, there are a number of equalisation methods used and the following are the two most common methods of implementing equalisation.

Series of Shares and Consolidation Method
This is widely acknowledged as the most user-friendly and the simplest of all the equalisation methods to understand. It requires the fund to issue a new series of shares each time there is a subscription. Every month, when calculating the

NAV per share, the correct incentive fee accruals, if any, are applied to each of the series separately. The first series of shares, which is issued when the fund is launched, is usually known as the "lead series". The objective is to consolidate each of the subsequent series issued into the lead series at the end of every accounting period, providing an incentive fee has been paid for each of the series, including the lead series. This may be quarterly, half-yearly, or annually. The following scenarios are used to illustrate this method.

Scenario 1: Rising Market

- Mr Big Investor buys 1,000 lead series shares at £1,000 per share.
- End of first month, GNAV per share has risen 10% to £1,100.
- NAV published at £1,080 (£1,100 less £20 incentive fee).
- Mr Little Investor now buys 1,000 series II shares at £1,000 per share.
- End of second month, value of fund has risen by further 10% so that:
  - GNAV of lead series is now £1,210 = NAV £1,168; and
  - GNAV of series II is now £1,100 = NAV £1,080.
- Investor C buys 1,000 series III shares at £1,000 per share.
- End of third month, fund value has again risen by 10% so that:
  - GNAV of lead series is now £1,331 = NAV £1,264.80;
  - GNAV of series II is now £1,210 = NAV £1,168; and
  - GNAV of series III is now £1,080.
- As it is the end of the quarter and a new high water mark (HWM) has been achieved, the incentive fees are paid.
- Series II and series III shares are then consolidated into lead series.m
- Thus:
  - Mr Little Investor exchanges 1,000 series II shares, now worth £1,168,000, for 923.466 lead series shares at £1,264.80 each;
  - Investor C exchanges 1,000 series III shares, now worth £1,080,000, for 853.890 lead series shares.

It is assumed that Mr Big Investor purchases 1,000 shares at the launch of the fund, at £1,000 per share. This will be the "lead series" of shares. (For this example we are assuming that the incentive fees are being paid quarterly).

It is also assumed that at the end of the first month the GNAV (the NAV before deduction of incentive fee) per lead share has risen to £1,100 and therefore the NAV will be £1,080, net of £20/20% incentive fee. At this time Mr Little Investor subscribes £1 million for 1,000 series II shares at, again, £1,000 each.

At the end of the second month, the value of the fund has risen by a further 10%, so that the GNAV for the lead series is now £1,210, whereas the GNAV for series II is now £1,100. The NAV for the lead series will now be £1,168 and that for series II £1,080, net of 20% incentive fee accrual. At this stage Investor C subscribes a further £1 million for 1,000 shares of series III at £1,000 per share.

It could be assumed that at the end of the third month the GNAV has, yet again, risen by a further 10%, so that:

▓ The GNAV per share of the lead series is £1,331, which translates to a NAV of £1,264.80;

▓ The GNAV of series II is £1,210, equalling a NAV of £1,168; and

▓ The GNAV for series III is £1,100, equalling a NAV of £1,080.

Thus at the end of the first quarter, because a new HWM has been reached and each of the series of shares has paid incentive fees, the series II and series III shares can now be consolidated into the lead series. This means that, in effect, the owners of series II and series III shares will sell, or exchange, their shares for lead series shares. Therefore, Mr Little Investor's shares are worth £1,168.00, which equates to 923.466 shares at the NAV of the lead series, at £1,264.80 each. Similarly, Investor C will liquidate their 1,000 shares of £1,080,000 and effectively invest the proceeds of that liquidation into the lead series at £1,264.80 per share, to receive 853.890 lead series shares.

Scenario 2: Volatile Market

▓ Mr Big Investor buys 1,000 lead series shares at £1,000 per share.

▓ End of first month, GNAV per share has risen 10% to £1,100.

▓ NAV published at £1,080 (£1,100 less £20 incentive fee).

▓ Mr Little Investor now buys 1,000 series II shares at £1,000 per share.

▓ End of second month, value of fund has risen by further 10% so that:

  ▓ GNAV of lead series is now £1,210 = NAV £1,168; and

  ▓ GNAV of series II is now £1,100 = NAV £1,080.

▓ Investor C buys 1,000 series III shares at £1,000 per share.

▓ End of third month GNAV has declined by 4% so that:

  ▓ GNAV of lead series is £1,161.60 = NAV £1,129.28

  ▓ GNAV of series II is £1,056 = NAV £1,044.80

  ▓ GNAV of series III is £960 = NAV £960.

▓ At this time an incentive fee is paid on the lead series and series II, but obviously not on series III.

▓ Therefore, series II will be consolidated into the lead series, but series III will have to wait until a new HWM has been achieved.

If, at the end of the third month, the value of the fund has declined by, say, 4% then the lead series and series II would still be profitable and could be consolidated. However, series III would be showing a loss, at GNAV of £960, and so would not be consolidated. Series III would remain in existence until a new HWM had been achieved which would put series III into profit.

The advantage of this system is that it is a relatively simple procedure and investors can understand how it works and can see that it is fair to all parties.

One of the disadvantages of this approach, however, is the fact that many funds only pay incentive fees once a year and this means that the Series of Shares and Consolidation Method can be quite cumbersome because if a fund is a heavily traded, expanding fund, then by the end of the year it could have 12 separate series in issue. And, of course, if it is a losing year then it is possible that this could go up to 24 series being issued before the next accounting period is finished.

The other obvious disadvantage of the Series method is that it is not possible to publish a single NAV per share because each series has its own NAV. Of course, there is no real problem in publishing several different NAVs but it could be confusing to some shareholders, particularly if they make several investments into the fund over a period of time and so end up with holdings that have different NAVs.

The third main drawback of issuing several series of shares occurs with funds whose shares are listed on a Stock Exchange, because it will probably be necessary to apply to list each share in issue. This is administratively time-consuming and therefore expensive and again there is the problem of having to publish the full list of NAVs.

Simple Equalisation

This procedure entails calculating the performance fee and allocating it fairly between each investor or group of investors at the end of each accounting period. As investors will have come in at different levels, this will mean calculating different NAVs per investor. However, in order to get a common NAV for all shares in the fund, the lowest of all the NAVs calculated, on an investor-by-investor basis, is selected to become the NAV of the fund.

Shareholders with a higher individual NAV per share are then issued "equalisation shares", so that the total number of shares issued to that investor (i.e. the original shares purchased plus any equalisation shares) multiplied by the new NAV of the fund, which we know is the lowest NAV calculated, will now enable the investment for those investors to be kept constant.

As an example, assume that, at launch, Mr Big Investor buys 1,000 shares at £100 to invest £100,000.

Scenario 1 – Rising Market

- Launch: Mr Big Investor buys 1,000 shares at £100 = £100,000.
- End month 1: GNAV = £110.
- Mr Big Investor NAV = £108 (£110 minus £2 incentive fee) = £108,000.
- Mr Little Investor buys 1,000 shares at £108 = £108,000.
- Total NAV of the fund = £216,000.
- End month 2: GNAV = £120.
- Mr Big Investor NAV = £116 (£120 minus £4 incentive fee) = £116,000.
- Mr Little Investor NAV = £117.60 (£120 minus £2.40 incentive fee) = £117,600.
- Published NAV = £116:
    - Mr Little Investor has 1,000 shares at £116 = £116,000
    - Mr Little Investor allocated 13.793 shares @ £116 = £1,600
      Total value= £117,600.

At the end of month one, the GNAV per share is £110, which gives us a NAV of £108 less £2 incentive fee. The shareholding is now worth £108,000.

Mr Little Investor buys 1,000 shares at £108 so the total NAV of the fund will now be £216,000.

143

At the end of month two, the GNAV per share has now risen to £120.

Mr Big Investor's NAV per share is now £116, which is £120 minus the £4 incentive fee.

Mr Little Investor's NAV per share is £117.60, which is £120 less the £2.40 incentive fee on the £12 profit between £108 and £120. This equates to £117,600 total NAV.

However, the published NAV per share will be the lowest NAV per share at £116.

Therefore, Mr Little Investor, who has 1,000 shares at £116, is short of £1,600. This is made up by allocating 13.73, effectively "notional", shares, at £116, which equals £1,600 to bring up the total value of his investment to £117,600.

What happens when the NAV subsequently declines?

Scenario 2 – Volatile Market

- End month 3: GNAV = £105.
- Mr Big Investor NAV = £104 (£105 minus £1 incentive fee).
- Mr Little Investor NAV = £105 (no incentive fee).
- Published NAV = £104:
    - Mr Little Investor has 1,000 shares at £104 = £104,000.
    - Mr Little Investor allocated 9.6154 shares at £104 = £1,000.
      Total value = £105,000.

Firstly, it is assumed that now, at the end of month three, the GNAV per share is £105, when there's the following situation.

Mr Big Investor's NAV per share is £104, that's £105 less £1 incentive fee, whereas Mr Little Investor's NAV per share is £105 because there is no incentive fee chargeable. The published NAV per share, therefore, will be the lowest at £104. Mr Little Investor now has 1,000 shares at £104 to give £104,000 and that's £1,000 short of the £105,000 NAV that he should receive. He will, therefore, be allocated 9.6154 shares at £104, which equals £1,000, to give him a full NAV value of £105,000.

If the NAV per share falls below the launch price or the previous high watermark, no incentive fee accrues on either of the shares and the NAV will be the same for each share in issue.

Scenario 3 – Falling Market

- End month 4: GNAV = £98.
- Mr Big Investor NAV = £98 – no incentive fee.
- Mr Little Investor NAV = £98 – no incentive fee.
- No equalisation shares issued because NAVs are equal.

For example, assume that at month four, the GNAV per share has declined to £98. There is no incentive fee due on either holding, therefore the NAV per share for both Mr Big Investor's and Mr Little Investor's holdings will be £98 and so, obviously, no "notional" shares will be issued to either investor.

The advantages of this system are that it is relatively simple to calculate the NAV for each shareholder and you end up with a single NAV per share for the fund.

However, there are two main disadvantages. Firstly, the NAV does not accurately reflect the fund performance because it is continually discounted and secondly, the addition of equalisation shares to investors' accounts on what, to many, probably seems an arbitrary basis, can confuse those investors.

Equalisation factor/ Depreciation deposit approach

The most common methods of equalisation are the "equalisation factor/depreciation deposit approach" and what is known as the "equalisation adjustment approach". They are both very similar.

Under the equalisation factor/depreciation deposit approach, each investor invests at the NAV, plus either the equalisation factor or the depreciation deposit, depending upon whether the NAV of the fund has increased or declined from the last high water-mark.

Industry experts believe that the equalisation factor method has been overtaken in the popularity stakes by the equalisation approach – so it is beneficial to briefly explain the first and show examples of the equalisation approach.

If the NAV has risen during the period, then a new subscriber would invest the equivalent of the GNAV in order to place the same amount of money at risk as the existing shareholders, the difference between the NAV and the GNAV being the equalisation factor. If the fund maintains its performance, the equalisation factor paid will be refunded in shares at the end of the incentive fee calculation period. If, however, the fund subsequently loses value, the equalisation will be lost for that period but is refundable, in the future, if the fund recovers. This avoids the clawback syndrome.

If, on the other hand, the fund's NAV is at a discount to the HWM at the time that an investor makes a subscription, then the investor will be required to pay a depreciation deposit equal to the incentive fee that would be payable if their shares rose to the HWM. If the fund starts to improve and recoup its losses, then the depreciation deposit becomes payable to the investment advisor as a performance fee. This avoids the "free ride" syndrome.

If the NAV declines, then the deposit is paid back to the investor upon redemption.

Equalisation Adjustment Approach

The equalisation adjustment approach is similar to the equalisation factor/ depreciation deposit method, in that the investor will subscribe at the GNAV but if the NAV, at the time of subscription, is above the previous HWM, then the investor will receive an equalisation credit for that portion of the NAV which represents the incentive fee accrual, (which the investor has paid within the GNAV). Like the equalisation factor, if, at the end of the accounting period, the NAV is still showing a profit or an increased profit, the investor will be paid their equalisation credit by way of an allocation of additional shares in the fund. If, however, the fund's NAV declines before the accounting period ends, then the equalisation credit will decline pro rata, but is recoupable if the NAV rises again.

Both the equalisation credit and equalisation factor methods enable all of the investor's money to be utilised in the fund.

If the investor subscribes during a draw down, or loss, period, they will still pay the GNAV (which, in this case, will be the same as the NAV), so that they have the same amount of capital risk as existing shareholders, but they will also receive what is described as an "equalisation deficit". If the fund subsequently increases in value by the end of the calculation period, a certain number of the investor's shares will be redeemed to equate to the equalisation deficit (or that part of it that is applicable) and the proceeds paid to the fund manager.

The following is an illustration of the equalisation adjustment approach.

- Launch at £100 per share.
- Mr Big Investor buys 1,000 shares at £100. Cost = £100,000.
- End month 1: GNAV = £120.
- Mr Big Investor NAV (£120 minus £4 incentive) = £116 Total = £116,000.
- Mr Little Investor subscribes GNAV (£120) for 1,000 shares. Cost =£120,000.
- This comprises:
  - 1,000 shares @ £116 NAV = £116,000
  - Equalisation credit = (incentive fee) = £ 4,000
  - Total subscribed = £120,000.
- End month 2: GNAV = £130.
- Mr Big Investor NAV = £124 (£130 − £6 incentive fee) Total = £124,000.
- Mr Little Investor NAV = £128 (£130 − £2 incentive fee) Total = £128,000.
- This will comprise:
  - Mr Little Investor = 1,000 shares at £124 = £124,000
  - Equalisation credit = £4,000
  - Total = £ 128,000.
- Total fund NAV = £252,000.
- Cross check:
  - GNAV (2,000 x £130) = £260,000
  - Total subscribed: Mr Big Investor = £100,000
    Mr Little Investor = £120,000
    Total subscribed = £220,000
    Add gross profit = £ 40,000
    GNAV = £260,000
    Deduct incentive 20% = £8,000
    Thus net profit = £32,000.
- Add net profit to sum subscribed NAV = £252,000.

It is assumed here that Mr Big Investor buys 1,000 shares at £100 per share at launch and at the end of month one the gross NAV has risen to £120.

Mr Big Investor's NAV will now be £116, that is £120 minus £4 incentive, so the value of his portfolio is now £116,000.

Mr Little Investor subscribes £120 for 1,000 shares at the GNAV for a cost of £120,000. This £120,000 comprises firstly 1,000 shares at the NAV of £116, which is £116,000, and an equalisation credit, which will equate to the incentive fee of £4,000, making up the total subscribed sum of £120,000.

It is now assumed that at the end of month two the GNAV has risen to £130.

Mr Big Investor's NAV is £124, that is £130 minus £6 incentive, whereas Mr Little Investor's NAV should be £128; that is £130 minus the £2 incentive on the £10 rise that he has had on the money he invested, which equals £128,000. This valuation will, in fact, be all-encompassing because the investor will receive a valuation showing 1,000 shares at the NAV of £124,000 plus his equalisation credit of £4,000 totalling £128,000. Thus at this stage the total NAV of the fund is £252,000.

To check this is correct, it can be viewed in another way – the GNAV of the fund at the end of month two is at £260,000; that is 2,000 shares at £130 each.

This comprises the total sums subscribed by Mr Big Investor of £100,000 and Mr Little Investor of £120,000 totalling £220,000. Add to that the gross profit, which is the £40,000, to bring it up to the total GNAV of £260,000. If an incentive fee is deducted off that £40,000, which would be £8,000, a net profit of £32,000 is achieved; add that to the sum subscribed and a total NAV of £252,000 is achieved, hence it all adds up.

If the price doesn't change before the end of the year then the £4,000 equalisation credit will be used to purchase additional shares at the NAV.

It is assumed that the fund isn't quite such a dramatically good performer and at the end of month two, the GNAV has fallen to £105 as shown in the illustration below.

Scenario 1 – Declining Market

- Mr Big Investor buys 1,000 shares at £100.
- Mr Little Investor buys 1,000 shares at £120, inclusive of £4 equalisation credit as before.
- End month 2: GNAV = £105.
- Mr Big Investor NAV = £104 (£105 – £1 incentive).
- Mr Little Investor NAV = £105
  Comprised of NAV: £104
  Equalisation credit: £1
  Total value: £105.
- End month 3: GNAV = £98.
- Mr Big Investor NAV = £98 (no incentive fee).
- Mr Little Investor NAV = £98 (no equalisation credit).

Mr Big Investor's NAV will now be £104, that's £105 less £1 incentive fee. Mr Little Investor's GNAV will be £105, which is comprised of the actual NAV (same as Mr Big Investor) at £104, plus an equalisation credit, which has now declined to £1, making £105 in total.

It could be assumed that at the end of month three, the GNAV has declined further to £98. Mr Big Investor's NAV will be £98, because there is no incentive fee involved and, similarly, Mr Little Investor's NAV will be £98, because there will be no equalisation credit left, as that will have been eaten up in the decline (although if the price was to recover, then Mr Little Investor could recoup his equalisation credit).

One difference between the equalisation deficit method and the equalisation depreciation deposit method is that, with the equalisation deficit method, the investor's money is fully invested in the fund, whereas under the depreciation deposit method, the deposit is usually invested in T-Bills, Money Market Funds, or some other passive low-risk investment, which means that the investor is not getting full exposure to the fund.

Choice of Equalisation Employed

The final problem, as far as equalisation goes, is the choice of which method is appropriate for a particular fund. This is usually dictated by a combination of market needs (for example, the choice as to whether to use the series method may be dictated by the fact that the shares are listed on the London Stock Exchange) and, to a large extent, the method that the fund manager is most comfortable with.

Another factor that must be seriously considered is the ability of the chosen administrator to calculate the NAV, utilising the equalisation method selected.

Conclusion

There are a number of other methods and variations on the methods described above, but the ones discussed are generally the most commonly used to date in the industry. Fund promoters usually outline the use of equalisation in the fund's prospectus, typically including an example to allow the potential investor to truly understand the calculation. There are simpler, less precise methods than those outlined above; however the more sophisticated investors will demand that equalisation be implemented, as when the amounts to be invested are large, such adjustments can be material to an overall return earned by an investment.

Derivatives and Hedge Funds

This chapter gives an overview of how hedge funds use derivatives and includes a case study on how the use of derivatives contributed to the high-profile failure of Long-Term Capital Managements.

Introduction

One of the more significant changes in financial markets in recent years has been the extraordinary rise of hedge funds and the growth of derivatives products, i.e. options, futures and other financial products whose value is derived from some other financial instrument. These financial products are perhaps the most misunderstood in the financial markets and, because of their growing importance, have aroused concern in some financial and policy circles.

The last two decades have witnessed an explosive growth in derivatives, fuelled by volatile interest rates, exchange rates and equity prices, as well as financial deregulation and intensified competition among financial institutions. The growth of the credit derivatives market, in particular, is due in part to investment by hedge funds in these financial instruments, which spread credit risk more widely rather than leaving it in the banking system. However, the use of derivatives has always been a controversial topic of discussion ever since the collapse of Long-Term Capital Management, which was blamed on the extensive use of derivatives.

Types of Derivatives

In Chapter 5 there was a discussion on credit derivatives, which are the most traded of all the derivatives products. However, there are other derivative products that are popular in the financial markets. Below are descriptions of some of these derivatives.

Some of the most basic forms of derivatives are futures, forwards and options.

Futures and Forwards
As the name suggests, futures are derivative contracts that give the holder the opportunity to buy or sell the underlying at a pre-specified price some time in the future.

They come in standardised form with fixed expiry time, contract size and price. Forwards are similar contracts but customisable in terms of contract size, expiry date and price, according to the needs of the user.

Options
Option contracts give the holder the option to buy or sell the underlying at a pre-specified price some time in the future. An option to buy the underlying risk known as a call option.

On the other hand, an option to sell the underlying at a specified price in the future is known as a put option.

In the case of an option contract, the buyer of the contract is not obligated to exercise the option. Options can be traded on the stock exchange or on the OTC market.

Other types of derivatives are swaps and warrants.

Swaps

A swap is an agreement between two or more parties to exchange a sequence of cash flows over a period in the future. There are different uses of swaps from speculation and arbitrage to hedging.

Warrants

A warrant is a derivative security that gives the holder the right to purchase securities (usually equity) from the issuer at a specific price within a certain time frame. Warrants are often included in a new debt issue as "sweeteners" to entice investors.

The main difference between warrants and call options is that warrants are issued and guaranteed by the company, whereas options are exchange instruments and are not issued by the company. Also, the lifetime of a warrant is often measured in years, while the lifetime of a typical option is measured in months. (Investopedia.com)

These types of derivative products are categorised according to the underlying asset that their value is derived from. For example, if the underlying asset of a particular derivative contract is a commodity then the derivative product is classed as a commodity derivative. The same applies to derivative products where the underlying asset class is equity, fixed income or currency.

There is a vast array of derivative products on the market and thus further discussion on types of derivative is outside the scope of this book. Derivatives will be adequately covered in "Business Knowledge for IT in Derivatives".

Use of Derivatives by Hedge Funds

Hedge funds use both exchange-traded and over-the-counter (OTC) derivative products to deliver superior returns for their investors. The principle of leverage and the ability to long and short mean that extensive use of exchange-traded derivative products is imperative for the hedge fund industry. Hedge funds are also among the dominant players in the multitrillion OTC derivatives market.

Obviously, derivatives are traded in two kinds of market: exchanges and OTC markets. Exchanges have traditionally been defined by "pit" trading through open outcry, but exchanges have recently adopted electronic trading platforms that automatically match the bids and offers from market participants to execute trades in a multilateral environment. The trading of derivatives (traditionally futures and options) in exchanges is conducted through brokers and not dealers.

The OTC markets are organised along several different lines. The first is called a traditional dealer market, the second is called an electronically brokered market and the third is called a proprietary trading platform.

The OTC markets have traditionally been organised around one or more dealers who "make a market" by maintaining the bid and offer quotes to market participants. The quotes and the negotiation of execution prices are generally conducted over the telephone, although the process may be enhanced through the use of electronic bulletin boards by the dealers for posting their quotes. The trading process of negotiating by phone, whether end-user-to-dealer or dealer-to-dealer, is known as bilateral trading because only two market participants directly observe the trading process.

OTC markets have also adopted new electronic and networking technologies for their trading needs. One use of technology is the formation of an electronic brokering platform, which is essentially the same as the electronic trading platforms used by exchanges, creating a multilateral trading environment.

In OTC markets organised through an electronic brokering platform, the firm operating the platform acts as a broker and does not take a position or act as counterparty to any of the trades made through the system. However, the situation changes if the electronic brokering platform adopts a clearing house. In this case, the clearing house assumes all the credit risk of trades that are made through the electronic brokering platform and reported to the clearing house.

Yet another type of trading arrangement found in OTC derivatives markets is a composite of the traditional dealer and the electronic brokering platform where the dealer sets up their own proprietary electronic platform. (Dood, 2002)

Hedge funds are major buyers of derivative products, using them to provide much needed liquidity, hedge against portfolio devaluation and mitigate financial risks. When used strategically they can also reduce transaction costs. Derivatives are not inherently bad, but they can be used very badly (see LTCM story in the latter part of this chapter). Derivative strategies in securities lending transactions must be consistent with the scope and objectives of the hedge fund manager's programmes. They should be applied on a case-by-case basis according to the individual investor's risk/return preferences. Some derivative strategies, though, may be perfectly acceptable to even the most conservative managers. Various types of floating-rate obligations, for example, add value by minimising interest rate risk. Other hedge fund managers, particularly those who currently use derivatives within their investment framework, can use derivative strategies to exploit market inefficiencies. Asset swaps and total rate of return swaps are two common techniques for identifying and taking advantage of arbitrage opportunities.

Any sort of derivative can be used by hedge funds and their presence is felt on derivatives desks in a big way. Many institutions have set up specific desks dedicated to the care and feeding of this sophisticated clientele. Some of the derivative products that hedge funds require, however, would stretch the hedging capabilities (and possibly the capital base) of all but the largest banks.

Direct demand from hedge funds for derivative products and ever more sophisticated product combinations, in turn boosted by increased institutional demand for hedge funds themselves, have seen the derivatives market boom. According to Celent, over the 2000 to 2006 period, credit default swaps grew the fastest at an annualised rate of 206% to US$34.5 trillion. This is not surprising given the extensive press coverage; commodities are next in line with a growth rate of 204% and a notional outstanding value of US$9.2 trillion. Equity derivatives grew to a notional value of US$7.2 trillion, with an annualised growth rate of 148%. Interest rates, the largest segment of the derivatives market with US$285.7 trillion notional outstanding, grew at an annualised rate of 147% over the six-year period. Foreign exchange grew at 126% to US$37.6 trillion.

There are hypotheses in the industry that underpin the use of derivatives by hedge funds as follows:

- Hedge funds with higher incentive fees are more likely to use derivatives.
- Hedge funds with longer lock-up and notice periods are less likely to use derivatives.
- Hedge funds with management ownership are more likely to use derivatives.
- Funds that use effective auditing services are associated with a greater incidence of derivatives use.
- Derivatives use should be related to investment style in a way consistent with potential savings on transaction costs.

According to Chen (2006), data collected from the Lipper TASS database as of June 2006 containing information about 6,877 individual hedge funds, of which 4,031 were live funds and 2,846 were defunct funds, provides statistics about hedge fund derivative use. Empirical findings based on this database show considerable variation in derivative use both within and across fund categories. Managed futures and global macro are two categories with the highest proportion of derivatives users, with 95% and 93% of such funds respectively using derivatives.[58] Meanwhile, equity market neutral funds show the least use of derivatives, with only 53% of these funds using derivatives. Across the derivatives categories, equity derivatives are more pervasively used, with 58% of the sample funds trading at least one of type of equity derivative. Commodity derivatives are the least popular category, with only 16% of sample funds in this category.

The overall pattern of participation in derivatives categories appears to sup-port the transaction-cost-saving hypothesis; equity-oriented funds are more involved in equity derivatives, bond-oriented funds in bond derivatives, and asset-allocation funds in multiple types of derivatives. For example, 79% of fixed income arbitrage funds trade interest rate derivatives or bond derivatives, but only 9% of them use equity derivatives. For global macro funds, 85% use foreign exchange derivatives. Convertible arbitrage funds show a high tendency to use both equity and bond derivatives. This is intuitive in that convertible arbitrage funds often buy the convertible bonds issued by small firms and sell short the equities of the small firms. Therefore, the choice of derivative category for each hedge fund style is consistent with the main underlying assets traded.

58 Source: Chen, Y. 2006 (12 December). Derivatives Use and Risk Taking: Evidence from the Hedge Fund Industry. Job Market Paper.

153

Figure 8.1 Percentage of Hedge Funds using Derivatives for 10 Fund Categories[59]

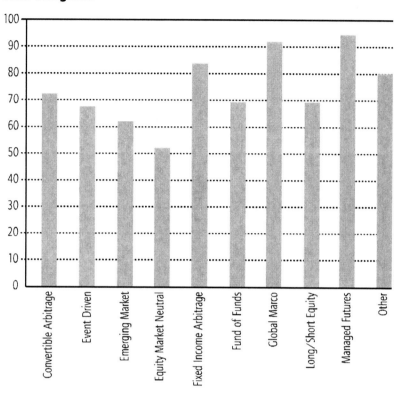

Hedge Funds Trades Associated with Particular Strategies

There are hedge fund trades that are typically associated with particular hedge fund strategies as shown in the following table. It should be noted that the definitions of the hedge fund strategies in this table are somewhat different from the definitions in Chapter 3. This is to create a better correlation between individual trade types and the associated strategy.

The Role of Derivatives in the collapse of LTCM

The collapse of Long-Term Capital Management in the 1990s exemplifies how not to use derivatives. It is usually cited as an event in the financial markets

59   Based on data from the TASS database as of June 2006.

Type of Fund (Strategy)	Definition	Typical Hedge Fund Trades
Aggressive growth	Usually investing in small/microcap stocks, which are expected to appreciate rapidly. Expected acceleration in growth of earnings per share.	Index options – puts mostly.
Distressed securities	Buying equity/debt of companies that are in or face bankruptcy, in the hope of company recovery.	Occasional market puts against sharp market drop.
Emerging markets	Investing in equity/debt of emerging markets. Strict definition of an emerging market is one with GNP (Gross National Product) of $7,620 or less in 1990 (World Bank).	Equities: most frequently used derivatives are index options. Fixed income: occasional interest rate swaps. Currency risk: options, futures and swaps.
Fund-of-funds	Manager invests with other money managers or pooled vehicles that may utilise a number of trading styles, thus creating a diverse instrument for investors.	Puts against market drops, used very infrequently.
Income	Investment with a focus on current income/yield rather than solely capital gains and appreciation over time.	Derivatives used for hedging primarily (although occasionally for investment). Some use of swaps and/or fixed income futures (e.g. T-bill futures).
Macro	Global or international investment that employs "top-down" approach, following major changes in global economies and hoping to realise significant shifts in global interest rates etc.	Broad use of most types of derivatives, depending on fund strategy. Liquidity constraints are a major concern. Derivatives tend to be used more for investment purposes vs hedging than in most other styles.
Market-neutral arbitrage	Manager focuses on obtaining returns with little or no market correlation. Typically buying/selling different securities issued by the same company and exploiting pricing discrepancies between them.	Often hedged with put options. For example, convertible arbitrage funds using put options when stock to short not available or too expensive.

155

Market timing	Large positions in one or two asset classes depending on market or economic outlook. Objective is to anticipate timing of when to be in or out of market.	Occasional use of index futures for quick market action.
Opportunistic	Manager changes from strategy to strategy as seems appropriate. Can use one or more disparate investment styles independent of approach or asset class.	Occasional use of puts vs shorting against individual stocks or market downturns.
Short sellers	Strategy consists of identifying overvalued companies and selling short their stock.	Occasional use of puts for shorting.
Special situations	Typically "event driven". Significant positions taken in a limited number of companies with "special situations", such as reorganisations, emerging bad news.	See opportunistic.
Value	Investing in stocks believed to be trading at a discount to their intrinsic or potential worth.	Limited use of stock and index options for hedging of individual positions or hedging of portfolios.

Source: Van Hedge Fund Advisors and Evaluation Associates

that has become the marker buoy for revealing shortcomings in the markets, in the hope that it may never occur again.

The use of leverage and derivatives has always been synonymous with the operations of the hedge fund industry and funds typically pursue trading strategies using complex derivative securities. Hedge funds leverage the capital they invest by buying securities on margin and engaging in collateralised borrowing. Better-known funds can buy structured derivative products without putting up capital initially but must make a succession of premium payments when the market in those securities trades up or down. In addition, some hedge funds negotiate secured credit lines with their banks, and some relative value funds may even obtain unsecured credit lines. Credit lines are expensive, however, and most managers use them mainly to finance calls for additional margin when the market moves against them. These practices may allow a few hedge funds, like Long-Term Capital Management (prior to its reorganisation), to achieve very high leverage ratios, but industry observers regard LTCM's practices as exceptional.

Industry experts opine that lessons have to be learned from the LTCM fiasco as activities of hedge funds are increasingly shaping the structure of the financial markets. To accentuate this point, the events leading to the failure of LTCM will be used as a case study.

Case Study[60]

John Meriwether, who founded Long-Term Capital Partners in 1993, had been head of fixed income trading at Salomon Brothers. Even when forced to leave Salomon in 1991, in the wake of the firm's treasury auction-rigging scandal (another marker buoy), Meriwether continued to command huge loyalty from a team of highly cerebral relative-value fixed-income traders, and considerable respect from the street.

Teamed up with a handful of these traders – two Nobel laureates, Robert Merton and Myron Scholes, and former regulator David Mullins – Meriwether and LTCM had more credibility than the average broker/dealer on Wall Street. It was a game, in that LTCM was unregulated, free to operate in any market, without capital charges and having only light reporting requirements to the US Securities & Exchange Commission (SEC). It traded on its good name with many respectable counterparties as if it was a member of the same club. That meant an ability to put on interest rate swaps at the market rate for no initial margin – an essential part of its strategy. It meant being able to borrow 100% of the value of any top-grade collateral, and with that cash to buy more securities and post them as collateral for further borrowing: in theory it could leverage itself to infinity. In LTCM's first two full years of operation it produced 43% and 41% return on equity and amassed an investment capital of $7 billion.

Meriwether was renowned as a relative-value trader. Relative value means (in theory) taking little outright market risk, since a long position in one instrument is offset by a short position in a similar instrument or its derivative. It means betting on small price differences which are likely to converge over time as the arbitrage is spotted by the rest of the market and eroded. Trades typical of early LTCM were, for example, to buy Italian government bonds and sell German Bund futures; to buy theoretically underpriced off-the-run US treasury bonds (because they are less liquid) and go short on on-the-run (more liquid) treasuries. It played the same arbitrage in the interest-rate swap market, betting that the spread between swap rates and the most liquid treasury bonds would narrow. It played long-dated callable Bunds against Dm swaptions. It was one of the biggest players on the world's futures exchanges, not only in debt but also equity products.

To make 40% return on capital, however, leverage had to be applied. In theory, market risk isn't increased by stepping up volume, provided you stick to liquid instruments and don't get so big that you yourself become the market.

Some of the big macro hedge funds had encountered this problem and reduced their size by giving money back to their investors. When, in the last quarter of 1997, LTCM returned $2.7 billion to investors, it was assumed to be for the same reason: a prudent reduction in its positions relative to the market.

But it seems the positions weren't reduced relative to the capital reduction, so the leverage increased. Moreover, other risks had been added to the equation. LTCM played the credit spread between mortgage-backed securities (including Danish mortgages) or double-A corporate bonds and the government

60 Source: IFCI Risk Institute. Reproduced with permission.

bond markets. Then it ventured into equity trades. It sold equity index options, taking big premiums in 1997. It took speculative positions in takeover stocks, according to press reports. One such was Tellabs, whose share price fell over 40% when it failed to take over Ciena, says one account. A filing with the SEC for 30 June 1998 showed that LTCM had equity stakes in 77 companies, worth $541 million. It also got into emerging markets, including Russia. One report said Russia was "8% of its book" which would come to $10 billion!

Some of LTCM's biggest competitors, the investment banks, had been clamouring to buy into the fund. Meriwether applied a formula which brought in new investment, as well as providing him and his partners with a virtual put option on the performance of the fund. During 1997, under this formula (see separate section below, titled UBS Fiasco), UBS put in $800 million in the form of a loan and $266 million in straight equity. Credit Suisse Financial Products put in a $100 million loan and $33 million in equity. Other loans may have been secured in this way, but they haven't been made public. Investors in LTCM were pledged to keep in their money for at least two years.

LTCM entered 1998 with its capital reduced to $4.8 billion.

A New York Sunday Times article says the big trouble for LTCM started on 17 July when Salomon Smith Barney announced it was liquidating its dollar interest arbitrage positions: *"For the rest of that month, the fund dropped about 10% because Salomon Brothers was selling all the things that Long-Term owned."* (The article was written by Michael Lewis, former Salomon bond trader and author of Liar's Poker. Lewis visited his former colleagues at LTCM after the crisis and describes some of the trades on the firm's books.)

On 17 August 1998, Russia declared a moratorium on its rouble debt and domestic dollar debt. Hot money, already jittery because of the Asian crisis, fled into high-quality instruments. Top preference was for the most liquid US and G-10 government bonds. Spreads widened even between on- and off-the-run US treasuries.

Most of LTCM's bets had been variations on the same theme: convergence between liquid treasuries and more complex instruments that commanded a credit or liquidity premium. Unfortunately, convergence turned into dramatic divergence.

LTCM's counterparties, marking their LTCM exposure to market at least once a day, began to call for more collateral to cover the divergence. On one single day, 21 August, the LTCM portfolio lost $550 million, writes Lewis. Meriwether and his team, still convinced of the logic behind their trades, believed all they needed was more capital to see them through a distorted market.

Perhaps they were right. But several factors were against LTCM:

■ Who could predict the time frame within which rates would converge again?
■ Counterparties had lost confidence in themselves and LTCM.
■ Many counterparties had put on the same convergence trades, some of them as disciples of LTCM.
■ Some counterparties saw an opportunity to trade against LTCM's known or imagined positions.

In these circumstances, leverage is not welcome. LTCM was being forced to liquidate to meet margin calls.

On 2 September 1998, Meriwether sent a letter to his investors saying that the fund had lost $2.5 billion or 52% of its value that year, $2.1 billion in August alone. Its capital base had shrunk to $2.3 billion. Meriwether was looking for fresh investment of around $1.5 billion to carry the fund through. He approached those known to have such investible capital, including George Soros, Julian Robertson and Warren Buffett, chairman of Berkshire Hathaway and previously an investor in Salomon Brothers (LTCM, incidentally, had a $14 million equity stake in Berkshire Hathaway), and Jon Corzine, then co-chairman and co-chief executive officer at Goldman Sachs, an erstwhile classmate at the University of Chicago. Goldman and JP Morgan were also asked to scour the market for capital.

But offers of new capital weren't forthcoming. Perhaps these big players were waiting for the price of an equity stake in LTCM to fall further. Or they were making money just trading against LTCM's positions. Under these circumstances, if true, it was difficult and dangerous for LTCM to show potential buyers more details of its portfolio. Two Merrill executives visited LTCM headquarters on 9 September 1998 for a "due diligence meeting", according to a later *Financial Times* report (on 30 October 1998). They were provided with *"general information about the fund's portfolio, its strategies, the losses to date and the intention to reduce risk"*. But LTCM didn't disclose its trading positions, books or documents of any kind, Merrill is quoted as saying.

The US Federal Reserve system, particularly the New York Fed which is closest to Wall Street, began to hear concerns about LTCM from its constituent banks. In the third week of September, Bear Stearns, which was LTCM's clearing agent, said it wanted another $500 million in collateral to continue clearing LTCM's trades. On Friday 18 September 1998, New York Fed chairman Bill McDonough made *"a series of calls to senior Wall Street officials to discuss overall market conditions"*, he told the House Committee on Banking and Financial Services on 1 October. *"Everyone I spoke to that day volunteered concern about the serious effect the deteriorating situation of Long-Term could have on world markets."*

Peter Fisher, executive vice-president at the NY Fed, decided to take a look at the LTCM portfolio. On Sunday 20 September 1998, he and two Fed colleagues, assistant treasury secretary Gary Gensler and bankers from Goldman and JP Morgan, visited LTCM's offices at Greenwich, Connecticut. They were all surprised by what they saw. It was clear that, although LTCM's major counterparties had closely monitored their bilateral positions, they had no inkling of LTCM's total off-balance-sheet leverage. LTCM had done swap upon swap with 36 different counterparties. In many cases it had put on a new swap to reverse a position rather than unwind the first swap, which would have required a mark-to-market cash payment in one direction or the other. LTCM's on-balance-sheet assets totalled around $125 billion, on a capital base of $4 billion, a leverage of about 30 times. But that leverage was increased tenfold by LTCM's off-balance-sheet business, whose notional principal ran to around $1 trillion.

The off-balance-sheet contracts were mostly nettable under bilateral ISDA (International Swaps & Derivatives Association) master agreements. Most of them were also collateralised. Unfortunately the value of the collateral had taken a dive since 17 August.

Surely LTCM, with two of the original masters of derivatives and option valuation among its partners, would have put its portfolio through stress tests to match recent market turmoil? But, like many other value-at-risk (VAR) modellers on the street, their worst-case scenarios had been outplayed by the horribly correlated behaviour of the market since 17 August. Such a flight to quality hadn't been predicted, probably because it was so clearly irrational.

According to LTCM managers, their stress tests had involved looking at the 12 biggest deals with each of their top 20 counterparties. That produced a worst-case loss of around $3 billion. But on that Sunday evening it seemed the mark-to-market loss, just on those 240-or-so deals, might reach $5 billion. And that was ignoring all the other trades, some of them in highly speculative and illiquid instruments.

The next day, Monday 21 September 1998, bankers from Merrill, Goldman and JP Morgan continued to review the problem. It was still hoped that a single buyer for the portfolio could be found – the cleanest solution.

According to Lewis's article, LTCM's portfolio had its second biggest loss that day, of $500 million. Half of that, says Lewis, was lost on a short position in five-year equity options. Lewis records brokers' opinion that AIG had intervened in thin markets to drive up the option price to profit from LTCM's weakness. At that time, as was learned later, AIG was part of a consortium negotiating to buy LTCM's portfolio. By this time, LTCM's capital base had dwindled to a mere $600 million. That evening, UBS, with its particular exposure on an $800 million credit, with $266 million invested as a hedge, sent a team to Greenwich to study the portfolio.

The Fed's Peter Fischer invited those three banks and UBS to breakfast at the Fed headquarters in Liberty Street the following day. The bankers decided to form working groups to study possible market solutions to the problem, given the absence of a single buyer. Proposals included buying LTCM's fixed income positions, and "lifting" the equity positions (which were a mixture of index spread trades and total return swaps, and the takeover bets). During the day, a third option emerged as the most promising: seeking recapitalisation of the portfolio by a consortium of creditors.

But any action had to be taken swiftly. The danger was that a single default by LTCM would trigger cross-default clauses in its ISDA master agreements, precipitating a mass close-out in the over-the-counter derivatives markets. Banks terminating their positions with LTCM would have to rebalance any hedge they might have on the other side. The market would quickly get wind of their need to rebalance and move against them. Mark-to-market values would descend in a vicious spiral. In the case of the French equity index, the CAC 40, LTCM had apparently sold short up to 30% of the volatility of the entire underlying market. The Banque de France was worried that a rapid close-out would severely hit French equities. There was a wider concern that an unknown number of market players had convergence positions similar or identical to those of LTCM. In such a one-way market there could be a panic rush for the door.

A meltdown of developed markets on top of the panic in emerging markets seemed a real possibility. LTCM's clearing agent, Bear Stearns, was threatening to foreclose the next day if it didn't see $500 million more collateral. Until now, LTCM had resisted the temptation to draw on a $900 million standby facility that had been syndicated by Chase Manhattan Bank, because it knew that the action would panic its counterparties. But the situation was now desperate. LTCM asked Chase for $500 million. It received only $470 million since two syndicate members refused to chip in.

To take the consortium plan further, the biggest banks, either big creditors to LTCM or big players in the over-the-counter markets, were asked to a meeting at the Fed that evening. The plan was to get 16 of them to chip in $250 million each to recapitalise LTCM at $4 billion.

The four core banks met at 7pm and reviewed a term sheet which had been drafted by Merrill Lynch. Then at 8.30 bankers from nine more institutions arrived. They represented: Bankers Trust, Barclays, Bear Stearns, Chase, Credit Suisse First Boston, Deutsche Bank, Lehman Brothers, Morgan Stanley, Credit Agricole, Banque Paribas, Salomon Smith Barney, and Societe Generale. David Pflug, head of global credit risk at Chase, warned that nothing would be gained a) by raking over the mistakes that had got them in this room, and b) by arguing about who had the biggest exposure: they were all in this equally and together.

The delicate question was how to preserve value in the LTCM portfolio, given that banks around the room would be equity investors and yet, at the same time, they would be seeking to liquidate their own positions with LTCM to maximum advantage. It was clear that John Meriwether and his partners would have to be involved in keeping such a complex portfolio a going concern. But what incentive would they have if they no longer had an interest in the profits? Chase insisted that any bailout would first have to return the $470 million drawn down on the syndicated standby facility. But nothing could be finalised that night since few of the representatives present could pledge $250 million or more of their firm's money.

The meeting resumed at 9.30 the next morning. Goldman Sachs had a surprise: its client, Warren Buffett, was offering to buy the LTCM portfolio for $250 million and recapitalise it with $3 billion from his Berkshire Hathaway group, $700 million from AIG and $300 million from Goldman. There would be no management role for Meriwether and his team. None of LTCM's existing liabilities would be picked up, yet all current financing had to stay in place. Meriwether had until 12.30 to decide.

By 1pm it was clear that Meriwether had rejected the offer, either because he didn't like it or, according to his lawyers, because he couldn't do so without consulting his investors, which would have taken him over the deadline.

The bankers were somewhat flabbergasted by Goldman's dual role. Despite frequent requests for information about other possible bidders, Goldman had dropped no hint at previous meetings that there was something in the pipeline.

Now the banks were back to the consortium solution. Since there were only 13 banks, not 16, they'd have to put in more than $250 million each. Bear Stearns offered nothing, feeling that it had enough risk as LTCM's clearing agent. (Their special relationship may have been the source of some acrimony: LTCM had an $18 million equity stake in Bear Stearns, matched by investments in LTCM of $10 million each by Bear Stearns principals, James Cayne and Warren Spector.) Lehman Brothers also declined to participate. In the end, 11 banks put in $300 million each, Societe Generale $125 million, and Credit Agricole and Paribas $100 million each, reaching a total fresh equity of $3.625 billion. Meriwether and his team would retain a stake of 10% in the company. They would run the portfolio under the scrutiny of an oversight committee representing the new shareholding consortium.

The message to the market was that there would be no fire-sale of assets. The LTCM portfolio would be managed as a going concern.

In the first two weeks after the bail-out, LTCM continued to lose value, particularly on its dollar/yen trades, according to press reports which put the loss at $200 million to $300 million. There were more attempts to sell the portfolio to a single buyer. According to press reports the new LTCM shareholders had further talks with Buffett, and with Saudi prince Alwaleed bin Talal bin Abdulaziz. But there was no sale. By mid-December 1998 the fund was reporting a profit of $400 million, net of fees to LTCM partners and staff.

In early February 1999 there were press reports of divisions between banks in the bailout consortium, some wishing to get their money out by the end of the year, others happy to "stay for the ride" of at least three years. There was also a dispute about how much Chase was charging for a funding facility to LTCM. Within six months there were reports that Meriwether and some of his team wanted to buy out the banks, with a little help from their friend Jon Corzine, who was due to leave Goldman Sachs after its flotation in May 1999.

By 30 June 1999, the fund was up 14.1%, net of fees, from the previous September. Meriwether's plan, approved by the consortium, was apparently to redeem the fund, now valued at around $4.7 billion, and to start another fund concentrating on buyouts and mortgages. On 6 July 1999, LTCM repaid $300 million to its original investors who had a residual stake in the fund of around 9%. It also paid out $1 billion to the 14 consortium members. It seemed Meriwether was bouncing back.

Post Mortem

A post mortem of the events should be included to highlight the inefficiencies that allowed this situation to deteriorate to the extent it did.

The LTCM fiasco naturally inspired a hunt for scapegoats:

1. First in line were Meriwether and his crew of market professors.
2. Second were the banks which conspired to give LTCM far more credit, in aggregate, than they would give to a medium-sized developing country. Particularly distasteful was the combination of credit exposure by the institutions themselves, and personal investment exposure by the individuals

who ran them. Merrill Lynch protested that a $22 million investment on behalf of its employees was not sinister. LTCM was one of four investment vehicles which employees could opt to have their deferred payments invested in. Nevertheless, that rather cosy relationship may have made it more difficult for credit officers to ask tough questions of LTCM. There were accusations of "crony capitalism" as Wall Street firms undertook to bail out, with shareholders' money, a firm in which their officers had invested, or were thought to have invested, part of their personal wealth.

3. Third in line was the US Federal Reserve system. Although no public money was spent – apart from hosting the odd breakfast – there was the implication that the Fed was standing behind the banks, ready to provide liquidity until the markets became less jittery and more rational. Wouldn't this simply encourage other hedge funds and lenders to hedge funds to be as reckless in future?

4. Fourth culprit was poor information. Scant disclosure of its activities and exposures by LTCM, as with many hedge funds, was a major factor in allowing it to put on such leverage. There was also no mechanism whereby counterparties could learn how far LTCM was exposed to other counterparties.

5. Fifth was sloppy market practice, such as allowing a non-bank counterparty to write swaps and pledge collateral for no initial margin as if it were part of a peer-group top-tier bank.

1. LTCM's risk management

Despite the presence of Nobel laureates closely identified with option theory, it seems LTCM relied too much on theoretical market-risk models and not enough on stress-testing, gap risk and liquidity risk. There was an assumption that the portfolio was sufficiently diversified across world markets to produce low correlation. But in most markets, LTCM was replicating basically the same credit spread trade. In August and September 1998, credit spreads widened in practically every market at the same time.

LTCM risk managers kidded themselves that the resultant net position of LTCM's derivatives transactions bore no relation to the billions of dollars of notional underlying instruments. Each of those instruments and its derivative had a market price which could shift independently; each was subject to liquidity risk.

LTCM sources apparently complained that the market started trading against its known positions. That seems like special pleading. Meriwether et al. must have been in the markets long enough to know they are merciless, and to have been just as merciless themselves. *"All they that take the sword shall perish with the sword."* (Matthew, xxvi, 52)

2. Risk management by LTCM counterparties

Practically the whole street had a blind spot when it came to LTCM. They forgot the useful discipline of charging non-bank counterparties an initial margin on swap and repo transactions. Collectively they were responsible for allowing LTCM to build up layer upon layer of swap and repo positions.

163

They believed that the first-class collateral they held was sufficient to mitigate their loss if LTCM disappeared. It may have been over time, but their margin calls to top up deteriorating positions simply pushed LTCM further towards the brink.

Their credit assessment of LTCM didn't include a global view of its leverage and its relationship with other counterparties.

A working group on highly leveraged institutions, set up by the Basle Committee on Banking Supervision, reported its findings in January 1999, drawing many lessons from the LTCM case. It criticised the banks for building up such exposures to such an opaque institution. They had placed a *"heavy reliance on collateralisation of direct mark-to-market exposures"* the report said. *"This in turn made it possible for banks to compromise other critical elements of effective credit risk management, including upfront due diligence, exposure measurement methodologies, the limit setting process, and ongoing monitoring of counterparty exposure, especially concentrations and leverage."*

The working group also noted that banks' *"covenants with LTCM did not require the posting of, or increase in, initial margin as the risk profile of the counterparty changed, for instance as leverage increased"*. (For full reports, see "Sound Practices for Banks' Interactions with Highly Leveraged Institutions" and "Banks' Interactions with Highly Leveraged Institutions".) Another report in June 1999 by the Counterparty Risk Management Policy Group, a group of 12 leading investment banks, suggested many ways in which information sharing and transparency could be improved. It noted the importance of measuring liquidity risk, and improving market conventions and market practices, such as charging initial margin.

3. Supervision

Supervisors themselves showed a certain blinkered view when it came to banks' and securities firms' relationships with hedge funds, and a huge fund like LTCM in particular. The US Securities & Exchange Commission (SEC) appeared to assess the risk run by individual broker dealers without having enough regard for what was happening in the sector as a whole, or in the firms' unregulated subsidiaries.

In testimony to the House Committee on Banking and Financial Services on 1 October 1998, Richard Lindsey, director of the SEC's market regulation division, recalled the following: *"When the commission learned of LTCM's financial difficulties in August, the commission staff and the New York Stock Exchange surveyed major broker-dealers known to have credit exposure to one or more large hedge funds. The results of our initial survey indicated that no individual broker-dealer had exposure to LTCM that jeopardised its required regulatory capital or its financial stability.*

"As the situation at LTCM continued to deteriorate, we learned that although significant amounts of credit were extended to LTCM by US securities firms, this lending was on a secured basis, with collateral collected and marked-to-the-market daily. Thus, broker-dealers' lending to LTCM was done in a manner that was consistent with the firms' normal lending activity. The collateral collected from

LTCM consisted primarily of highly liquid assets, such as US treasury securities or G-7 country sovereign debt. Any shortfalls in collateral were met by margin calls to LTCM. As of the date of the rescue plan, it appears that LTCM had met all of its margin calls by US securities firms. Moreover, our review of the risk assessment information submitted to the commission suggests that any exposure to LTCM existed outside the US broker-dealers, either in the holding company or its unregistered affiliates."

The sad truth revealed by this testimony is that the SEC and the NYSE were concerned only with the risk ratios of their registered firms and were ignorant and unconcerned, as were the firms themselves, about the market's aggregate exposure to LTCM.

Bank of England experts note the absence of any covenant between LTCM and its counterparties that would have obliged LTCM to disclose its overall gearing. UK banks have long been in the habit of demanding covenants from non-bank counterparties concerning their overall gearing, the Bank of England says.

4. Was there moral hazard?

The simple answer is yes, since the bailout of LTCM gave comfort that the Fed will come in and broker a solution, even if it doesn't commit funds. The Fed's intervention also arguably tempted Meriwether not to accept the offer from Buffett, AIG and Goldman. The offer, heavily conditional though it was, shows that the LTCM portfolio had a perceived market value. A price might have been reached in negotiations between Buffett and Meriwether. Meriwether's argument (and the Fed's) is that Buffett's deadline of 12.30 didn't give Meriwether time to consult with LTCM's investors: he was legally unable to accept the offer.

It is possible to argue that a market solution was found. Fourteen banks put up their own money, regarding it as a medium-term investment from which they expected to make a profit. From a value-preservation point of view it was an enlightened solution, even if it did seem to reward those whose recklessness had created the problem.

Federal Reserve chairman Alan Greenspan defended the Fed's action at the 1 October hearing in the House Committee on Banking and Financial Services as follows: *"This agreement [by the rescuing banks] was not a government bailout, in that Federal Reserve funds were neither provided nor ever even suggested. Agreements were not forced upon unwilling market participants. Creditors and counterparties calculated that LTCM and, accordingly, their claims, would be worth more over time if the liquidation of LTCM's portfolio was orderly as opposed to being subject to a fire sale. And with markets currently volatile and investors skittish, putting a special premium on the timely resolution of LTCM's problems seemed entirely appropriate as a matter of public policy."*

The true test of moral hazard is whether the Fed would be expected to intervene in the same way next time. Greenspan pointed to a unique set of circumstances which made an LTCM solution particularly pressing. It seems questionable whether the Fed would act as broker for another fund bailout unless there were also such wide systemic uncertainties.

5. Was there truly a systemic risk?

Since there was no global meltdown, it is difficult to prove that there was a real danger of such a thing that September. But if the officers at the US Federal Reserve had waited to see what happened, no-one would have thanked them after the event. In the judgement of this writer, the world financial system owes a lot to the prompt action of Greenspan, McDonough, Fisher and others at the Fed for their willingness to meet the problem fair and square. One shudders to think what the Bank of England (FSA) might have done, given its "constructive ambiguity" during the Barings crisis.

But the counter-argument is also valid. Those Wall Street firms, once they knew the size of the problem, had only one sensible course of action: to bankroll a co-ordinated rescue. They had the resources to prevent a meltdown and it took only a night and a day to pool them. Mutual self-interest concentrates the mind wonderfully.

It seems that in the developed world, since the early 1990s, financial firms have built up enough capital to meet most disasters the world can throw at them. Their mistakes in emerging markets were costly both for them and for the countries concerned, but they haven't threatened the life of the world financial system. It seems the mechanisms for restructuring and acquisition are so swift that the demise of a financial firm simply means it will be stripped of the trash and carved up. In a down-cycle, however, the outcome could be very different. Moreover, the social costs of this financial overreach, followed by cannibalism, could be considerable.

Systemic, no. Ripe for concerted private and public intervention, yes.

On 29 September 1999, six days after the LTCM bailout, US Federal Reserve chairman Alan Greenspan cut Fed fund rates by 25 basis points to 5.25%. On 15 October 1999 he cut them by another quarter. His critics associate these cuts directly with the bailout of LTCM: it was an extra dose of medicine to make sure the recovery worked. Some sources attribute the cut to rumours that another hedge fund was in trouble.

The more generous view is that if the financial markets were in disarray, we ain't seen nothing yet! Bruce Jacobs, who has followed the systemic implications of the 1929, 1987 and subsequent mini-crashes, fearful of the dangers of globally traded derivatives, writes in a new book: *"Had LTCM not been bailed out, the immediate liquidation of its highly leveraged bond, equity, and derivatives positions may have had effects, particularly on the bond market, rivalling the effects on the equity market of the forced liquidations of insured stocks in 1987 and margined stocks in 1929. Given the links between LTCM and investment and commercial banks, and between its positions in different asset markets and different countries' markets, the systemic risk much talked about in connection with the growth of derivatives markets may have become a reality."* (Capital ideas and market realities, Blackwell, 1999, page 293)

Corrective Response

The Basle Committee on Banking Supervision's report on highly leveraged institutions (HLIs) in January 1999 suggests that supervisors demand higher capital charges for exposure to highly leveraged institutions where there is no limit to overall leverage: *"Possibly all exposures to all counterparties not covered by covenants on leverage should carry a higher weight."* It further considers the possibility of extending a credit register for bank loans in the context of HLIs. *"The register would entail collecting, in a centralised place, information on the exposures of international financial intermediaries to single counterparties that have the potential to create systemic risk (i.e. major HLIs). Exposures would cover both on- and off-balance-sheet positions. Counterparties, supervisors and central banks could then obtain information about the overall indebtedness of the single counterparty."*

The Losers

Among the investors who lost their capital in LTCM (according to press reports) were:

- LTCM partners – $1.1 billion ($1.5 billion at the beginning of 1998, offset by their $400 million stake in the rescued fund)
- Liechtenstein Global Trust – $30 million
- Bank of Italy – $100 million
- Credit Suisse – $55 million
- UBS – $690 million
- Merrill Lynch (employees' deferred payment) – $22 million
- Donald Marron, chairman, PaineWebber – $10 million
- Sandy Weill, co-CEO, Citigroup – $10 million
- McKinsey executives – $10 million
- Bear Stearns executives – $20 million
- Dresdner Bank – $145 million
- Sumitomo Bank – $100 million
- Prudential Life Corp – $5.43 million

There were no reported numbers for the following organisations:

- Bank Julius Baer (for clients)
- Republic National Bank
- St Johns University endowment fund
- University of Pittsburgh

UBS Fiasco

The biggest single loser in the LTCM debacle was UBS, which was forced to write off Sfr950 million ($682 million) of its exposure. The UBS involvement with LTCM pre-dated the merger of Union Bank of Switzerland and Swiss Bank Corporation in December 1998. Various heads rolled, including that of chairman Mathis Cabiallavetta (formerly chief executive of Union Bank of Switzerland), Werner Bonadurer, chief operating officer, Felix Fischer, chief risk officer, and Andy Siciliano, head of fixed income (who had been with SBC).

UBS's deal with LTCM was a variation on other attempts to turn hedge funds into a securitised asset class with a protected downside. However, in this case UBS was protecting the downside and LTCM was taking a good deal of the upside. The sweetener for UBS was a structure that looked more like an option than a loan, turning any income into a capital gain, and an opportunity to invest directly in LTCM.

For a premium of $300 million, UBS sold LTCM a seven- year European call option on 1 million of LTCM's own shares, valued then at $800 million. To hedge the position – the only way it could be done – UBS bought $800 million worth of LTCM shares. UBS also invested $300 million (most of the $266 million premium income) directly in LTCM. Such an investment had to be held for a minimum of three years.

This transaction was completed in three tranches in June, August and October 1997. The deal was calculated so that the $300 million premium was equivalent to a coupon of Libor plus 50 basis points over the seven years.

Assuming that LTCM performed well, the deal provided UBS with a steady, tax-efficient return plus a share in the upside, through its $266 million stake.

But if ever its hedge looked like falling below the $800 million strike price, it was looking at a loss. The only way to hedge it would have been to sell LTCM shares.

But there were various impediments to this. UBS could not just dump the shares. It was obliged to convert any shares it sold into a loan at par value, maturing in 2004.

Shares in hedge funds aren't liquid, and LTCM's were no exception. It was impossible to mark them regularly to market. LTCM reported to shareholders only monthly. If UBS did sell LTCM shares in a falling market, and then LTCM's performance picked up again, there was no guarantee it could rehedge its position. No one was making a market in LTCM shares.

Theoretically there was a volatility cap on the arrangement: if the fund's volatility exceeded a certain level, a cash sum would be reckoned in UBS's favour, payable at the end of year seven. But it is not clear how that would have left UBS market-neutral.

In the climate of mid-1997, it is understandable how UBS risk managers might have overlooked the horrible implications of a worst-case LTCM scenario. LTCM had a fantastic reputation for big-number but low-risk arbitrage. (There is a parallel in the reputation that Nick Leeson enjoyed at Barings before March 1995.)

But it is clear now that UBS risk managers never faced the possibility of a collapse of LTCM, which would have left them with $766 million exposure ($800 million hedge, $266 million investment, less $300 million option premium). That is, they didn't wake up to it, apparently, until around April 1998, in a post-merger review when it was too late to do much about it.

Credit Suisse Financial Products, which did a similar deal for $100 million, set that as the maximum it was prepared to lose.

An interesting aspect of the UBS deal is to consider it from LTCM's point of view. LTCM secured $800 million of new investment capital at Libor plus 50 basis points. It had a call on all returns above that level. UBS's obligation, to convert any shares it wanted to sell into a loan, provided LTCM with a synthetic seven-year put on its own performance. Was this an added incentive to roll the dice? It was a cheap gambling stake.

Common Systems Used in the Hedge Fund Industry

9

This chapter contains information on systems commonly used in the hedge fund industry and a brief overview of the hedge fund technology market.

Introduction

As far as technology goes, there has never been a better time to be a hedge fund manager. There is an array of applications on the market from mobile order entry to sophisticated modelling; most within the budget of even the smallest hedge fund start-up.

A recent development in the financial technology market space is the increasing number of solutions being designed specifically for hedge fund managers rather than the cut-down versions of applications designed for trading desks that they had to make do with in the past, which is an added bonus.

Demand for cutting-edge systems from the leading vendors in the hedge fund industry is driven by various factors including greater transaction volumes, increased requirements from institutional investors and the need for multiple prime broker support. But in a fiercely competitive marketplace, all managers are obviously aware that they need the right tools to generate the returns their investors require while avoiding the pitfalls of inadequate risk management.

Another factor driving demand for software solutions is the diversity of hedge fund activity. At one extreme, the funds that are now quite mature are, in effect, behaving almost exactly like "grown-up" asset management firms; they have multiple clients to manage, they are watching the markets, creating investment strategies and taking positions like mainstream asset management firms. At the other extreme there are hedge funds that behave in a radically different way; some are almost private equity firms, taking direct shareholdings in unlisted business, or acting as arbitrage traders. This shows that there some extremes in investment behaviour in the hedge fund universe.

While divergence has come to characterise the hedge fund market as a whole, the convergence between the larger hedge funds and the traditional asset management space is beginning to drive technological change.

What do hedge fund managers use these systems for?

- **Trading** – this is an area where every hedge fund manager would demand the best-of-breed systems as it is the "bread and butter" of their business.
- **Risk Management** – this is becoming increasingly important in the face of stricter regulations and compliance requirements and fund managers need systems that can help them manage risk efficiently. Furthermore, investors are becoming far more demanding and actually want to see the risk management and reporting systems in place before they part with their capital. They are no longer prepared to take this on trust or on the basis of the manager's reputation. Nor are they prepared to accept the basic risk analysis traditionally provided by hedge fund administrators.
- **Analysis** – this is another important area of the business of hedge fund management. Fund managers need applications with analytic features to detect interdependence within groups of securities and to predict the future movement of one security in the group by analysing the behaviour of others. In addition, these applications need to detect periodic behaviour in markets and to build predictions of future directions.

■ **Interest rate modelling** – hedge fund managers require applications that can integrate interest-rate modelling with other features, so that one database and one implementation system can handle all product types (i.e. range of instruments that they trade) and cross-reference between them.

■ **Marketing** – because of their client demographic, hedge fund managers often spend a considerable amount of time on the move, making presentations to clients. Handheld devices that provide real-time prices and allow order entry are consequently of interest. They may also want to provide clients with a range of pre- and post-trade services available to them via a selection of portable devices, including Blackberrys and PDAs.

■ **Transaction management** – functionality that provides comprehensive transaction management including trade tickets, confirms, SWIFT interface, cashflow management and even a global swap resetter would be desirable to hedge fund managers.

Figure 9.1 Typical Interfaces required by a Hedge Fund

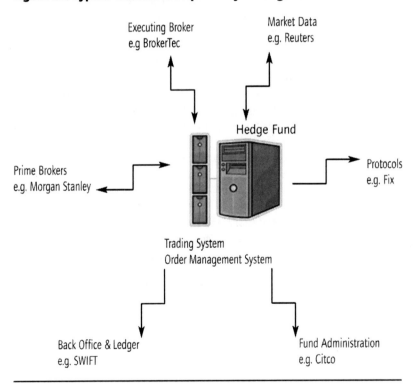

The Hedge Fund Technology Market

Hedge funds are ramping up their use of technology to cope with increased financial regulations and lower profit margins. As a result, global hedge fund investment in IT is set to reach $3.3bn by 2009, according to a study by analyst Datamonitor.

As for prime brokers and fund administrators, most of the IT spending will be focused on Asia and Europe in the next few years. Industry watchers estimate it will reach $414m and $194m respectively by 2009 as these service providers attempt to enhance their margins and stock lending systems as well as upgrading settlement systems to process higher volumes, and the more complex instruments being traded by hedge funds. Technology solutions will continue to be driven by the need to retain and capture order flow.[61]

To Build or To Buy

Operational and administrative processes have been set up for better running of the funds in the wake of the rapid growth experienced in the hedge fund industry. However what is missing right now is the proficiency to take care of the technology associated with the processes. Until now, hedge fund managers have relied heavily on third-party technology infrastructures to carry on their activities.

Their prime focus is on asset management and they leave no stone unturned in order to get the best investment talent in the industry. But the technology that they use is generally an extension of the one offered by prime brokers. The source transactions flow through these units. Considering the huge size of the industry, the reliance of hedge funds on outsourced technology is surprising.

While most of the hedge funds are small to mid-level and cannot afford to maintain an in-house technology, some hedge funds are reaching the scale of growth and complexity where they perhaps would consider recruiting their own Chief Technology Officer, more so because of the inability of prime brokers to offer such diversity. For prime brokers, hedge funds are a big chunk of their business, something they just cannot ignore. For example, hedge funds are estimated to be providing an average of 35% of the daily transaction volumes through the major exchanges in Europe.

It is no surprise, then, to see these brokers bending over backwards to provide whatever the hedge funds demand. They have been known to provide a variety of services in securities transaction services including research, secured lending, trade execution, risk management, transaction processing, clearing, settlement and custody to their "prime clients". For this they charge an individually structured and agreed fee.

But the question still remains, should the hedge funds invest in their own technology set-up? The question becomes more relevant for those fund managers who manage several funds at one time. For them, the additional responsibility of making the third-party technology work seamlessly is an additional burden.

61 Source: "Hedge funds turn to technology", www.banking-business-review.com.

For prime brokers, this is good business. Not only are the volumes large, but hedge funds come with minimal financial regulations. Hence the "soft commissions" are definitely permitted. Also to be noted is the fact that the disclosure of commercial, reciprocal arrangements with the prime brokerage units is at the complete discretion of the hedge fund manager. What it means is that if the fund does not want to disclose its dealings with the prime broker to its investors, it is free to do so. IT Director reports:

"New financial products are the lifeblood and success ingredients for some funds. Technology is required to ensure that fund managers can deliver them efficiently and at the necessary scale for commercial success."

Trading Systems

What is a trading system?
Trading systems' vendors provide front-office to back-office software systems for trading, risk and processing. These systems are designed to capture, store and process data – trades – and allow that data to be subjected to various kinds of analysis, accessed through user-friendly interfaces and passed around the organisation efficiently. Trading systems are not designed primarily to price derivatives – that is a separate large area of technological spending. However, many systems include pricing functions, or are designed to work with certain pricing models.

Trades are captured in the front office, and here staff can use various functions such as product structuring, analytics and position management.

Risk components typically include "what if" analysis, VaR analysis, P&L analysis, limit management and hedge recommendations.

The other part of a trading system is workflow management between the front and back office, and between the back office and external parties for confirmation, payments and settlement. Accounting functions also form part of a trading system.

Trading systems come with development tools and programming interfaces to allow modifications and extensions, often using C/C++ or Java APIs, or using COM or CORBA interfaces. Alternatively, systems can be supplied with built-in scripting engines and extension tools.

What is a Multi-class Trading System?
Multi-class trading systems are systems that are security neutral. These are solutions that facilitate the workflow of any type of security instrument – not with workarounds but rather with security and trade-specific screens, relatively few clicks, and well-displayed data, forming a dynamic, scalable instrument model that allows full customisation of the security within the solution. Many technology solutions do not offer a fully built-out system with the ideal breadth of solution functionality for hedge fund firms. Depending upon their point of origin, vendor solutions can fall short on derivative processing, advanced risk analytics, connectivity, or functions critical to the buy side, such as flexible workflow, trading, compliance, performance measurement and client reporting.

173

Two of the distinguishing attributes of today's multi-asset-class platforms are as follows:

- Advanced risk analytics: analytics such as securities valuation, multiple flavours of VaR, stress testing, scenario analysis, yield curve analysis, and the greeks[62] common to hedge fund analysis, such as delta, gamma, and rho.
- Securities valuation: vendors offer standard pricing models and the ability for clients to modify these and upload proprietary models. Further, some vendors offer professional services with financial engineers to develop custom models.

Order Management Systems/ Process

An order management system is a software-based platform that facilitates and manages the order execution of securities, typically through the FIX protocol. An order management system can instantly provide a firm with an increased level of straight-through processing in the front-to-middle office environments, enabling more efficient operations almost immediately.

Order Management Systems

In a simple world, when a hedge fund manager places a trade order over the phone, the order goes to a broker. The broker then looks at the size and availability of the market to decide which path is the best way for it to be executed. A broker can attempt to fill an order in a number of ways:

- **Order to the floor** – For assets trading on exchanges, the broker can direct the order to the floor of the exchange.
- **Internalisation** – This occurs when the broker decides to fill the order from the inventory of financial assets that the brokerage firm owns. This type of execution is usually accompanied by the broker's firm making additional money on the spread.m
- **Order to third market maker** – For assets trading on an exchange, the brokerage can direct the order to what is called a third market maker. A third market maker is likely to receive the order if they provide the broker with an incentive to direct the order to them or the broker is not a member firm of the exchange to which the order would otherwise be directed.
- **Electronic Communications Network (ECN)** – ECNs automatically match buy and sell orders. These systems are used particularly for limit orders be - cause the ECN can match by price very quickly.

---

62 Dimensions of risk involved in taking a position in an option (or other derivative). Each risk variable is a result of an imperfect assumption or relationship of the option with another underlying variable. Various sophisticated hedging strategies are used to neutralise or decrease the effects of each variable of risk.

■ **Order to market maker** – For over-the-counter orders, the broker can direct the trade to the market maker in charge of the stock the customer wishes to purchase or sell. Some brokers make additional money by sending orders to certain market makers.

Once the appropriate order routing path has been identified, the broker needs to bring the request to the appropriate market in order to find a party wishing to assume the opposite position. Once both parties are found, the second portion of the transaction occurs, which is commonly referred to as clearing. While all brokers maintain their own books recording the entire amount of buy and sell orders transacted by clients, the actual act of clearing all these transactions is handled by a clearing institution.

Figure 9.2 Trade Transaction Flow

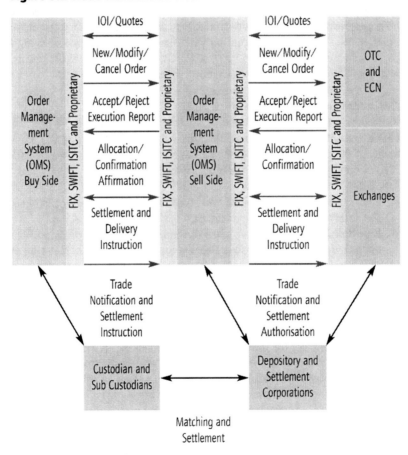

Source: Hexaware Technologies

Common Systems

System: Beauchamp

Vendor: Linedata

Beauchamp focuses on delivering software and services that allow fund managers and traders to concentrate on their core competences, whatever and wherever they are trading. Its solutions help clients to manage the increasingly heavy load of operational risk management and reporting, and include a P&L analysis engine.

The Beauchamp suite covers front, middle and back offices, so clients benefit from seamless processing – from electronic trading, straight through to reconciliation and reporting, every aspect of workflow becomes easier, faster and more efficient, reducing errors and costs.

The increased concentration on compliance issues has become a burden for many hedge fund managers. It can soak up valuable time that could be spent more profitably on managing portfolios. Beauchamp Fund Manager can give the fund manager back that time.

Trades are reflected immediately in reports, reconciliations, and optionally in communications to prime brokers, fund administrators and other service providers, and NAV can be monitored in real time. There is a complete audit trail, and no trade can be amended or cancelled without leaving a clear trace.

In addition to the in-built catalogue of Core Reports, developed by fund managers for fund managers, hedge fund managers can easily create drag-and-drop report configurations with user-defined aggregation across asset classes, filtering and ordering levels.

The product suite is designed to grow and adapt with the fund manager, from an ASP service for smaller managers who want minimal infrastructure and maintenance overheads, to fully and locally installed systems with a complete range of add-on modules.

About Linedata Services

Linedata Services is a leader in the financial technology market, delivering global software solutions for asset management, savings & insurance, and leasing & credit finance.

Linedata's asset management offerings encompass a complete, global set of best-of-breed software products from front to back office. Their solutions address the specific requirements of mutual and institutional funds, alternative and hedge funds, fund administrators, prime brokers and private wealth companies.

Linedata acquired Beauchamp Financial Technology in December 2005. Beauchamp had been building, marketing and supporting trading and portfolio management software products for hedge fund managers since 1997.

The company is working on some initiatives to ensure that they *"stay in the vanguard of solutions providers"* to the hedge fund community including:

- **further work on scalability:**
  - a new P&L engine, including support for parallel processing;
  - archiving functionality, to manage dataset growth.
- **asset class coverage:**
  - extend native support for OTC derivatives;
  - additional interfaces to external valuation services for illiquid OTC positions;
  - extend internal valuation capabilities using well-established models;
  - standard interfaces to STP utilities, to minimise operational risk for both listed and OTC products.

System: FlexTRADER

Vendor: FlexTrade Systems Inc.

Algorithmic trading is the touchstone of FlexTRADER. It is a fully customisable execution management system (EMS) with predefined trading strategies and tactics for portfolio and single-stock trading. The platform provides organically developed pre-trade, real-time and post-trade analytics as well as risk- and cost-optimised portfolio trade scheduling (FlexPTS); advanced integrations with major OMSs; bunching of orders and complex real-time allocations; a Reg NMS-compliant[63] smart router; a sophisticated dark pool router;[64] 1,400 message per second throughput; proprietary fundamental data calculations; commission management; complete transaction and IOI[65] quality management (FlexTQM); and a dynamic strategy matrix.

For buy-side institutions, FlexTRADER can leverage confidential information such as stock-specific alpha expectations and portfolio holdings in conjunction with market conditions to vary the execution time horizons of individual names and achieve desired portfolio characteristics. It also provides automatic commission management across multiple brokers by optimising the broker execution capabilities and liquidity availability vs difficulty and urgency of trading individual names.

Additionally, the ability to easily write and revise customised analytics and quantitative trading strategies within the system makes it an ideal choice for those engaged in agency trading, index arbitrage and other proprietary and standard strategies, such as VWAP, transition trading, pairs and long/short trading. From a single neutral platform, orders are routed automatically to various points of execution, including approximately 80 broker-dealers, as well as all leading ECNs and primary exchanges.

---

63 Regulation promulgated by the United States Securities and Exchange Commission (SEC).
64 Technology scans hidden pools of liquidity, finds the best price and executes trades anonymously.
65 Indicator of interest.

Key features

- It has the ability to process 1,400 transactions per second while analysing market data on a tick-by-tick basis within an automated strategy.
- It can control multiple portfolios comprised of several sub-accounts over many global destinations from one comprehensive trading blotter. Diagnostics such as cash constraints, trade cost estimates, transaction cost monitoring, sector and industry exposure, as well as custom calculations are available on the front-end.
- Automated trading strategies available include VWAP, volume participation, random slicing, momentum, mean reversion, adapting pricing and best efforts. Each may be configured to a trader's preferences for aggressiveness and expediency, or placed into a larger strategy, such as dollar neutral/sector neutral, to manage portfolio characteristics, risk or cash restraints.
- Arbitrage strategies include convertible arbitrage, index arbitrage, exchange traded funds (ETF) arbitrage, cross-border arbitrage (with the ability to hedge FX exposure automatically) and risk arbitrage (as part of the pairs trading module).
- It has comprehensive portfolio analytics that direct strategies based on historical and real-time information, such as volume profiles, volatility, spread and pricing data.
- It contains a customisable Reg NMS-compliant smart router, dark pool router, and order replacement templates as well as a full suite of rule-writing capabilities.

Advanced features

- Clients can use the platform's optimal trading curve or create their own based on execution objectives. They can also rescale a stock's curve, as necessary, during the trading day.
- A strategy matrix enables the segregation of each portfolio into separate execution strategies while maintaining portfolio-level control.
- It can access global equity, FX, options and futures market centres electronically.
- Clients can write their own trading and arbitrage strategies using the platform's formula-building template.
- There are comprehensive APIs in Java, C, C++ and C#/.Net.
- It monitors broker performance, response time and commission levels on an intra-day and historical basis.
- It can be implemented on-site or as a fully hosted global ASP solution via data centres in New York, London, Geneva, Paris and Singapore.
- It is configurable for multiple traders over a network, and runs on SunSolaris, Linux and Windows network operating systems.

About FlexTrade Systems Inc.

Founded in 1996, FlexTrade Systems Inc. is the industry pioneer and global leader in broker-neutral algorithmic trading platforms and execution management systems for equities, foreign exchange and listed derivatives. With in

North America, Europe and Asia, FlexTrade has a worldwide client base spanning more than 130 buy- and sell-side firms, including many of the largest investment banks, hedge funds, asset managers, commodity trading advisors and institutional brokers. Clients include Bank of America, Bank of New York, Barclays Global Investors, HSBC Investment Bank, Jefferies & Company Inc., Sanford C. Bernstein & Co., LLC, UBS Global Asset Management and Wachovia.

System: VALUE

Vendor: Sophis

Sophis VALUE is a cross-asset, front- to back-office platform made up of four integrated modules: front office; risk management; middle/back office; and data management. It provides sell-side-level financial and technological capabilities with the user-friendliness, connectivity and ease of implementation required by the buy-side. VALUE has been adopted by more than 80 institutions worldwide, from start-up hedge funds to large investment management companies, to handle the entire range of funds:

- equity funds
- fixed income funds
- monetary funds
- structured funds
- alternative and hedge funds
- funds of funds

Sophis VALUE references include the following hedge funds:

- AlgebramArgent
- Blue Crest
- Elliot Adviser
- Maple Leaf
- New Star
- Reech
- Robeco
- Sutton Brook

About Sophis

Founded in 1985, Sophis has more than 15 years' experience in supplying portfolio and risk management technologies to the world's leading financial institutions. Sophis designs flexible, open and scalable solutions that support fully automated processing of transactions across all asset classes. Sophis' technologies are developed by a highly qualified R&D department, including a dedicated quant team, to rapidly meet the changing needs of a demanding client base.

Sophis is present in the key financial centres with more than a hundred clients worldwide and with offices in Paris, Frankfurt, London, Dublin, New York, Hong Kong, Tokyo, Singapore and Dubai.

System: CognityFoF

Vendor: FinAnalytica Inc.

The Cognity post-modern portfolio framework uses probability models that accurately model extreme asset returns, combined with informative and mathematically justified downside risk measures and downside risk-adjusted performance measures. The framework enhances these core capabilities with modern methods for modelling volatility clustering, robust outlier treatment, and quantitative Bayesian use of portfolio manager knowledge. Consequently, Cognity enables more efficient use of information and more accurate modelling of portfolios under conditions of volatility and extreme events. Using Cognity, active and absolute returns asset managers achieve significantly higher risk-adjusted returns while achieving the same downside risk of conventional portfolio optimisation methods, and reduced risk of catastrophic loss.

Fully featured technology platform

Using state-of-the-art Java and XML technology, Cognity simplifies installation and accelerates deployment through its plug-in component architecture. User interfaces, data connectors, analytical algorithms and pricing calculators are all independent modules to a common integrated data and computation management platform. Browser-based access to one centralised location makes Cognity easy to manage, rapidly extensible and highly scalable, with reduced ownership and support costs. Cognity offers a rich set of graphics and reports based on XSL style sheets, providing maximum flexibility, visualisation and reporting options. Cognity is offered as an in-house server-based solution as well as an ASP solution.

CognityFoF (fund of funds)

Fund-of-funds managers have historically relied primarily on thorough due diligence and other qualitative analysis in manager selection. Increasingly, institutional investors are demanding more quantitative approaches to risk measurement and portfolio construction. However, fund-of-funds quantitative methods have been hampered by limited return histories that exhibit strong non-normality and influential outliers, unequal return history lengths and serial correlation, unreliable mean returns estimates and performance uncertainties that impede accurate risk management and asset allocation through optimisation. Using CognityFoF, fund-of-funds managers can now for the first time enhance their qualitative manager selection process with new quantitative methods. CognityFoF enhances the entire FoF investment process through application of the latest advances in statistical and financial analyses and modelling methods. FoF managers achieve superior performance through full use of prior information, improved asset allocation and more accurate risk assessments. Protecting against downside performance while capturing upside opportunities, CognityFoF reduces the chance of extreme loss by combining analyst reports with cutting-edge analyses that detect hidden movements in funds and fund-style groups. CognityFoF maximises actionable information delivered to analysts, portfolio managers and investment committee members. Features include:

- in-depth, visual manager analysis and screening;
- full risk reporting including downside expected tail loss (ETL) measures;
- full historical and scenario-based optimisation;
- robust correlations and covariances for outlier detection in manager and group returns;
- extensive risk factor data;
- classical and robust time series factor models;
- automatic robust risk factor selection in factor models;
- visual and statistical crisis period detection;
- crisis period stress testing with factor models;
- full use of analyst forecasts with Black-Litterman.[66]

About FinAnalytica

FinAnalytica Inc. is a privately held company incorporated in the state of Washington in the USA. The company was founded in 2003 when it purchased the assets of the Bravo Information Group, a technical team based in Sofia, Bulgaria. FinAnalytica has recently completed on a $5 million venture capital investment from New Europe Venture Equity (NEVEQ), primarily in order to grow the customer-facing part of the business. With offices in New York, Seattle and Sofia, FinAnalytica develops the Cognity suite of post-modern portfolio construction and risk management software products and markets them to investment management companies in the USA and Europe. The Cognity suite of solutions includes CognityRisk (market risk), CognityOpt (portfolio optimisation) and CognityFoF (fund-of-funds).

Other Systems

System	Vendor	Uses
Tradar Insight	Tradar Ltd	Portfolio management and fund accounting
Hedge Rx	Reval	Front-to-back office processing and FAS 133and IAS39
Eagle Star	Eagle Investment Systems LLC	Global investment accounting
Calypso	Calypso Technology Inc.	Cross-asset trading and risk management

---

66 Black-Litterman is a tactical asset allocation model and a tool for blending implied returns and investor returns.

H-Fund	Financial Tradeware	Front, middle and back office trading
Sales Logix for Buy-Side firms	Infinity Info Systems	CRMsystems
Egar Focus	Egar Technology	Position keeping and risk management
Sparta	Stockbridge Systems	Recording portfolio, general ledger, customer accounting and credit information
Clienteer Group	Imagineer Technology	Client relationship management
ProTrak Advantage	ProTrak International	Investor profiling and High Net Worth and Institutional sales and marketing
Unilogic, Inc	FundsTOTAL	Trading and position keeping
Advantage Fee System	Interactive Technologies	Billing and revenue administration
AspenHedge	FNX Solutions	Trading and risk management
Unity Performance	Confluence	Performance reporting
Intuitive Trading Solutions	RipTide	Trading and order management
Apama	Progress Software	Algorithmic trading platform for leveraging proprietary trading strategies
Trinity	Brady Plc	Trading and risk management

Source: "Hedge funds turn to technology" www.banking-business-review.com.

IT Projects in Hedge Funds

This chapter contains a list of IT projects as well as discussions of the implementation of trading systems, service-oriented architecture and data management.

Introduction

As seen in previous chapters, times are changing for hedge fund managers. The greater focus on regulation in the industry is forcing funds to think more about transparency and audit trails, and in turn to examine the capabilities of their IT infrastructure. At the same time, the increasing number of new funds entering the highly competitive landscape compels managers to focus on the actual return of their funds.

Hedge fund managers have to look for new ways to generate better returns and these may require trading a wider variety of financial instruments and more complex strategies, which could pose a challenge to the managers' IT infrastructures. In the meantime, as it is common practice nowadays for hedge funds to deal with a number of prime brokers as opposed to one, they need to ensure that their IT systems are capable of dealing with the additional operational complexities.

The need for effective operational controls and risk management has been accentuated by a handful of recent high-profile setbacks for hedge funds. Notable examples include the collapse of Amaranth Advisers in September 2006 after losing roughly US$6 billion in a single week on natural gas futures. The failure was the largest hedge fund collapse in history. Spectacular losses such as these have turned the spotlight on the organisation of hedge fund managers and their investment processes, risk management systems, and ability to monitor positions through real-time data.

In addition, as institutional investors are increasingly pouring money into hedge funds, managers are under additional pressure to ensure that their technological infrastructure is capable both of handling larger investment flows and of standing up to the due diligence examinations that these more demanding investors insist on.

Furthermore, in order to win the acceptance of these investors, hedge funds have to demonstrate a greater degree of transparency, which means new requirements have to be drawn up. The managers also have to increase their frequency of reporting to the requirements of the investors. Traditionally, funds have been used to reporting what they wanted when they wanted, but they must now adapt if they want to attract big pension funds and other institutions, which require evidence of a solid operational infrastructure to be convinced of a fund's capabilities.

Given the new requirements and challenges that hedge funds are faced with, these firms are embarking on a number of new IT projects to ensure long-term survival of their business.

List of Project Types

The relative size of hedge fund management firms to other financial services firms means that the IT projects undertaken are not as grandiose as the ones in these other firms. That said, hedge fund management firms use cutting-edge trading and order management systems and therefore the projects that involve implementation of these systems require highly technical staff that are on top of their game. Furthermore, given the complexity of the hedge fund business model and the interfaces with prime brokers and fund administrators, project staff should apply the associated business concepts to ensure effective use of these systems.

Which kinds of IT projects are undertaken at hedge fund management firms?

- Implementation of trading systems
- Building of interfaces to prime brokers' systems
- Building of interfaces to fund administrators' systems
- Upgrades of trading systems
- Implementation of order management systems
- Connection of internal systems to electronic exchanges
- Desktop and server upgrades

While the list above is not exhaustive, it provides a guideline to the types of IT projects that aspiring IT professionals to the hedge fund industry will be involved in.

Trading Systems

Trading systems have been defined in the last chapter but in this chapter a more relevant definition that is suited to software development concepts will be offered.

A trading system is simply a group of specific rules, or parameters, that determine entry and exit points for a given security. These points, known as signals, are often marked on a chart in real time and prompt the immediate execution of a trade. (Investopedia, 2006)

Fundamental role of a trading system
A front-office trading system is essentially a key element of the technical infrastructure of a hedge fund that supports traders by processing their executions. Traders use trading systems to:

- capture deals;
- keep track of their positions, both in terms of absolute numbers as well as derived numbers, i.e. P&L;
- monitor risk of their trading desk in conjunction with risk analysts;
- enable compliance of their trading operation with regulatory or internal rules and market conformity.

Merits of adopting a trading system
- **Allows for trading without emotions** – trading and emotions are not widely regarded as good bedfellows. Traders who second-guess their decisions

185

because they are unable to cope with losses end up losing money. Using a pre-developed system eliminates the need to make any decisions. A fully developed and established system automates the trading process thereby eliminating human inefficiencies and allowing traders to make more profit.

- Time saving – traders save a lot of time by using fully developed and optimised trading systems as actual trading is automated, freeing the trader from spending time on analysis and making trades.

Demerits of adopting a trading system

- **Complexity** – in order to develop a trading system, a developer has to have a solid understanding of technical analysis, the ability to make empirical decisions and a thorough knowledge of how parameters work.
- **Development can be a time-consuming task** – getting a developed trading system running and working properly takes up a lot of time. There are usually a considerable number of iterations of backtesting and paper trading in real time involved to ensure reliability.

Implementation of Trading Systems

Implementation of trading systems usually entails the generic phases of analysis, designing, building, testing and deployment.

Analysis

The analysis phase of the implementation of trading systems involves identifying financial instruments, workflows and trade lifecycles of the systems and the asset classes covered. Systems architects[67] create a high-level systems architecture showing modules of the system and the interfaces to the system. Business analysts liaise with traders to capture requirements in line with the specification of the system to be built or customised.

Designing Trading Systems

The design of trading systems requires knowledge of markets that are suited to system trading. The following are some design considerations for equity, foreign exchange and futures markets.

Trading in Different Markets

Foreign Exchange Markets

The foreign exchange or forex market is the largest and most liquid market in the world. The market is a global, technology-based marketplace in which banks,

67 Given the relatively small size of hedge funds, this role could be carried out by an external consultant.

governments, corporations and institutional investors trade forex around the clock. Hedge funds, in the quest for alpha, have begun to treat FX as an asset class in its own right. They have found that they can successfully apply the same trading methods in FX to generate alpha as they have historically applied to equities, bonds and other asset classes.

Design Considerations

- ▓ The liquidity in this market – due to the huge volume – makes trading systems more accurate and effective.
- ▓ Profits are made in this market through spreads; there are no commissions. This makes it easier to make any transactions without increasing costs.
- ▓ In contrast with other asset classes, like commodities and equities, there is a limited number of currencies to trade. The range of volatility is, however, not limited given the availability of "exotic currency pairs", i.e. currencies from smaller countries.
- ▓ The types of trading systems best suited to the forex market are those that follow trends or systems that buy or sell on breakouts.[68]

Equity Markets

The equity market is the perhaps the most common market to trade in. Traditional value and growth investing are known to be the common strategies for trading in the equity markets.

Design Considerations

- ▓ The wide variety of equities available – from extremely volatile over-the-counter stocks to non-volatile blue-chips – allows traders to test systems on many different types of equities.
- ▓ Unlike the FX markets, there are commissions to be paid on successful equities trades which can eat into profits generated. OTC equities usually incur additional fees.
- ▓ The low levels of liquidity of some equities can limit the effectiveness of trading systems.
- ▓ The types of trading systems best suited to the equity market are those that look for value, i.e. systems that are parameterised to determine the undervaluation of a security when compared to its past performance, its peers, or the market in general.

Futures Markets

Futures trading takes place in commodity, equity and forex markets. Futures markets are usually considered to be the markets with the widest range of trad-

---

68 These are price movements through an identified level of support or resistance, which is usually followed by heavy volume and increased volatility. Traders will buy the underlying currency when the price breaks above a level of resistance and sell when it breaks below support.

ing opportunities. They are characterised by the organisational form of the futures exchanges, the types of contracts that are traded, and the ways in which futures exchanges compete with each other for business.

Design consideration
- High amount of leverage is a key attraction.
- High levels of liquidity and volatility as well as the amount of leverage can amplify gains or losses.
- Trading systems that are able to capitalise on the futures market require a relatively greater amount of customisation, and development time can be protracted.

In conclusion, it can be assumed that with the advent of multi-asset trading systems from leading vendors being deployed at most hedge funds, these considerations have been factored in. However, if a hedge fund specialises in specific asset classes or would rather have the system built by an in-house development team, then these considerations could inform the choice of the developers.

Generic design elements
- Portfolio/book structure
- Static data specification
- Specification of workflow and trade lifecycle events
- GUI customisation
- Modelling of interest rate curves, spread curves
- Specification of Profit and Loss and risk measures
- Access control

Building Trading Systems

There are a number of key considerations for developers to think about before starting to build trading systems. They are as follows:

- **Data set-up** – live and historical data are essential, as backtesting (see below) will be required during the building process. Such data can be integrated into trading systems development software, or be used as a separate data feed.
- **Development tools**– there are a number of fully featured toolboxes used to create trading systems. These toolboxes have features that enable the trader to do the following:
    - Automatically place trades: this usually requires access to the broker's end as a constant connection must be in place between the tool and the brokerage. Traders must ensure that trades are executed immediately and at exact prices in order to ensure compliance.
    - Code a trading system: the tool must allow for implementation of a proprietary programming language that facilitates easy building of rules.

- Backtesting the strategy: the tool should contain a simple backtesting application that allows for definition of data sources, inputting account information and backtesting for any amount of time with the click of a mouse.
- Report generation: a report should be generated within the tool that outlines the specifics of the results of the backtest. This should include profit, number of un/successful trades, consecutive days down, number of trades and other bits of information that can aid in the troubleshooting of the system.
- **Trialling** – backtesting and paper trading[69] are integral parts of the trialling process during development of a trading system. During trialling, several backtests are run on different time periods and it is essential to ensure that results are consistent and satisfactory. Paper trading the systems is also required until consistent profitability is achieved. Several iterations of trialling are essential as it is imperative that consistent profit is made in most markets and conditions. To ensure that unforeseen circumstances are included in the trials ,transaction costs should be factored in. Real commissions should be used and something extra to account for inaccurate fills (difference between bid and offer prices). Risk should also be factored in as it is important to have ways to limit losses (otherwise known as stop-losses) and ways to lock in profits.

Three-phase Evolution of Electronic Trading

The global market trading environment is in the midst of a fundamental paradigm shift. Historically, there has been a clear separation between the roles played by the buy side, their sell-side brokers and the exchanges. But nowadays these lines are being redrawn, and the distinctions between the parties blurred. Buy-side firms, like hedge funds, are assuming ever greater control over the execution of their trades, encroaching on the territory that was once the sell-side's preserve. Meanwhile, the market structure itself is changing rapidly, in the shape of merger-driven consolidation of exchanges in some regions and the ongoing emergence of alternative trading systems (ATSs).

At the junction of all these changes stands the buy-side trader, whose role increasingly resembles that of a sell-side trader as the industry grapples with achieving the concept of "best execution".[70]

69 Paper trading (sometimes also called "virtual trading") is a simulated trading process in which would-be investors can practise investing without committing real money.
70 Best Execution refers to the obligation of an investment services firm executing orders on behalf of customers to ensure that the prices those orders receive reflect the optimal mix of price improvement, speed and likelihood of execution. In order for an investment services firm to determine its compliance with the Best Execution requirement, the firm must evaluate the orders it receives from all customers in the aggregate and assess which competing markets, market makers, or electronic communications networks (ECNs) offer the most favourable terms of execution.

189

These changes are apparent on the hedge fund trader's desktop. Not so long ago, these traders performed their job with a traditional order management system (OMS) and market data feed. Their new execution-focused role, the super-fragmented structure and the best execution requirement now mean that today's world is more complex. It is not uncommon for a trader to have multiple front-ends on their desktop comprising tools such as execution management systems (EMSs), direct market access (DMA) systems, algorithmic trading systems, transaction cost analysis tools and risk management systems, all used in conjunction with their OMS. Managing an order through such a collection of disparate technologies is onerous, particularly as there are interoperability issues to contend with.

Advent software has identified the evolution of electronic trading in three phases. The company predicts that tomorrow's trading platforms to the buy side will be firms that are successful in removing the integration complexity of today's tools away from the trader, while at the same time enabling the achievement of best execution.

The phases are described here.

Phase One – Componentised Complexity
To date, brokers and software vendors have focused on creating ad hoc components to help buy-side traders to do their jobs. The problem is that these components only address specific pieces of the puzzle. Firms today can buy a range of best-of-breed tools, but together they create an unwieldy patchwork of applications, which leaves the traders either managing the different parts manually by "swivel chair" integration, or attempting to stitch them together using the FIX protocol.

Phase Two – The One-Stop Shop
The next phase – evidence of which is already emerging – will be characterised by a broker-provided "one-stop shop", in which agency brokerage capabilities are combined with various software tools that support pre-trade analysis, order management, execution and post-trade analytics. Such models, with their suites of tightly integrated products, offer a compelling alternative to the buy side's hitherto disparate system environments, by taking the integration complexity off the buy-side trader's hands and replacing it with a unified solution. This approach is made even more attractive since most of these tools are offered at no upfront cost.

Phase Three – Broker-Neutral Trading Platform
Successfully balancing the demand for reduced technology complexity while simultaneously satisfying traders' best execution requirements will therefore depend on the emergence of an alternative approach. In phase three, true broker neutrality is combined with the functionality of today's order management and execution management systems. Such open systems, provided by independent software vendors with no broker conflicts, will thus offer a clean separation between access and execution services.

According to Advent, although the vision exists, the technology capability is not yet there. Instead, the different trading components currently in place will require significant alteration before the requisite buy-side trader environment can become reality:

- **OMS/EMS**: These platforms will provide the architectural backbone to support the emergence of phase three in the trading evolution. Traditionally, order management and execution management systems have existed separately, operating on different workflows. But going forward, the functions of the two will blend, forming the core application into which various tools will plug.
- **Algorithms**: The first generation of algorithms, predominately volume-weighted average price (VWAP) or arrival price, were rudimentary – basically slicing up orders over a certain timeframe – and thus not suited to illiquid stocks. New formulations will be liquidity seeking, portfolio based and adaptive.
- **Transaction Cost Analysis**: At the moment TCA tools tend to be broker-specific and do not offer a complete picture of the quality of execution across multiple brokers. These systems are also constrained by the quality of the data collected and fed into them. This situation will change as independent vendors begin to enter the space and the tools become more integrated with trading platforms.
- **Crossing Networks**: Today's crossing networks suffer from low execution rates and a certain amount of information leakage. In the future, crossing networks will boost their execution rates by merging their models with other liquidity sources.[71] In addition, portfolio-based crossing networks will be able to handle baskets of securities.

Electronic Trading Implementation

Success factors

A key consideration in the move to electronic trading is whether the business model changes and the extent to which it will change. When implementing an electronic trading system, it is critical to address this issue.

Another issue that needs to be considered is the suitability of different models to different markets, at least for hedge funds with a multi-asset strategy. For example, crossing systems used in equities markets are unlikely to be suited to FX products, at least in the early stages of electronic trading. This is because of credit limits. Many FX transactions are subject to limit checking, and limits will

---

71 These are financial marketplaces where fund managers can negotiate large blocks of equities directly and anonymously with each other across one integrated trading venue, bypassing all exchanges and intermediaries. An example is Liquidnet. Streaming liquidity providers and partners will be discussed in Business Knowledge for IT in Trading and Exchanges.

Figure 10.1 Schematic diagram of a Crossing System

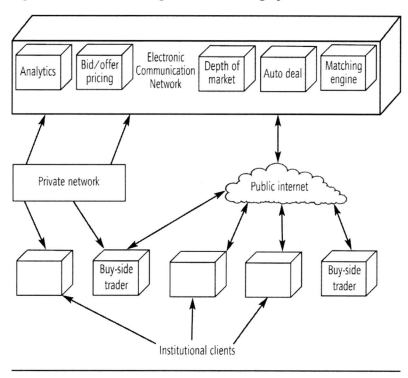

vary according to the quality of the counterparty. The main crossing systems, on the other hand, are designed to provide equal access to all.

Implementation

Implementation of an electronic trading system requires consideration of both technology and business issues. The business model dictates the way and manner in which technology will be used. However, the sticking point is the possibility of integrating a new electronic system with existing technology.

Algorithmic Trading

Algorithmic trading – in which traders rely on computers and software designed to automate not just the worldwide execution of their trades, but in some instances much of the thinking behind those trades – is reshaping world financial markets in amazing ways, and with amazing speed.

The hedge fund industry is also undergoing a major transition – large firms are turning into financial services franchises and small firms are struggling both to raise assets and run a successful fund. The competition to produce high returns has become fierce and survival depends on it. The largest funds are able to leverage their size to lower their costs in securities lending and diversify into multiple asset classes. The challenge for the smaller funds, and even some large fundamental shops, is to effectively use their assets to match or surpass their larger competitors. Cutting-edge technology such as algorithmic trading affords them this rare opportunity.

There are four basic types of algorithmic trading.

Statistical

These are trading strategies that seek to make money over time based on analysis of historical time-series data. Examples include relative-value trading, statistical arbitrage, macro-economic models and trend-following algorithms. These strategies generate trading requirements when they spot opportunities and operate at different frequencies such as:

- low frequency – a few actions a day;
- medium frequency – dozens of action a day;
- high frequency – thousands of actions a day.

Auto-hedging/ Position Hedging

This involves dynamic monitoring and management of risk levels that generate hedging orders to get to a desired risk position; for example, setting trading rules to reduce a position when the size reaches a certain threshold or to pass undesired risk to the market. Another example is automatically adjusting positions in response to information such as flows or news that has historically been correlated with market moves.

Algorithmic Execution Strategies

These involve finding the optimum way for a trade to fulfil the execution objective such as:

- match TWAP[72] or VWAP;[73]
- minimise market impact (passive strategy);
- execute quickly (active strategy).

These strategies entail analysis of current market conditions and previous statistical history of execution characteristics to individually and dynamically work the order in pieces across multiple trading platforms. Strategies are deemed passive when they add liquidity to a market, active where they remove liquidity from the market, or a combination of the two. Historical statistics may be used to optimise the execution which is normally processed through direct market access.

---

72 Time Weighted Average Price is the average market price over a particular time interval.
73 Volume Weighted Average Price is the weighted average price if there is participation in every transaction during a specific period of time.

Direct Market Access

Direct market access (DMA) optimises buy-side traders' access to liquidity pools and multiple execution venues directly, without intervention from a broker's trading desk. It is a useful tool for aggregating liquidity. By assuming the market risk of executing with the venues directly, traders can achieve improvements in speed and cost that yield the degree required to make their strategies profitable. The real motivation for a hedge fund to pursue aggressive DMA trading is cheaper commissions.

Latency

The word "latency" is always associated with algorithmic trading and speed is of the essence in the algorithmic trading market. For the algorithm to result in a successful trade, there are massive quantities of real-time market data streaming through these systems. The primary concern of traders is the speed of this data. High throughput. Low latency. These are two key terms in the ongoing battle for faster market data. Realistically, a matter of milliseconds (1/1000 of a second) can be the difference between a successful trade and an unsuccessful trade. So, slow market data (by no more than a few hundred milliseconds) means the difference between a hedge fund, whose system is running only thousandths of a second faster, executing successfully, and other competitors losing opportunities to profit.

As yet, it appears there has not been an industry definition of latency measurement to ensure that trading venues, systems and infrastructure are all judged by a common standard.

What is Latency?

Latency can be defined as the time it takes to get a deal done, cancel an order or know what is happening in the market.

Latency is a statistical function that can be impacted by:

- a hedge fund's systems and architecture;
- the architecture and construction of the venue to which the hedge fund is connecting;
- the connection between the two.

The goal of every successful algorithmic trading firm is zero, or near zero, latency. Hedge funds will be looking for ways to reduce delays in the transmission of information. One way to accomplish this is to eliminate the middle man. Consolidated market-data providers like Reuters and Thomson are continually working to lower latency. Still, if an algorithmic platform provider can get the feed directly from the source, aggregate it, and provide that to its customers, that model will always be faster since the data is making one less stop on its journey. And latency is increasingly becoming as important an issue as the data itself. Getting data from the source provides an immediate shortcut

The next challenge for hedge funds will be to achieve near-zero latency in their internal messaging platforms. Messaging platforms push data around

194

internally. Usually these systems operate under a "publish/subscribe" model, where the internal applications and systems receive only relevant data. These could be the basis of a project that could greatly enhance their algorithmic trading capability.

Case Studies

The following case study is about the implementation of Geneva, a real-time portfolio accounting system, by BizFund Global Fund Services, a fictional fund company that provides administrative and accounting services to hedge funds.

Geneva is part of the product offering of Advent software, a multinational firm that provides solutions to hedge funds among other financial services companies.

BizFund Global Fund Services is based on the Isle of Man in the middle of the Irish Sea and administers some $13 billion in hedge fund and fund of funds assets from its headquarters, as well as regional offices in New York, Chicago and the Cayman Islands.

With clients throughout Europe and North America investing in a myriad of currencies and instruments, often through multiple brokers, BizFund needed an accounting system that could handle the complexities of global hedge funds on a 24/7 basis.

Administering hedge funds for clients as far away as Turkey, Scandinavia and North America leaves no margin for inaccuracy or inefficiency. Fund managers want and expect access to the most current, accurate fund data to help them make decisions and implement sophisticated investment strategies. BizFund felt that the Geneva global accounting platform was the perfect engine to make it possible to meet their demands.

The Geneva system was hosted on a server in the Cayman Islands office and accessed over the internet via a secure connection. The Managing Director and Chief Information Officer felt it was a robust system in terms of the types of securities that their clients traded and an enabler for the company to handle complex accounts.

Prior to the implementation of Geneva, accounting for different currencies within the same portfolio was a complex chore requiring a patchwork of systems and manual data transfer, which slowed the process and increased the risk of error. With Geneva, real-time multi-currency processing on a single platform is possible.

This reinforces the view held by industry experts that hedge fund administrators have to be able to handle multiple currencies. In fact, on the European side most clients will be dealing outside the US dollar in a lot of euro-denominated securities. In addition, the company has clients that are investing in emerging markets hence the need to deal in a wide variety of currencies.

Not only do global hedge funds operate in many currencies, but their strategies also involve a wide range of equity and fixed-income instruments, as well as hedging with derivatives. Geneva supports a broad range of securities with comprehensive reference data, specialised transaction types, industry-standard accounting calculations and workflow automation that streamlines the management of complex instruments, which the staff and hedge fund clients find invaluable.

Adding another layer of complexity to global hedge funds is the fact that managers tend to allocate their trades among multiple brokers. The complexity is mitigated by Geneva's architecture that streamlines the reconciliation process. This means that the administrator has a choice between taking data from the hedge fund client and then reconciling it to the broker or taking data from the broker and reconciling to the hedge fund client. Either way, there are three different parties involved – the hedge fund, the broker and the administrator – with each party pretty much on the same page as possible.

Given that hedge funds and fund administrators are regulated in some jurisdiction around the world, it is the norm that the fund administrator will be independent of the fund manager and will produce an independent set of numbers every month, reconciled to the broker and to the client. The auditors will access the administrator's records; they won't access the fund manager's records. An accounting system should therefore help ensure a high level of accuracy and data integrity that will satisfy auditors.

Use of SOA in Hedge Funds

Companies in the financial services industry have historically searched for better ways to cost-effectively integrate large-scale business processes. But in recent times they appear to have found a solution in service-oriented architecture (SOA) concepts. The SOA concept is relatively straightforward: applications and automated processes access information resources through standard service interfaces without requiring programming and knowledge of lower-level systems. Web services, in particular, provide the open standards needed to implement ubiquitous, reusable business functions, which enable complex business processes to be broken down and implemented as simplified, manageable entities.

The following are SOA principles and their associated benefits that are enablers for collaboration and agility:

- **Specialisation** – best-of-breed applications and processes can be developed by experts, and deployed in a fashion that makes them accessible by developers in other areas.
- **Alignment of IT with business requirements** – Management gains better visibility into business processes by defining the services they need while implementation consultants retain control over service implementation.
- **Shielding complexity**– Developers need not understand low-level systems in order to build and maintain composite processes. Applications can be maintained and modified independently since low-level functions can be masked behind high-level services.

196

- **Enabling collaboration** – By shielding the details of application implementation from other applications, standard interfaces allow otherwise incompatible applications to cooperate as they perform tasks needed in higher-level business processes.m
- **Broadly adopted services** – any application or process can provide services to any other applications or processes, allowing broad reuse of existing software and the design of innovative solutions for business problems.

The successful deployment of a new application or process, utilising SOA constructs and making its resources available through services, requires a basic understanding of SOA principles. The design of services must be accomplished in such a way as to provide the required functionality while eliminating dependencies on low-level application interfaces as much as possible. When properly designed, a service becomes usable over any established service channel in the enterprise. Industry experts suggest that limiting services to Web services is a strategic mistake: services should be available using a variety of interfaces, including J2EE Connector Architecture (JCA), XML, Simple Object Access Protocol (SOAP), Web Service Definition Language (WSDL) and message queuing – or combinations of these standards. In addition, services should be reusable with existing proprietary application and integration technologies, which often require specialised plug-ins.

Hedge funds that have chosen to migrate to SOA can choose from a variety of platform and developer tools offered by software vendors. The term "enterprise service bus" or ESB has been adopted in the IT industry to indicate a collection of functionality needed to create an SOA, including the following:

- **Transformation** – When applications work together to respond to events or provide services, a sophisticated transformation engine must provide the mapping between their different representations of business entities.
- **Intelligent routing** – Service calls and other events enable collaboration by stimulating action in applications and other parts of the enterprise, which requires a comprehensive mechanism for identifying message types, recognising data values in them, knowing the possible endpoints for messages, and routing messages to where they are needed – without burdening developers with the complexity of communication mechanisms or application manipulations.
- **Optimised runtime engine** – A scalable, distributed service engine must run on a variety of operating platforms and offer customisation for unique business needs.
- **State management** – Although SOA advocates agree that services in an SOA should be stateless, long-running business processes that use these services require a state management capability such as that provided by the Business Process Execution Language (BPEL) engine.
- **Advanced capabilities** – Certain types of services fit more effectively into the distributed architecture than they would in other platforms, such as extending services to partners and enabling simplified enterprise searches.

197

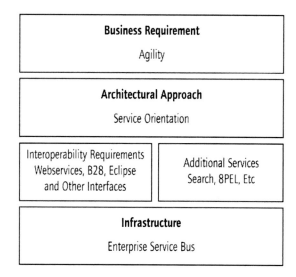

Business Requirement
Agility

Architectural Approach
Service Orientation

| Interoperability Requirements Webservices, B28, Eclipse and Other Interfaces | Additional Services Search, 8PEL, Etc |

Infrastructure
Enterprise Service Bus

Source: iWay Software

The adoption rate of SOA among hedge funds is expected to increase as more firms find themselves operating in complex technology and market environments. This view is validated by a report by TowerGroup in 2006, which notes that a number of the largest investment managers have already embarked on SOA projects – breaking down siloed applications into component services "reusable" for other related functions within their organisations.

TowerGroup expects that SOA adoption rates in the near future will increase among mainstream buy-side managers, as well as hedge funds due to convergence of complexities/drivers:

■ use of sophisticated strategies and instruments;
■ multiple applications and operating systems;
■ complicated counterparty networks.

Given that hedge funds are moving out of the "alternative" realm into the mainstream, it should be expected that their adoption rate of SOA will also be on the increase. A snag, however, is the impact that the implementation of SOA has on a hedge fund's operations and technology strategy. But a properly implemented SOA for hedge funds with multiple applications provides a viable way of making infrastructures more efficient.

Data Management

As hedge funds continue to grow, they require a technology infrastructure that can sustain continuous operations and protect critical operational systems in the wake of growing transaction volumes and reporting requirements. They appear to be gravitating towards storage area networks (SANs) to fulfil these requirements.

The following are drivers for the increasing adoption of SANs by hedge funds:

- The exponential growth of a hedge fund's files, email, instant messages and databases are creating a continual need for storage.
- The addition of more and more electronic and algorithmic trading technologies, research management systems and advanced OMS and EMS systems requires more storage capacity.
- Increasing institutionalisation of the hedge fund industry requires fund managers to maintain overall transparency and compliance.

What is a SAN?

A SAN is a device filled with large disk drives that allows data stored on many different servers to consolidate into one location. Resources are virtualised and presented over high-speed networks specifically designed for data storage.

SANs often utilise a fibre channel fabric topology – an infrastructure specially designed to handle storage communications. They deliver enhanced data protection through "snapshots" of advanced applications and deliver storage at disk rather than data level. Snapshots work by capturing a block-level image of a volume taken on a customisable schedule that keeps the data as it was when the snapshot was created, even if the original data changes. This allows firms to go back to a specific point in time and regain the information, meaning that all failed updates or upgrades can be undone and re-attempted.

Furthermore, SANs recover data much faster than off-site back-ups. Overall flexibility is also enhanced when hedge funds utilise a SAN because storage resources share performance across all disks and can be resized on the fly at multiple recovery points. One other benefit of SANs is the self-managing capabilities that include the ability of the SAN to automatically send notifications to the manufacturers and system manager in the case of failed events or parts.

Medium and larger hedge funds (AUM[74] greater than $500m) typically prefer to adopt a SAN for its efficient and reliable data replication between units, which facilitates failover should an outage occur, and simplifies data management.

Infrastructure projects that involve implementation of SANs can be carried out for reasons including archiving data, ensuring local and remote disaster recovery, reducing development times for new applications, and improving application performance. Other reasons include a response to increased regulation that may require many firms to modify their retention policies, therefore increasing storage requirements.

74 AUM stands for Assets Under Management.

High-Performance Computing

High-performance computing (HPC) can be described as the use of (parallel) supercomputers and computer clusters; that is, computing systems comprising multiple (usually mass-produced) processors linked together in a single system with commercially available interconnects. This is a branch of computer science that involves research into systems design and programming techniques to extract the best computational performance out of microprocessors. In essence, HPC is about running applications and business processes faster and more reliably than before.

Hedge funds, in a bid to comply with current and future regulations, will have to manage and analyse their data quicker than ever before. The data volumes are expected to grow in size and complexity and the analysis involved will challenge even the most ardent financial analysts. These challenges in data and analytics management make the need for greater computing power within the firm compelling. The solution lies in the deployment of a high-performance computing platform.

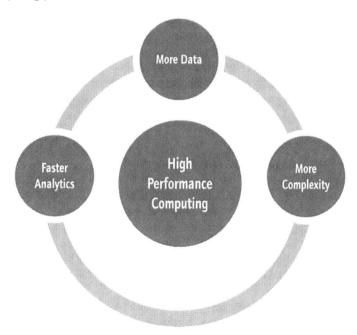

Another compelling reason for adopting HPC is the intense competition in the hedge fund sector. From a commercial standpoint, the rewards of quicker time-to-market for a new product or service than that of the competition are huge and whenever faster calculation, improved end-user productivity and operational efficiency provides a competitive edge, then it stands to reason that the use of HPC will be beneficial.

The following are some commercial drivers for the implementation of HPC.

Algorithmic Trading, Speed and Data Volumes

Algorithmic trading activity is on the increase and, as a result, trading volumes are on the increase given that more trades are implemented in smaller transaction amounts across multiple trading venues. Other factors responsible for the growth in trade volumes include changes in exchange quoting methods and regulations such as MiFID and RegNMS in the USA that have led to the search for price transparency and liquidity, causing algorithmic trading products to search across a greater number of trade execution venues.

Trading opportunities based around techniques such as statistical arbitrage, whereby traders search for "alpha" from intraday opportunities, are also leading to increases in trade volumes. Traders are increasingly interested in intraday tick data given that equity markets have matured and there are fewer opportunities for arbitrage trading by using end-of-day data.

Credit Derivatives and Product Complexity

The increasing use of credit derivatives such as credit default swap (CDS) and the creation of more complex credit products require extensive use of Monte Carlo simulation methods given that the pricing techniques in the credit derivatives market are relatively new and less mature than those of other more established and better understood asset classes.

Currently, there is intensive competition among hedge funds and with other financial markets for a slice of the credit derivatives market. To achieve this, a great deal of consideration should be given to scalability across business processes, which may provide a competitive edge. HPC is a veritable technology that is an enabler for scalability and faster pricing of existing and new types of exotic derivatives.

Hedge Fund Valuation and Risk Management

As hedge funds continually use derivatives and complex investment strategies to generate better returns for their investors, they require better risk management and derivatives valuation. HPC can enable effective generation of alpha and well as returns that are less correlated with mainstream markets.

Application of HPC in Hedge Funds

Backtesting, Data Mining and Complexity in Algorithmic Trading

As algorithmic trading practices evolve, strategists in hedge funds will be looking for new ideas to develop and backtest in production-like environments as quickly as possible in order to achieve faster time-to-market. This task could be time-consuming and involve much iteration of rewriting and retesting in an automated trading environment that is production worthy.

In addition, the growth of the automated trading market will necessitate the use of more complex algorithms that combine real-time statistical analysis of real-time intraday and historic data. The degree of complexity is likely to increase considering the new asset classes that might fall into the realms of auto-

201

mated trading, resulting in the requirement for real-time pricing for derivatives and fixed-income pricing within all algorithmic trading solutions. As execution latency makes the difference as to whether an algorithm is profitable or not, and is increasingly viewed as the current key technology for algorithmic trading, processing power will be essential for success in this market.

Given the growing complexity of algorithmic trading, there will be the attendant difficulty in analysing huge volumes of stored real-time data, which will present a challenge to traders.

To overcome this data analysis challenge, hedge funds need scalable, fault-tolerant server-side tools that emit processing power which traders can use to try new ideas and strategies quickly and easily. The advantage to be derived is faster time to market for new trading strategies that is enabled by faster parameterisation, faster backtesting, faster repricing of derivatives and faster data analysis.

Derivatives Trading

Hedge fund traders use "what if" scenarios for market risk analysis at both instrument and portfolio level. This is because they need to manage and hedge the position of each instrument, after pricing the instrument and trading with a counterparty, within the context of a wider portfolio of derivatives, underlying securities and hedge instruments.

Faster revaluation of their portfolios and analysis of more complex scenarios in shorter periods of time is the advantage that the processing power of HPC offers traders. They are also able to carry out more vigorous hedging and, in addition, analyse pre-trade opportunities more quickly.

Risk Management

Risk measures such as Value at Risk (VaR) have been gaining popularity among hedge fund risk managers, despite the view taken by industry experts that there is no universally accepted VaR model in the hedge fund industry. This is attributed to the fact that hedge fund returns, unlike traditional asset classes, exhibit rather unstable statistical properties as hedge funds can also migrate from one strategy to another.

Nevertheless, the two main techniques used to estimate VaR are historical simulation and Monte-Carlo simulation. Monte-Carlo simulation is used to value and analyse instruments, portfolios and investments by simulating the various sources of uncertainty affecting their value, and then determining their average value over the range of resultant outcomes. Historical VaR involves running a current portfolio across a set of historical price changes to yield a distribution of changes in portfolio value, and computing a percentile (the VaR).

These two methods involve intensive computations and in order to reduce calculation time, it will be beneficial to spread this large compute load across multiple servers and processors. Furthermore, given that VaR is calculated as part of an end-of-day process, the growth in portfolio will be accompanied by longer processes which could make a mockery of the concept of overnight reporting, as there might not be any allowance for reruns in the event of process failure or anomalous results that may require further investigation.

A number of notable software giants including Sun and Microsoft are already offering HPC platforms as it is evident that as financial institutions face the challenging journey towards real-time pricing, trading and risk management across asset classes, they will need high-performance computing.

The deployment of HPC into the IT infrastructure of hedge funds will be the basis of many projects in these firms in the years to come.

11

Common Terminology Used in Hedge Funds

This chapter contains a list of commonly used terminology in the hedge fund industry.

Introduction

The terminology commonly used in the hedge fund industry is similar to that used in investment banking and the capital markets in general. However, there are naturally variations given the peculiar nature of the hedge fund industry.

It is imperative that IT professionals have a firm grasp of the terminology as they will be working closely with time-poor hedge fund managers who will have little room for expatiating on the financial jargon that is second nature to them.

The terminology listed below is by no means exhaustive and readers are advised to look through other sources such as the Internet and on our partner website www.bizle.biz when it is fully operational.

Absolute-return fund A typical market-neutral hedge fund whose primary objective is to produce positive returns, rather than outperform a particular benchmark. Such vehicles serve as a source of capital protection in falling markets. Because they are designed to be less volatile than the overall financial markets, absolute-return funds often have trouble keeping pace during strong bull markets.

Accredited investor An institution or high-net-worth individual that meets the specified criteria for investing in hedge funds.

Active order This is an order that immediately matches when it enters a continuous order matching system. These orders remove liquidity from the book.

Activist investment strategy An approach in which a manager buys stakes in companies and seeks to become their most influential shareholder.

Administrator A service provider that hedge funds hire to calculate fund performance, oversee shareholder relations and perform other record-keeping functions. US-based fund managers that run offshore funds employ local administrators to handle back-office functions for those entities in order to win the tax advantages available to truly offshore vehicles.

Aggressive growth investment strategy An approach that aims to produce the highest-possible returns by investing in relatively risky assets, employing high leverage or making speculative investments that aren't fully hedged.

Alpha Measures the value that an investment manager produces by comparing the manager's performance to that of a risk-free investment (usually a Treasury bill). For example, if a fund had an alpha of 1.0 during a given month, it would have produced a return during that month that was one percentage point higher than the benchmark Treasury. Alpha can also be used as a measure of residual risk, relative to the market in which a fund participates.

205

Alternative assets A category of investments that includes arbitrage vehicles, commodities, distressed securities, hedge funds, managed funds, oil-and-gas partnerships, private equity, real estate, timber, venture capital or other assets whose returns aren't correlated to the stock and bond markets.

Annual rate of return The compounded gain or loss in a fund's net asset value during a calendar year.

Arbitrage investment strategy An approach that aims to exploit price differentials that exist as a result of market inefficiencies. Arbitrage plays typically involve purchasing a security in one market, while selling an instrument with similar performance characteristics in another market, earning returns that far exceed the risk incurred.

Assets under management Includes all investments, leveraged and unleveraged, including cash that are overseen by a fund manager.

At risk An investment that an investor can lose. For a limited partnership, this usually equals the paid-in investment. Either owner can contract to commit additional funds if necessary, which raises the amount at risk.

Average annual return (annualised rate of return) Cumulative gains and losses divided by the number of years of an investment's life, with compounding taken into account. The measure is used to compare returns on investments for periods ranging from partial to multiple years.

Average monthly return Cumulative gains and losses divided by the number of months of the investment's life, with compounding taken into account.

Average rate of return The mean average of a fund's returns over a given number of periods. It is calculated by dividing the sum of the rates of return over those periods by the number of periods.

Backtest Attempts to determine the effectiveness of an investment model by applying the system to past periods and comparing those results with the actual performance of other strategies. Usually considered an inferior method of projecting future performance.

Beta Gauges the risk of a fund by measuring the volatility of its past returns in relation to the returns of a benchmark, such as the S&P 500 index. A fund with a beta of 0.7 has experienced gains and losses that are 70% of the benchmark's changes. A beta of 1.3 means the total return is likely to move up or down 30% more than the index. A fund with a 1.0 beta is expected to move in sync with the index.

Bond-futures arbitrage investment strategy An approach that aims to profit from pricing inefficiencies between bonds and corresponding bond futures.

Bottom-up investment strategy An approach that seeks to identify investments that will produce strong returns, before assessing the influence that economic factors will have on those assets.

Capital-structure arbitrage investment strategy An approach that seeks to exploit discrepancies in the valuations of various securities that a particular company offers, based on their seniority. For example, such funds might take a long position in a company's senior bank debt, while shorting its stock.

Clearing The process of reconciling details of a securities trade that are provided by various parties to the transaction, prior to settlement. Clearing can be a highly lucrative business for securities firms, partly because the function is often linked to margin-lending activities.

Clearing house A firm that works with the exchanges to handle confirmation, delivery and settlement of transactions. Also called clearing corporations or clearing firms.

Closed fund A hedge fund or open-end mutual fund that has at least temporarily stopped accepting capital from investors, usually due to rapid asset growth. Not to be confused with a closed-end fund.

Closed-end fund A mutual fund with a fixed number of shares outstanding that are publicly traded at a premium or discount to the fund's net asset value.

Collateralised debt obligation (CDO) A leveraged investment vehicle that issues notes to fund the purchase of pools of bonds, loans, preferred stock, hedge fund shares or other CDOs. Also defined as a securitisation of other bonds, loans and financial instruments. Principal and interest payments on the underlying assets fund the principal and interest payments owed to holders of CDO notes. Based on the type of their underlying assets, CDOs can take a variety of forms including collateralised bond obligations (CBOs), which are backed almost entirely by other debt securities, collateralised loan obligations (CLOs), which are backed entirely by corporate loans, and collateralised fund obligations (CFOs). Despite the similarity of the term, collateralised mortgage obligations are not part of the CDO category.

Collateralised fund obligation (CFO) A type of collateralised debt obligation (CDO) that is backed by zero-coupon bonds to fund the purchase of shares in hedge funds, private equity funds or multi-manager vehicles known as funds of funds. From the fund manager's standpoint, such issues serve as a source of long-term capital and behave much like funds of funds that purchase shares of their vehicles. Fund managers can earn arbitrage profits on the returns that are eft after CFO holders have been made whole. CFOs are often structured as zero-coupon bonds that make lump sum payments by redeeming the underlying fund-of-fund shares at maturity. Others have been arranged as convertible issues.

Commodity trading advisor (CTA) A person or entity providing advice to others on investments in commodity futures, options and foreign-exchange contracts – or invests in those instruments on behalf of others. Most CTAs must register with the Commodity Futures Trading Commission, unless they are exempt from the registration requirements.

Compounded monthly return The average monthly increase that, when compounding is taken into account, would have produced a fund's total return over any period of time. For example, if a fund had a one-year return of 20%, its compounded monthly return would be 1.53% – the amount it would have needed to gain in each of 12 months to achieve that full-year result.

Convergence investment strategy An approach that exploits discrepancies in the values of securities that have historically been almost identical – and assumes that they will ultimately become fairly priced and their values will converge.

Convertible arbitrage investment strategy A conservative, market-neutral approach that aims to profit from pricing differences or inefficiencies between the values of convertible bonds and common stock issued by the same company. Managers of such funds generally purchase undervalued convertible bonds and short-sell the same issuer's stock. The approach typically involves a medium-term holding period and results in low volatility.

Convertible bonds A corporate bond that can be exchanged, at the option of the holder, for a specific number of the company's common or preferred shares.

Country-specific investment strategy An approach that involves a heavy concentration of investments, usually stocks, in one country, or a few countries within a geographical region.

Correlation A statistical measure of how two securities move in relation to each other. Correlations range from 1 to -1. A correlation close to 1 means that the two assets or fund managers tend to move in opposite directions. Correlation close to zero means that the two series of returns move independently of one another.

Custodian A bank, trust company or other financial institution that holds and protects a fund's assets and provides other services, including collecting money from investors, distributing redemption proceeds, maintaining margin accounts, registering investments and exercising options.

Dedicated short bias fund Type of hedge fund that predominantly shorts stocks with minimal long exposure to stock prices.

Delta The ratio comparing the change in the price of the underlying asset to the corresponding change in the price of a derivative. Sometimes referred to as the "hedge ratio".

Derivative A financial instrument whose performance is linked to a specific security, index or financial instrument. Typically, derivatives are used to transfer risk or negotiate the future sale or delivery of an investment. Derivative instruments come in four basic forms: forward contracts, futures contracts, swaps and options.

Discretionary account (managed account) A vehicle in which investors give a manager or broker discretion to buy and sell securities, futures or other assets on their behalf, either unconditionally or with restrictions.

Distressed securities investment strategy Purchasing deeply discounted securities that were issued by troubled or bankrupt companies. Also, short-selling the stocks of those corporations. Such funds are usually able to achieve low correlations to the broader financial markets. The approach generally involves a medium- to long-term holding period.

Diversification Generally refers to the variety of investments in a fund's portfolio. Risk-averse fund managers seek to combine investments that are unlikely to all move in the same direction at the same time.

Downside variance A version of statistical variance that ignores positive deviation from the mean. This measure of risk ignores positive differences from the mean (profits) and accumulates only negative differences (losses).

Drawdown The percentage loss that a fund incurs from its peak net asset value to its lowest value. The maximum drawdown over a significant period is sometimes employed as a means of measuring the risk of a vehicle. Usually expressed as a percentage decline in net asset value.

Due diligence Research aimed at satisfying that an investment is not fraudulent or inappropriate. The research is primarily concerned with whether the risks are reasonable and much less concerned with the prospects for trade.

Efficient frontier The combination of securities that maximises the expected return for any level of expected risk, or that minimises expected risk for any level of expected return.

Efficient market viewpoint The body of thinking that includes two main ideas: financial markets are efficient, and the rational investor should hold a portfolio that is efficiently diversified.

209

Emerging markets investment strategy Investing in stocks or bonds issued by companies and government entities in developing countries, usually in Latin America, Eastern Europe, Africa and Asia. Such funds typically employ a short- to medium-term holding period and experience high volatility.

Event risk The likelihood that an investment's value will change as the result of unexpected events, such as corporate restructurings, takeovers, regulatory shifts or disasters.

Equity pairs trading fund A type of hedge fund specialising in arbitrating between nearly identical securities issued by the same company.

Exposure The extent to which a hedge fund is vulnerable to changes in a given financial market. Exposure can be measured on a net or gross basis. Net exposure takes into account the benefits of offsetting long and short positions and is calculated by subtracting the percentage of the fund's equity capital invested in short sales from the percentage of its equity capital used for long positions. For example, if a fund is 125% long and 50% short, its net exposure would be 75%. Gross exposure is calculated by adding the percentage of the fund's equity invested in short sales to the percentage of its equity used for long positions. In both cases, the exposures often exceed 100% because they don't account for the use of leverage.

Fair value The price at which a single unit of a security would trade between parties that don't have interests in the issue. Fair value does not take into account various premiums or discounts that would be assessed for large or illiquid positions.

Family office The accounts of several affiliated investors run by a private investment counsellor.

FAS133 Statement from the Financial Accounting Standards Board requiring that derivative securities be marked to market and establishing whether a related cash asset must also be marked to market.

Finder's fees Allocation of management and incentive fees to third-party hedge fund marketers.

Fixed-income investment strategy An approach in which the manager invests primarily in bonds, annuities or preferred stock. The investments can belong positions, short sales or both. Such funds are often highly leveraged.

Fixed-income arbitrage investment strategy An approach that aims to profit from pricing differentials or inefficiencies by purchasing a bond, annuity or preferred stock and simultaneously selling short a related security. Such funds are often highly leveraged.

Flow-through entity A business unit that pays no tax; instead, all taxable items are allocated to owners and reported on the investors' tax returns.

Forward contract A private, over-the-counter derivative instrument that requires one party to sell and another party to buy a specific security or commodity at a pre-set price on an agreed-upon date in the future. Similar to a futures contract, which is traded on an exchange.

Front running To place an order to buy or sell a security in front of a known order for additional securities.

Fund of funds (multi-manager vehicle) An investment vehicle whose holdings consist of shares in hedge funds and private-equity funds. Some of these multi-manager vehicles limit their holdings to specific managers or investment strategies, while others are more diversified. Investors in funds of funds are willing to pay two sets of fees, one to the fund-of-funds manager and another set of (usually higher) fees to the managers of the underlying funds.

Fundamental analysis investment strategy An approach that relies on valuing stocks by examining companies' financials and operations, including sales, earnings, growth potential, asset size and quality, indebtedness, management, products and competition.

Futures contract An exchange-traded agreement to buy or sell a particular type and quantity of a commodity or security for delivery at an agreed-upon place and date in the future. Futures, which are popular hedging tools, can be derivatives of agricultural products, metals, petroleum products, government securities and individual issues of common stock. They are similar to forward contracts, which are traded privately.

General partner The individual or firm that organises and manages a limited partnership, such as a hedge fund. The general partner assumes unlimited legal responsibility for the liabilities of a partnership.

Global-macro investment strategy An approach in which a fund manager seeks to anticipate broad trends in the worldwide economy. Based on those forecasts, the manager chooses investments from a wide variety of markets – i.e. stocks, bonds, currencies, commodities. The approach typically involves a medium-term holding period and produces high volatility. Many of the largest hedge funds follow global-macro strategies. They are sometimes called "macro" or "global directional-investment" funds.

Grandfathered fund A Section 3(c)(1) hedge fund that can convert to a Section 3(c)(7) fund without removing existing shareholders who aren't "qualified investors". As many as 100 investors who don't meet the qualified-investor criteria may continue to hold shares in a grandfathered fund, provided their investments were made on or before 1 September 1996.

211

Haircut The amount by which a lender discounts the actual market value of collateral pledged by a borrower.

Hedge fund A private investment vehicle whose manager receives a significant portion of their compensation from incentive fees tied to the fund's performance – typically 20% of annual gains over a certain hurdle rate, along with a management fee equal to 1% of assets. The funds, often organised as limited partnerships, typically invest on behalf of high-net-worth individuals and institutions. Their primary objective is often to preserve investors' capital by taking positions whose returns are not closely correlated to those of the broader financial markets. Such vehicles may employ leverage, short sales, a variety of derivatives and other hedging techniques to reduce risk and increase returns. The classic hedge-fund concept, a long/short investment strategy sometimes referred to as the Jones Model, was developed by Alfred Winslow Jones in 1949.

Hedged equities investment strategy An approach that seeks to reduce investors' exposure to volatility in the stock market by offsetting a portfolio of common stocks with short positions and index options.

High-water mark A provision serving to ensure that a fund manager only collects incentive fees on the highest net asset value previously attained at the end of any prior fiscal year – or gains representing actual profits for each investor. For example, if the value of an investor's contribution falls to, say, $750,000 from $1 million during the first year, and then rises to $1.25 million during the second year, the manager would only collect incentive fees from that investor on the $250,000 that represented actual profits in year two.

Hurdle rate The minimum return necessary for a fund manager to start collecting incentive fees. The hurdle is usually tied to a benchmark rate such as Libor or the one-year Treasury bill rate plus a spread. If, for example, the manager sets a hurdle rate equal to 5%, and the fund returns 15%, incentive fees would only apply to the 10% above the hurdle rate.

Hypothecate To pledge an asset.

Incentive fee (performance fee) The charge – typically 20% – that a fund manager assesses on gains earned during a given 12-month period. For example, if a fund posts a return that is 40% above its hurdle rate, the incentive fee would be 8% (20% of 40%) – provided that the high-water mark does not come into play.

Inception date The day on which a fund starts trading.

Initial margin Margin required by a clearing corporation for a future or future options.

International investment strategy Purchasing securities issued by companies that are located in developed countries, as opposed to emerging markets.

Joint back office A clearing operation that a hedge fund jointly owns with a prime broker for the purpose of exceeding the Federal Reserve's Regulation T limits on margin borrowing. By assuming an ownership stake in such a clearing operation, a fund can effectively render all transactions with its prime broker as internal transfers – giving the prime broker the ability to reduce margin loan requirements substantially, under Section 220.7(c) of Regulation T. By setting up a joint back office, a hedge fund can borrow an amount equal to many times its equity capital. Most other US investors can leverage only half of their investments, under Reg T.

Jones model An investment approach developed by former journalist Alfred Winslow Jones, who is said to have created the first hedge fund in 1949. Unlike traditional long-only mutual funds, the Jones model involved a limited partnership that employed a long/short investment strategy – thus hedging the portfolio against market fluctuations. Jones, who was committed to capital preservation, targeted absolute returns rather than a return that was correlated to the broad stock market. He charged investors a performance fee equal to 20% of annual gains. He also invested his own money in the fund.

Layered tax allocation Form of tax allocation in which each lot of each asset is treated as if the investor individually bought or sold a portion of asset directly (outside the partnership).

Leverage The borrowed money that an investor employs to increase buying power and increase their exposure to an investment. Users of leverage seek to increase their overall invested amounts in hopes that the returns on their positions will exceed their borrowing costs. The extent of a fund's leverage is stated either as a debt-to-equity ratio or as a percentage of the fund's total assets that are funded by debt. Example: if a fund has $1 million of equity capital and it borrows another $2 million to bring its total assets to $3 million, its leverage can be stated as "two times equity" or as 67% ($2 million divided by $3 million). Ratios of between two and five to one are common. Leverage can also come in the form of short sales, which involve borrowed securities.

LIFO layering Layered tax allocation using last-in, first-out matching of realised gains and losses to investor's gains and losses.

Limited partnership Many hedge funds are structured as limited partnerships, which are business organisations managed by one or more general partners who are liable for the fund's debts and obligations. The investors in such a structure are limited partners who do not participate in day-to-day operations and are liable only to the extent of their investments.

213

Liquidity The ease with which an investment product can be sold in large volumes, without impacting its price. Hedge funds typically offer quarterly or annual liquidity, meaning that they allow investors to redeem their shares that often.

Liquidity risk The potential that an investor will be unable to convert their holdings into cash quickly and in large quantities without having to accept a substantial discount. The term also refers to the potential that a securities buyer will not have enough money to pay for the purchase.

Lock-up The period of time – often one year – during which hedge-fund investors are initially prohibited from redeeming their shares.

Long position This is a position that will make money if the price of the asset goes up.

Long-biased investment strategy An approach taken by fund managers who tend to hold considerably more long positions than short positions.

Long-only investment strategy An approach that involves no short positions. While most mutual funds hold only long positions, the strategy is uncommon for hedge funds.

Long/short investment strategy An approach in which fund managers buy stocks whose prices they expect will increase and take short positions in securities (usually in the same sector) whose prices they believe will decline. The strategy, also known as the Jones Model, is designed to generate profits during bullish periods in the overall stock market, while serving as a source of capital protection in a falling stock market.

Macaulay duration Present value weighted to maturity.

Managed futures A vehicle in which an investor gives a commodity trading advisor – usually a manager or broker – discretion or authority to buy and sell futures contracts, either unconditionally or with restrictions. A type of discretionary account.

Management fee The charge that a fund manager assesses to cover operating expenses. Investors are typically charged separately for costs incurred for outsourced services. The fee generally ranges from an annual 0.5% to 2% of an investor's entire holdings in the fund, and it is usually collected on a quarterly basis.

Margin loan A line of credit from a broker that provides an investor with capital for the purpose of purchasing securities. The loan usually finances up to 50% of the securities purchase and is secured by stock owned by the client. Hedge funds can usually leverage themselves far more than that through other means, such as joint back offices. Like any form of leverage, a margin loan allows investors to boost their buying power, while at the same time increasing their risk. The value of the securities an investor holds in a margin account must be maintained above a minimum level in order for the loan to remain in good standing. If the value of the collateral falls below the threshold, the investor will get a margin call, also known as a Regulation T (Reg T) call.

Margin call Occurs when a broker demands that the holder of a margin loan puts up extra cash or securities as collateral for that loan, usually because the value of the securities purchased with the loan has declined. When such a Regulation T call is made, an investor has the option to put up cash to reduce the loan amount, add more securities to the margin account to raise the portfolio value or sell securities in the account to reduce the loan balance.

Market-neutral investment strategy An approach that aims to preserve capital through any of several methods and under any market conditions. The most common followers of the market-neutral strategy are funds pursuing a long/short investment strategy. These seek to exploit market discrepancies by purchasing undervalued securities and taking an equal, short position in a different and overvalued security. Market-neutral funds typically employ long-term holding periods and experience moderate volatility.

Market-neutral option arbitrage investment strategy An approach that seeks to exploit pricing differentials between options contracts or warrants and the stocks to which they are tied. Those following the strategy typically purchase options or warrants, while taking short positions in the underlying stocks.

Market timer A hedge fund manager that selects asset allocations in anticipation of movements in the broad market.

Merger arbitrage investment strategy Trading the stocks of companies that have announced acquisitions or are the targets of acquisitions. Seeks to exploit deviations of market prices from proposed exchange formulas.

Minimum investment The smallest amount that an investor is permitted to contribute to a hedge fund as an initial investment.

Mortgage-backed securities arbitrage investment strategy An approach that seeks to exploit pricing differentials between various issues of mortgage-related bonds.

Multi-strategy An investment style that combines several different approaches. The term often applies to funds of funds that allocate capital to a diverse group of hedge fund managers.

215

Net asset value (NAV) The market value of a fund's total assets, minus its liabilities and intangible assets, divided by the number of its shares outstanding. The measure is used to determine prices available to investors for redemptions and subscriptions. Hedge funds typically calculate their NAVs at the end of every business day, but report them to investors on a monthly basis. Mutual funds report their NAVs daily.

Net fee requirement A Securities and Exchange Commission rule in the USA stating that hedge fund managers and other types of investment advisors must deduct "advisory fees" they charge from any performance figures they present to prospective investors.

Netting The process of adjusting a gross amount, usually by subtracting. The term usually applies to the deduction of fees and taxes from an investment's return.

Non-ledger data Types of data that cannot be conveniently preserved within the double-entry books.

Notice The amount of time an investor must allow before a request to withdraw will be honoured.

Operational risk Measures the probability that investment losses will result from factors other than credit risk, market risk or liquidity risk, such as employee fraud or misconduct, errors in cash-flow models, incorrect or incomplete documentation of trades or man-made disasters.

Opportunistic investment strategy An approach that seeks to produce the greatest possible returns by making aggressive investments in the most efficient products at a given time. Such funds typically hold their investments for five to 30 days, based on the momentum of the investments' values. They usually experience low volatility.

Opportunistic value investment strategy An approach that seeks to produce the greatest possible returns by assuming long-term positions in the most efficient products at a given time. Such funds, which often pursue long/short investment strategies, may hold a variety of investments, including stocks, bonds, options and warrants, as well as distressed securities.

Option A contract that gives parties the right to buy, or sell, a specific asset or security at a specified strike price by a pre-set date. It falls under the derivatives category and comes in the form of calls (options to buy) and puts (options to sell). The cost of an option is generally a fraction of the cost of its underlying security.

Options arbitrage investment strategy An approach that seeks to exploit pricing differentials between similar option contracts or between the price of an option contract and its associated securities.

Options investment strategy Any of a number of approaches in which the manager invests in options contracts.

Pairs trading investment strategy An approach that seeks to identify similar companies whose securities are trading at a wide differential. The manager of such a fund would assume a short position in the overvalued security, while taking a long position in the undervalued one.

Passive Order This is an order that doesn't match when it enters a continuous order matching system. These orders add liquidity to the book.

Payment netting (netting by novation) A form of netting in which multiple payments between two parties are combined into a single "master agreement" that allows for one payment on a specified date, and in a specified currency. The practice is common in the foreign exchange market, where parties often have large numbers of offsetting payments due on the same day and in the same currency.

Performance trigger The point at which a hedge fund's losses cause specific contractual provisions designed to insulate investors from further losses.

Pooled investment vehicle Any limited partnership, trust or company that operates as an investment fund and is exempt from SEC registration under the Investment Company Act of 1940.

Portfolio manager A company or individual that runs capital on behalf of an investment fund, such as a hedge fund. The portfolio manager is often the general partner of the fund's limited partnership. It may be an employee of the fund management firm, or an external entity with which the hedge fund makes a passive investment.

Portfolio turnover rate The rate of trading activity in a hedge fund or mutual fund, expressed as a percentage of the portfolio's size, that is bought or sold each year. Calculated by dividing the lesser of purchases or sales by average assets during that year.

Prearranged trade A futures or futures option trade executed between buyer and seller without giving other exchange members a chance to bid, offer, or participate.

Price-weighted duration Nominal change in price for a 1 per cent (100 basis point) change in yield. Price-weighted duration is equal to modified duration times price (as a percentage of $1 face value).

Principal-protected note Structured securities that promise hedge fund returns without risking an investor's principal. Investors receive hedge fund returns, minus a 1% to 2% fee required by a financial institution to guarantee buyers' principal amounts. Principal-protected notes give investors a safe haven from stock- or bond-market volatility, while providing a way for risk-averse investors – such as insurance companies and endowments – to invest in hedge funds that would otherwise be off-limits to them. The issues are often sponsored by a bank guarantor, with proceeds going to a group of hedge funds. To protect its own position, the guarantor bank reserves the right to redeem shares from any or all hedge funds in the pool when the combined net asset value of the funds' shares falls below certain levels.

Private equity fund Entities that buy illiquid stakes in privately held companies, sometimes by participating in leveraged buyouts. Like hedge funds, the vehicles are structured as private investment partnerships in which only qualified investors may participate. Such funds typically charge a management fee of 1.5% to 2.5%, as well as an incentive fee of 25% to 30%. Most private equity funds employ lock-up periods of 5 to 10 years, longer than those of hedge funds.

Qualified investor Any individual whose investment portfolio is valued at a certain amount of money or more, or any company that owns or manages at least a value of investments that meets the criteria of a hedge fund.

R-squared A measure of the degree to which a hedge fund's returns are correlated to the broader financial market. A figure of 1 would be a perfect correlation, while 0 would be no correlation and -1 would be a perfect inverse correlation. Any figure below 0.3 is considered non-correlated. The result is used to determine whether a hedge fund follows a market-neutral investment strategy. Sometimes referred to as "R".

Rate of return The annual appreciation in the value of a fund or any other type of investment, stated as a percentage of the total amount invested. Sometimes referred to as simply the "return".

Realised gain/loss A gain/loss that results from a closeout of an opening purchase or sale.

Rebate Interest paid on cash used to collateralise stock loan trades. Rebate (for stocks) is the same as repo interest (for bonds).

Recognised gain/loss Any realised or unrealised gain or loss that is acknowledged in the accounting and/or tax records.

Redemption fee A charge, intended to discourage withdrawals, that a hedge fund manager levies against investors when they cash in their shares in the fund before a specified date.

Redemption notice period The amount of advance notice that an investor must give a hedge fund manager before cashing in shares of the fund. Notification is usually required in writing.

Redemption Liquidation of shares or interests in an investment fund.

Regional investment strategy An approach in which the fund manager invests in instruments that are issued by companies or governments in a specific geographical region.

Relative-value investment strategy A market-neutral investment strategy that seeks to identify investments whose values are attractive, compared to similar securities, when risk, liquidity and return are taken into account.

Reporting agent A third-party individual or company that verifies a fund's performance figures.

Risk arbitrage investment strategy Purchasing stocks of companies that are likely takeover targets, while assuming short positions in the would-be acquiring companies. Risk arbitrage players can employ an event-driven investment strategy or merger arbitrage investment strategy, seeking situations such as hostile takeovers, mergers and leveraged buyouts. Such funds typically experience moderate amounts of volatility.

Risk-free rate The theoretical return on a risk-free investment, usually a US security.

Scalability The ability to increase the assets under management for a hedge fund strategy without reducing the returns.

Sector investment strategy Limiting investments to securities issued by companies that operate in a particular industry sector, such as finance, energy, health care or high-tech. Some managers pursue multi-sector strategies that involve more than one sector.

Settlement Synonymous with a transaction's closing when, after clearing has taken place, securities are delivered and payment is received.

Short-biased investment strategy An approach that relies on short sales. Such funds tend to hold larger short positions than long positions.

Short-only investment strategy An approach that seeks to profit exclusively by short sales – taking short positions in securities whose values the fund manager believes will fall. Such funds typically employ medium-term holding periods and experience high amounts of volatility.

Short position A short position is a position that makes money if the price of an asset goes down.

Short sales The process of borrowing securities or futures contracts from a broker and "selling them short" with the expectation that the same asset can later be purchased at a lower price. The sale is covered by buying back the securities (hopefully at a lower price) and returning them to the lending broker.

Short-term trading strategy An approach in which the fund manager focuses on opportunistic trades, holding investments for only brief periods. Such funds often engage in "day trading".

Small-cap/micro-cap investment strategy Purchasing stocks issued by small companies. Small-cap companies generally have $250 million to $1 billion of market capitalisation, while micro-cap companies have less than $250 million of market capitalisation.

Soft dollars Credits that can be used to pay for research and other services that brokerage firms provide to hedge funds and other investor clients in return for their business. Those credits are accumulated through soft-dollar brokers, who channel trades to multiple securities brokers.

Sophisticated investor Any investor who is capable of assessing the risks involved with a hedge fund – either alone, or with the help of an investment advisor.

Special situations investment strategy An event-driven investment strategy in which the manager seeks to take advantage of unique corporate situations that provide the potential for investment gains.

Specialised hedged financing An approach in which the hedge fund manager purchases privately placed junk-rated securities and then hedges against the risk that those securities will default. Because the investments are typically in danger of defaulting, they tend to sell at deep discounts and carry unusually high yields.

Spread The difference in price or yield between two securities. Most often used to describe the difference between the yield on a Treasury security and the yield on another type of bond. It also refers to the return from a given investment product, such as a hedge fund, versus the return of a benchmark such as the S&P 500 index.

Standard deviation For an investment portfolio, it measures the variation of returns around the portfolio's mean-average return. In other words, it expresses an investment's historical volatility. The further the variation from the average return, the higher the standard deviation.

Statutory representation A market-neutral investment strategy that seeks to simultaneously profit and limit risk by exploiting pricing inefficiencies identified by mathematical models. The strategy often involves short-term bets that prices will trend toward their historical norms.

Sticky Adjective describing capital unlikely to be removed from the fund for a significant period or following poor performance.

Stock-futures arbitrage investment strategy An approach that seeks to take advantage of differences between a stock's current price and its expected future price by buying a group of stocks and shorting futures contracts in the corresponding index – or by purchasing the futures contracts and short-selling the stock.

Subscription agreement Legal document filed as part of an investment in a hedge fund, creating a contract between the investor and the fund.

Survivorship bias An over-estimation of historic returns for the hedge fund industry that results from the tendency of poor-performing hedge funds to drop out of an index while strong performers continue to be tracked. The result is a sample of current funds that includes those that have been successful in the past, while many funds that underperformed are not included.

Swap contract An agreement by two or more parties to exchange currencies, commodities, interest payments, investment returns or cash flows, either presently or at a future date. Swaps are a form of derivatives. Interest-rate swaps, which are usually used to convert a fixed-rate investment into a floating-rate instrument, and vice versa, are the most common example of a swap. Credit-default swaps and rate-of-return swaps are used to ensure specific returns on investments, with the swap counterparty assuming the risk.

Top-down investment strategy An approach that seeks to assess the influence of various macro-and micro-economic factors before identifying individual investments.

Traditional investments Products whose performances closely track the broader stock and bond markets.

Value-investment strategy An approach that involves purchases of stocks that the manager deems to be priced below their intrinsic values, or are out of favour with the market but are still fundamentally solid. Such funds typically employ long-term holding periods and experience low volatility.

Value at risk (VaR) A measure of the potential change in value that a fund's portfolio may experience during that vehicle's holding period. It is usually expressed as a percentage, which is referred to as a confidence level.

Value-added monthly index (VAMI) The value that $1,000 allocated to an investment fund on its inception date would currently have, assuming that all profits and distributions were reinvested.

Variation margin Adjustment to futures account reflecting changes in price of established positions. Additional margin must be satisfied with cash deposits only. Excess variation margin can be withdrawn.

Venture capital Money given to corporate start-ups and other new high-risk enterprises by investors who seek above-average returns and are willing to take illiquid positions.

Volatility The likelihood that an instrument's value will change over a given period of time, usually measured as beta.

Volatility arbitrage investment strategy An approach by which a manager seeks to take advantage of fluctuations and inefficiencies in financial markets, usually the stock market. A common form of volatility arbitrage is an options arbitrage investment strategy, which can be carried out as a market-neutral investment strategy or with a long bias toward volatility. The returns are generally expected to have low correlation to those of the stock or bond markets.

Warrant A contract that gives an investor the right to purchase a security at a specific price (usually above the current price) on a future date. It is usually issued with a bond or preferred stock to provide additional incentive to the buyer. Warrants are similar to options contracts, but unlike options, they can stay in effect for a period ranging from a few years to eternity.

Window dressing Making changes to positions at an accounting statement period to make state-ments more desirable. This product often involves leverage.

The Future

This chapter contains a discussion on the future of IT and business in the hedge fund industry..

The Future: What does it hold for Hedge Funds in Business and IT?

As the impact of hedge funds continues to be felt in the financial markets, the future of the industry has been under the microscope. Much has been said in the press and among industry watchers about how sustainable the hedge fund business model is and whether hedge funds can come out of the alternative investment realm into the mainstream of the investment market space.

The fact that the hedge fund industry, which is now massive, witnessed sedate growth in the 1950s and 1960s has led its critics to dismiss hedge funds as mere "casinos". Their perception should not be disregarded, however, since by the end of the second quarter of 2006, there were around 9,000 hedge funds in existence managing assets valued at $1,225bn. And because these funds characteristically use substantial leverage, they play a far more important role in the global securities markets than the size of their net assets indicates. In 2004, market makers on the floor of the New York Stock Exchange, for instance, estimated that hedge funds accounted for more than half of the daily volume of shares changing hands.

To buttress the casino argument, it is widely acknowledged that past performance is no guide to the future and it would make sense not to assume that hedge funds will always perform well in the future. Industry experts believe that past hedge fund performance may have been overstated and that intensifying competitive pressures are driving returns down.

Another issue with hedge funds that could potentially cast doubts on their long-term survival is the biases that can exist in the published indices of hedge fund returns. Unlike mutual funds, which must report their periodic audited returns to regulators and investors, hedge funds provide information to the database publishers only if they desire to do so. Managers often establish a hedge fund with seed capital and begin reporting their results at some later date if the initial results are favourable, but the results of fund start-ups that are dismal are not submitted. This bias is often called an "incubation" bias.

Despite all that has been said above, the future could indeed be very bright for hedge funds. Hedge fund management firms will be looking into the future, concentrating on the following key areas of IT and business.

Globalisation of Hedge Funds

In order to maximise returns on capital, especially in light of falling management fees, the hedge fund management company of the future will need to become a global, multi-strategy, absolute-return institution. This will require the wherewithal to provide investment management services to as large an asset base as possible at as low a cost as possible.

What will differentiate hedge fund management companies of the future will be the ability to attract not only the pension funds, high net worth investors and endowments, but retail investors as well.

The globalisation of hedge funds will gather pace in the near future since as they are unregulated, they can borrow considerable amounts of money and, as a consequence, invest amounts way above the real amount originally invested. These amounts can be invested in almost every sort of asset class (currency, real estate, commodities) in emerging markets and developing economies because of the liberalisation of monetary flows.

The globalisation of hedge funds will have a destabilising effect on the world's financial markets for two major reasons. On one hand, the investment capacity of these funds is amplified by the use of leverage (borrowing). This increased investment capacity has a direct positive impact on the financial markets owing to the increase in liquidity. However, a hedge fund's quest for pure economic return in the short term can upset the stability of the markets, resulting in increased volatility in currency and commodities.

It should be recalled that hedge funds were implicated in the 1992 crisis that led to major exchange-rate realignments in the European Monetary System, and again in 1994 after a period of turbulence in international bond markets. Concerns mounted in 1997 in the wake of the financial upheavals in Asia. And they were amplified in 1998, with allegations of large hedge fund transactions in various Asian currency markets, such as those of Hong Kong SAR and Australia, and with the failure of Long-Term Capital Management (LTCM).

It remains to be seen whether hedge funds can still wield this much power in future as government authorities all over the world are considering whether new policies or regulations are needed to control the activities of hedge funds.

Hedge Fund Capacity Expansion

In order for the hedge fund industry to expand, hedge fund managers have to adopt innovative approaches by entering into investment strategies that are new to hedge funds and entering both newly established and emerging markets.

New Markets for Capacity Expansion
Below are a number of strategy sectors that will offer future opportunities for expansion:

- **Energy** – an increasing number of hedge funds are specialising in the energy sector as shown in Chapter 5. It was estimated that by the end of 2005 there were well over 300 energy-specific funds with some posting extraordinary returns.

  Energy investments include established commodities such as oil futures, new energy derivatives such as spread options and storage swaps, and direct investments in power-generating plants and pipelines.

  Hedge funds are attracted to the energy sector for the following reasons:
  - Energy markets are both inefficiently priced and deep.
  - Volatility is on the increase.
  - Arbitrage opportunities are readily available.

225

- Hard assets such as power plants are relatively inexpensive.
- Prices are rising.The energy industry provides opportunities for hedge funds to expand their capacity in the future.
- **Real estate** – hedge funds are increasing their activity in real estate. Some invest exclusively in real estate while others invest in it opportunistically. The main driver for investing in real estate was the liquidity offered by REIT securities. But a lot of hedge funds are now investing in hard real-estate assets.

  Examples of major hedge funds that are investing opportunistically include Perry Capital and Farallon Capital Management. Others are likely to follow suit in the future.
- **Asset-backed financing** – some hedge funds have been active in the asset-backed financing market for years while others have just begun to enter it.

  Funds active in asset-backed financing either do auto financing or trade financing.
- **Exchange-traded funds (ETFs)** – ETFs have been growing in popularity since they were first introduced in 1993. They represent a new, user-friendly investing mechanism and therefore extend the range of products that are at managers' disposal.

New Areas or Strategies for Capacity Expansion
The following are the world economies that could potentially offer capacity expansion for hedge funds.

Developed economies
There are various developed economies that do not have significant hedge fund investment. These economies provide growth opportunities for US and European hedge funds and may well provide capacity for growth of hedge funds within the countries themselves. These countries include some European countries and Canada.

Developing economies
Not so long ago, wealthy families and large domestic insurance companies were the only Asian hedge fund investors. Nowadays, there is a proliferation of Asian hedge funds and hedge fund investors in the region, either within the Asian countries or as investors in Asia from outside. In 2005, the hedge fund population in Asia comprised over 500 funds; 300 funds out of this number were Asia-based hedge funds. There has also been increasing growth of investment in Asia by funds outside the area. Hong Kong, Taiwan, Singapore and Korea are also witnessing increasing hedge fund activity from within and from outside.

Volatile local equity markets, overvalued bonds, and low dollar interest rates are among the drivers for the increase in investor activity in Asia. However, there are deterrents to hedge fund growth as follows:

- the inability to short sell in some markets;

▦ a lack of futures and options markets and index derivatives;
▦ lack of liquidity;
▦ laws prohibiting local investors from investing in hedge funds in South
Korea, Thailand and Malaysia.

The future capacity for hedge funds in Europe and Asia (excluding China and India) is expected to come mainly from Russia, while in Africa it is South Africa and in Latin America it is Brazil.

By and large, "the BRICs" (Brazil, Russia, India and China) are touted as the most important emerging economies for future hedge fund capacity. The table shows the projected GDP levels for BRICs compared with that of the USA over a 50-year timeline.

	Brazil	Russia	India	China	USA
2000	762	391	469	1,078	9,825
2010	668	847	929	2,998	13,271
2020	1,333	1,741	2,104	7,070	16,415
2030	2,104	2,980	4,935	14,312	20,833
2040	3,740	4,467	12,367	26,439	27,229
2050	6,074	5,870	27,803	44,453	35,165

Source: Van Hedge Fund Advisors

Economists such as Goldman Sachs have projected that within 20 years the BRIC GDP will be half that of the G6.[75] In about 40 years, the BRIC GDP is expected to exceed that of the G6.

As the table shows, the BRIC GDPs (and therefore their hedge fund capacity, all other things being approximately equal) are expected to increase significantly. However, in comparison with the population bases of China and India, those of Brazil and Russia are relatively small. Furthermore, Brazil has a high debt rate and macro instability. Russia's population is shrinking.

According to a Goldman Sachs study, the economic leaders of the future are expected to be China, the USA, India, Brazil and Russia in that order.

Hedge fund investments in India and China have existed in relatively small quantities for some time. As evidenced above, this activity is expected to grow at an increasing rate.

China's GDP, according to experts, is expected to exceed that of Germany within 5 years, that of Japan within 10; and that of the USA in less than 40 years. At that point, China will have the world's largest economy. The impact of China's growth is already being felt in world markets as its economy demands commodities, for example, as it builds its infrastructure.

75 G6 countries are the USA, EU, Australia, Japan, India and China.

India

There are clear indications that the hedge fund industry will grow rapidly in India. India's GDP is expected to exceed that of Italy in 10 years; of France in 15; of Germany in 20 and of Japan in 30 years.

India's already-large capacity of hedge funds will be expanded by the country's economic growth. As mentioned above, India's GDP is projected to be the third largest in the world in less than 30 years from now.

In order to assess India's future impact on the hedge fund industry, it is useful to understand its recent economic and political developments.

The BJP-led government (Bharatiya Janata Party), which maintained power for its full five-year term from 1999 to 2004, increased foreign direct investments and achieved the highest levels of reserves to date in India.

The BJP's economic reforms were instrumental in the transformation of India's socialistic, closed economy to a more market-based economy. The following factors were essential to the turnaround:

- lower trade barriers;
- lessened restrictions on foreign investments;
- divestment by the government of many of its publicly owned, inefficient companies.

On the economic front, industry experts are united in their opinion that India will have the fastest growing economy over the next few decades. In addition, financial institutions such as The Asian Development Bank expect growth of 7.4%.

India has 23 stock exchanges with 90% of the trading volume being handled by the Bombay Stock Exchange and National Stock Exchange. Both have expanded rapidly since market reforms were introduced.

It is clear from the above that hedge funds based in India will thrive and the same is expected of funds that invest in India from other countries.

China

China, like India, will offer enormous capacity for hedge funds. This is unsurprising given that it is the most populous country in the world. It also has the fourth largest GDP. Various industry sectors including education and IT are growing rapidly. China's leaders' stance against collectivism has led to the continual introduction of market reforms, reforms that are driven by the terms of China's agreement with the World Trade Organisation.

Politically, China is transforming itself from a communist, centrally planned economy to a bureaucratic market economy. Economic wealth is getting more widespread and members of the People's Congress are increasingly educated and independent. They are getting equipped more with the necessary electoral power to vote on more issues than in the past.

It is increasingly accepted that China is moving towards a free market. A major plus for China, in economic terms, is the decision to allow Hong Kong to continue under a separate system.

Chinese people are, by nature, very hard-working and entrepreneurial. The sea change that has seen nationals who have prospered in foreign countries returning to their native land, as seen in India, will also gain a foothold in China.

Eminent economists expect China to experience growth rates of 6.5% to 7.5% until 2020. It is also expected to have the largest GDP in the world by 2050.

It is evident from the above that a fully viable economic marketplace in China should provide a huge and excellent business environment for hedge funds in the future.

Dubai

Industry experts are divided in their opinion of Dubai as fertile ground for hedge funds. While some firmly believe that hedge funds in the region will flourish, others are less optimistic, citing the perception that the rate of expansion in Dubai is slow and that the service infrastructure needs a boost to speed up growth.

From our perspective, the future is bright for the fledgling industry, provided all care is taken to nurture and grow it so that it can appeal not only to investors from the region, but to global investors as well.

This is the reason behind the setting up of the Dubai International Financial Centre (DIFC), the first and only regulatory body in the world to have instituted a regulatory framework for the hedge fund industry – not only for products but also for managers.

The DIFC introduced the new Collective Investment Law in April 2006, setting out the framework for regulating funds. The law permits the operation of various types and categories of collective investment vehicles including hedge funds.

Although statistics are not readily available as yet about the size of the hedge fund industry, those that are positive about the growth potential believe it is enormous. Several major factors justify their belief in this potential for growth and the following are some of the factors:

- **Size of AUM in MENA** – experts estimate the size of the total assets under management in the Middle East North Africa (MENA) will grow by close to a quarter every year over the next five years to reach $200bn by 2012. A significant part of that is expected to find its way into the hedge fund sector.
- **Familiarity of Middle Eastern investors with hedge funds** – the Middle East is not totally new to hedge fund investors. Sophisticated Middle East investors have been using hedge funds to park a portion of their assets into non-equity co-related classes to reduce their level of risk, especially after the global stock market correction in 2000. And institutional investment in hedge funds in the Gulf is estimated at 35%.

   Hedge funds, as an alternative asset class that can lower the risk across a portfolio of investments, are an increasingly attractive option for all investors in the Middle East, especially in the wake of the 2006 downturn in the region's stock markets, particularly in the UAE.

229

▧ **Steady liberalisation of the markets in MENA** – the steady liberalisation of the markets in this region coupled with a programme of reform and renewal is attracting the attention of hedge fund managers to the region.

▧ **Expansion of wealth creation** – a recent world wealth report by Cap Gemini and Merrill Lynch revealed that wealth creation is expanding rapidly in the Middle East. According to the report, in the UAE alone – which has a population of just four million – millionaires expanded their community in 2006 by 15.4% to 68,100.

▧ **Opening of the DIFX** – the opening in 2005 of the Dubai International Financial Exchange (DIFX), a subsidiary of DIFC, is also a major plus. DIFX is the region's first international exchange, trading securities, bonds and derivatives.

▧ **Location** – the location of Dubai is also a major advantage. It is unique in the sense that it lies on both sides of a time zone not covered by any market – the closest in the East being Singapore and in the West, Frankfurt. This presents enormous opportunities for hedge fund managers for trading and wealth creation after Tokyo or Singapore go to bed and before Frankfurt or London wake up. However, this is also a challenge since firstly they have to understand the region and regional investors and secondly, have a regional platform from which to meet those needs. Experts believe the DIFC provides that platform.

Restructuring of Fee Structures

As shown elsewhere in this book, hedge fund managers charge investors a 1% to 2% asset-based fee and at least a 20% profit participation fee. The fee structure of many funds involves higher charges and funds of funds charge an additional layer of fees. Hedge fund investors were not averse to paying these fees when returns were high. But in a chaotic market environment, with more average returns and less overall volatility in the equity markets, investors would baulk at the thought of paying a large percentage of total fund returns that will reduce returns to them to unattractive levels.

Additionally, the intensifying competition in the hedge fund market space as a result of the proliferation of new managers entering the arena will eventually drive the fees down in order to entice investors. Furthermore, institutional investors, who have great buying leverage and are not accustomed to paying fees that they cannot negotiate, would demand fee concessions for large capital commitments. Emerging managers, unlike established managers, would have to yield to demands for fee compression, which could result in a trend towards a new and lower fee structure with which those who follow will have to comply. This is analogous to the trend in the institutional money management business where increased competition and consolidation created a more efficient market that resulted in a precipitous decline in fees. It is expected the hedge fund industry will follow this trend as it matures.

Increased Transparency

As the attraction of institutional investors to hedge funds shows no sign of abating, increased transparency will increasingly be demanded of hedge fund management companies. Investing on faith will no longer be accepted by investors investing in hedge funds. The days when a closely guarded or exclusive strategy gave the hedge fund manager a competitive edge are long gone.

With the calls for transparency in most jurisdictions in the post-LTCM era, it is surprising that another spectacular blow-up in the hedge fund industry – Amaranth Advisors – occurred.

In the future, investors will demand detailed information on the nature of the assets in the fund and how returns are generated. More investors will make these demands in the face of misleading, and in some cases fraudulent, activity, news of which finds its way into the popular press on a regular basis. As a result, many funds, especially newer emerging funds, will be forced to deliver full transparency if they wish to raise substantial assets.

Rising Barriers to Entry

It is indisputable in the current hedge fund business environment that the bigger players are getting bigger and the smaller players are either morphing into niche players, being merged with larger players or closing down. This trend is likely to continue in the foreseeable future. It is now seen as unwise for a distinguished trader to leave the comfort and security of a large investment bank to start up a hedge fund with a comparably low value of assets under management of, say, $50m or less.

In the past few years, the increasing maturity of the hedge fund industry has led to a raised barrier to entry. Institutional investors have become more enlightened and discerning with the assets they control. In addition, pioneer hedge fund managers have now taken up roles as service providers and investors and, given their inside knowledge of the workings of hedge funds, have raised the bar on operational due diligence.

They are aware from experience that the recipes for failure in the industry include fraud and operational inefficiencies and thus make more demands of the due diligence process. Regulators are also partly responsible for raising the bar as they are making changes to registration requirements, focusing on best execution and numerous other developments in the area of compliance around the world. Despite the perception of the regulation of hedge funds as being "light touch", it is surely going to raise the cost of doing business in the industry in the foreseeable future.

231

Convergence of Hedge Funds with Private Equity

It appears that hedge funds managers are beginning to encroach on the territory of private equity managers. This recent development can be attributed to the search for higher returns by the hedge fund managers, who are realising that the markets they operate in are getting more efficient, resulting in lower returns.

The differences between hedge funds and private equity firms were discussed elsewhere in this book but in order to illustrate their convergence, their business models have to be discussed.

The hedge fund model usually involves an open-ended fund, meaning a fund whereby the investors may enter and withdraw at some stated and rather frequent interval, i.e. monthly, quarterly, annually, etc. The assets in the fund generally consist of marketable securities, making subscriptions and redemptions easy because the net asset value (NAV) is easily determined. Fees are keyed to NAV and billed at intervals during the life of the investment. The subscriptions are made in cash (or sometimes marketable securities). Lastly, the deal is not subject to a stated term of years, although this is unnecessary because investors can redeem at will, subject to any lock-up.

The private equity model starts and ends in a different place. First off, many private equity deals are commitment deals in the sense that the manager can request committed cash from investors as and when needed. By nature, private equity deals do not invest in liquid assets therefore private equity managers would rather not have cash without having first identified the investment, as cash is deemed a drag on performance. These deals are basically closed ended – the investor signs up at the start (or almost at the start)[76] of the deal and signs the commitment at the time.

Between 2005 and 2007 there was a raft of cases of hedge funds bidding in the larger capitalisation private equity market. Most of these deals took place in the USA, and notable examples include Cerberus Capital Management leading a consortium of hedge funds in the auction of Texas Genco, and Cerberus's $5.5 billion offer for Toys "R" Us, both bids losing out to a consortium of private equity funds – although Cerberus was successful in its $2.3 billion buyout of MeadWestvaco. In Europe, Fortress bought out German housing group Gagfah for $3.5 million and Perry Capital offered to acquire Drax Group, owner of Europe's largest coal-fired power station. The UK also witnessed the first Mergers and Acquisitions (M&A) transactions to be led by hedge funds: the acquisition of WestLB's interests in TV rental company Boxclever by Cerberus and Fortress, the £404.4 million management buyout deal of discount clothing retailer Peacock Group by Perry Capital and Och-Ziff, and the involvement of

76 Sometimes there is a rolling start – investment, say, over the initial six-month ramp-up period and sometimes with an interest component charged to cash coming in after day one.

hedge funds including Och-Ziff in the buyout of Manchester United football club.

Industry experts are of the opinion that out of the estimated 9,000 hedge funds worldwide, 20% are reported to be contesting in the $1 billion-plus enterprise buyout market. With a number of these having over $10 billion in capital to deploy, they represent both a fertile alternative source of financing for companies and a serious threat to the traditional pastures of the private equity houses.

Why are Hedge Funds now operating in the Private Equity Market?

The intensifying competition in the hedge fund marketplace coupled with the massive inflows of capital into the industry has brought down the returns, forcing hedge fund managers to look elsewhere for new sources of return. Private equity has consistently outperformed the public markets in recent times and offers an opportunity for hedge funds to achieve alpha, i.e. maximise their outperformance. Industry experts are maintaining that there is a blurring of the line between hedge funds and private equity, driven primarily by these reasons.

One of the major developments that underscore the convergence of private equity and hedge funds is the activities of some activist hedge funds aiming to build up significant equity stakes to effect shareholder-led changes in corporate management or corporate governance. A notable example is the influence of two hedge funds in recently forcing Deutsche Borse to abandon its potential bid for the London Stock Exchange and instead agree to return cash to shareholders, and in reshaping the Deutsche Borse management – a move that is more private equity than hedge fund.

Eager to deploy this considerable amount of capital, hedge funds have also been active providers of subordinated debt in the leveraged buyout market – notably second-lien[77] and mezzanine debt,[78] and payments-in-kind (PIK) securities. A high-profile example of this was the 2005 takeover of Manchester United, which entailed financing by a consortium of hedge funds by taking PIK securities in one of the acquisition vehicles.

Two notable contributing factors to the evolution of hedge funds operating in the private equity market are the experience that managers of distressed or activist hedge funds have in influencing and controlling companies, and the familiarity of hedge fund managers that have provided, or participated in, lever-

---

77 Debts that are subordinate to the rights of other, more senior, debts issued against the same collatoral or a portion of the same collatoral. If a borrower defaults, second-lien debts stand behind higher-lien debts in terms of rights to collect proceeds from the debt's underlying collatoral.

78 Debt that gives the lender the rights to convert to an ownership or equity interest in the company if the loan is not paid back in time and in full.

aged financing with the private equity market. In addition, hedge funds have lately been pursuing a wider range of investment strategies, incorporating not just shareholder activism and distressed debt, but venture capital, distressed private equity and private equity control. 2006 saw hedge funds clubbing together in a bid to acquire corporate targets, in a similar manner to private equity firms who have been doing this for years.

Ironically, the convergence of private equity and hedge funds goes beyond hedge funds competing in private equity auctions. Notable private equity houses have established hedge funds (Carlyle, Texas Pacific via TPG-Axon Capital, Bain via Sankaty Advisors and Blackstone), which puts these buyout houses on a par with hedge funds in terms of speed, access to capital and investment flexibility.[79]

Effects of Convergence

The following are some of the future ramifications of the convergence of private equity and hedge funds:

- Convergence is creating options for buyer and seller and is presenting additional partners to co-invest with.
- The overlap will result in greater competition and higher prices for acquisitions as well as greater competition for limited partners' capital.
- Hedge funds are aiming for quicker liquidity events in their private equity investments.
- Private equity firms who get involved in hedge fund investing will take a longer-term approach than most hedge funds.
- Convergence may result in lower returns for private equity firms.

Challenges for hedge fund managers

Hedge fund managers that are contending for private equity face some unique challenges, in particular the perception (perhaps the reality) that they do not have sufficient experience in running companies and the creation of value over the medium to long term. Some have mitigated this by hiring buyout specialists, and their annual performance fee payouts enable them to compensate employees in some cases more favourably than private equity houses.

According to industry experts there are also several structural tensions that hedge fund managers have to grapple with, in particular the following:

- **Liquidity** – allowing investors an opportunity to exit the fund on any calendar quarter is feasible if the fund's assets are readily realisable at their market price, but not when those assets are illiquid shares in unquoted companies.

79 Further information about private equity can be found in "Business Knowledge for IT in Private Equity".

■ **Valuation** – the accurate valuation of assets is crucial both to the calculation of the annual performance fee, and to the price at which investors subscribe to and redeem from the fund.

The Future

Industry experts believe that the convergence between hedge funds and private equity is likely to continue in the short term. However, the principal focus of hedge funds will likely continue to be strategies involving liquid securities and debt providers, rather than as buyers of controlling equity positions in buyout transactions. A likely trend is the emergence of more hybrid funds, i.e. hedge funds with private equity components. These funds will probably have an investment sector bias with much trading in the public markets but will reserve the right to invest in private deals within the strategy or sector.

In conclusion, it remains to be seen how hedge funds will change the buyout landscape. And, given that successful private equity investments can only be judged on some exit years later, it will be quite some time before hedge funds can be adjudged successful in their attempts to translate their advantages into higher returns for their investors.

Figure 12.1 The Convergence of Hedge Funds with Private Equity and Traditional Fund Management

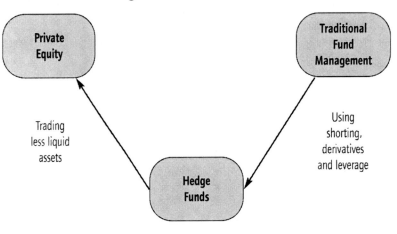

Interestingly some of the bigger hedge funds are also making a big push into traditional fund management to diversify their customer base – part of a growing trend towards the convergence of hedge funds with traditional fund management. Industry experts expect that their product base will be aimed at institutional investors who want conventional money management, but with the ability to sell short up to a certain level.

Focus on Niche Strategies

As more managers flock to the hedge fund space, investors are likely to seek out those funds with a definable niche, which run strategies that are difficult to replicate and have performance that is more likely to persist.

The bulk of the more than 9,000 currently registered hedge funds follow traditional strategies such as long/short, global macro and merger arbitrage, but the hedge funds that investors will gravitate towards in the future are the ones that use esoteric forms of technical analysis. One of the niche strategies that could be gaining traction among hedge fund managers in the future is high-frequency finance.

High-frequency finance hedge fund managers use tick-by-tick market data as input to their statistically driven quantitative models and to optimise timing of their trades. Hedge fund managers that use the methodology of high-frequency finance have a different risk return profile to the other hedge fund managers. They have the capability to build models that are far more adaptive to changing market environments. In addition, their models have a much longer lifetime than traditional models developed on the basis of low-frequency data.

In future, there will be a growing number of high-frequency finance hedge fund managers, significantly more than in the past few years. Progress of high-frequency hedge fund managers has traditionally been slow due to the high start-up costs and the secretiveness. These managers have achieved success with the trading technology to the extent that they do not need to do any active marketing which would reveal any information to the public. As a result, only a small group of investors know about the technology and this gives anonymity to the high-frequency hedge fund managers. The managers therefore gain a competitive edge by taking advantage of the calm before the storm.

Industry experts have opined that the unique risk-adjusted returns of high-frequency finance managers will result in a high demand for their products. It is expected to increase in the future.

Role of Technology

Hedge fund management companies of the future, in a bid to minimise operational costs as well as attract the best talent, will need to adopt the best technology possible. This will involve using a combination of purpose-built, integrated professional portfolio accounting systems, order management systems, pre-trade compliance systems, risk systems and execution tools.

This software will need to handle trade capture, processing and reporting for every instrument under the sun, as well as every aspect of hedge fund balance-sheet management, counterparty reconciliation and trade settlement.

Various types of connectivity to multiple executing brokers, fund administrators and prime brokers will be required. In addition, hedge fund management companies of the future, in the quest for globalisation, will need a global presence, both to capitalise on investment opportunities around the world and to attract investors. This means they will need operational infrastructures that will extend seamlessly across currency markets and time zones.

One of the key developments in hedge fund technology that hedge funds of the future will embrace is the concept of an application service provider (ASP). Outsourcing certain aspects of their operational infrastructure to specialist companies will be essential, giving them room to focus on what they do best, i.e. investing.

Operational efficiency will be the key focus when these firms adopt technology in the future. This means the technology infrastructure will need to be more flexible than that of the past, thereby facilitating the reduction of the cost/income ratio. Adoption of electronic trading will continue to reduce transaction costs. Borrowing costs will also be reduced by detailed balance-sheet management. Ticket fees and other ancillary charges will be eliminated by standard interfacing, reporting and reconciliation between counterparties. Given that there will be less human involvement in any particular transaction, the cost of human error will be less. In the meantime, portfolio management and risk analysis tools will continue to enhance fund managers' ability to focus on delivering alpha.

Technology will play a critical role in ensuring that hedge fund management companies of the future are leaner, meaner, global multi-strategy machines offering a wider variety of products to every type of investor.

Rise and Rise of Algorithmic Trading

The rise of algorithmic trading is accentuated by the increasing use of algorithms by traders to execute block trades. Algorithmic trading is set to grow in the near future as barriers between markets fall and trading across asset classes becomes more prominent globally.

It is currently estimated that about 40% of trades on the London Stock Exchange are executed by algorithmic trading systems. Some industry experts predict that the figure could rise to 60% in the next few years. According to Celent, the US research house, it is expected that more than 25% of global trading volumes will be executed by algorithmic trading systems.

Predicted trends that will affect algorithmic trading in future include:

▨ **The rise of the buy-side as an algorithmic powerhouse**
   Experts unanimously predict that the explosion of the hedge fund market will alter the competitive landscape, prompting sell-side institutions to optimise their client services. At the same time, the buy-side is demanding increased anonymity and control over their traditional trading strategies. With algorithmic trading being adopted by firms of various shapes and sizes, the need for technology that supports unique trading techniques will continue grow.

▨ **Broad asset class adoption of algorithmic techniques**
   It is well documented that equities was the first asset class to adopt algorithmic trading. But other asset classes like FX have followed suit and so will

other asset classes during the next few years. Some hedge funds are already algorithmic trading not only equities, but also FX, futures and options and fixed income.

The optimal combination of algorithms

According to experts, pre-trade and execution analytics will be combined in the future to create new strategies that give a competitive edge. An example is a strategy that uses VWAP[80] techniques for historic volume-based slicing, but simultaneously hedges each slice with an FX position if the instrument is a foreign currency, which can create an innovative package of trades. In tandem, the sophistication of these new combinations requires detailed simulation and careful testing. Modern algorithmic trading plat-forms provide the tools to backtest, profile and tune new strategies in advance of deployment.[81] The ability to test new algorithms against historical market conditions and simulate the impact on the market can help a hedge fund manager to explore the prospective performance of strategies.

Managing the evolution of algorithmics

The adoption of the latest in algorithmic technology can aid in the automation and development of new trading strategies for hedge funds. Cutting-edge tools in the current market can help to identify the cause and effect of trading techniques to teach lessons from profit and loss, and to identify interesting market patterns and suggest new combinations of algorithms. Consistent use of these tools over time enables the "genetic tuning" of algorithmic trading systems. In comparison with Darwin's survival of the fittest theory, algorithmic traders can run thousands of permutations of an algorithm, swap out the least profitable and replace them with more effective approaches.[82]

Use of algorithms to meet regulatory requirements and monitor compliance

In the coming years, the latest in algorithmic trading technology will be a boon to hedge funds as their trades will need to comply with future regulations. The key issues they will need to consider will be how to calculate the best price and how market depth, risk and hidden liquidity factors are factored into the calculation of best price. In addition, they will need to accommodate automated surveillance used by regulators for the monitoring of trading operations for patterns of abuse.

Algorithmic trading to replace human traders?

It has been predicted that algorithmic trading will reduce the number of traders in the financial services industry over the coming years. Most hedge

---

80 VWAP is a trading acronym for Volume-Weighted Average Price, the ratio of the value traded to total volume over a particular time horizon (usually one day). It is a measure of the average price a stock is traded at over the trading horizon.

81 Source: Bates, J. and Palmer, M. 2006 (December). "Ten Algorithmic Trading Trends in the Lead-up to 2010". Financial Intelligence Guides.

82 Ibid.

fund management firms will be increasing the capacity of their systems to cope with a big increase in algorithmic trading. While speed is one of the biggest advantages that these systems have over human traders – as well as the ability to operate around the clock, without wages – it is unlikely that they will ever completely replace human traders. In addition, the threat of being replaced may be smaller for higher-level traders who take strategic risk positions that computer systems are less able to determine.

Algorithmic "auto-trading" will complement human traders and make them more effective. But traders will also need to be more sophisticated to survive in the near future and by automating low-value, high-volume deals they can concentrate on designing new algorithmic techniques.

The Future
Hedge funds will react to the evolution of the algorithmic landscape by re-evaluating and evolving their views on information technology, trading techniques, asset-class mix, trading strategy and their human resources strategy.

In conclusion, algorithms are set to revolutionise the hedge fund landscape and present an opportunity for those who are willing to innovate, and those that are unwilling remain so at their peril.

Future of Hedge Funds in the Wake of US Subprime Crisis

Hedge funds will be stepping up their investment in new markets in the wake of the US subprime problems. It is expected that capital inflows will be experienced in markets that were hitherto deemed too small or unattractive in terms of yields.

The US subprime market, which caters for borrowers with poor credit histories, hit lenders as homeowners fell behind with mortgage payments, forcing dozens of firms out of business or into bankruptcy.

Hedge funds, which tend to have fewer investment restrictions than other kinds of institutional funds, already have minor interests in some relatively small mortgage-backed markets, and are now increasing their interest.

A case in point is Mexico's mortgage industry that is looking attractive in comparison with the gloomy US sector. This market is reported to be expanding rapidly. According to Reuters, as at July 2007, outstanding mortgage-backed bonds (debt) in Mexico stood at $6billion, having grown remarkably from virtually nil in 2003. Industry experts expect the market to double in size by 2010.

By comparison, US companies placed about $300 billion in mortgage-backed debt in 2006. This was on the assumption that this type of debt, which normally carries a high credit rating because it is backed by underlying loans, would generate decent returns. The spate of foreclosures in the US housing market meant that these returns failed to materialise.

Given that there is no end in sight for the subprime crisis and that no one can form any conclusions about the knock-on effects in the financial markets, it

239

is expected that international investors will continue to pour money into promising markets that can offer yields which are more favourable than the US market.

Conclusion

The factors described above, which will shape the hedge fund industry in the future, provide a glimpse of the opportunities that abound for those IT professionals who want to advance their career or gain a foothold in an industry has undoubted potential. As the industry matures further, it will require the brightest and the best IT staff that can help to grow the business as well as ensure the requisite operational efficiencies to survive.

The time has come to gain the knowledge that will fulfil these aspirations and earn a sustainable living whilst doing so.

Appendix

The Hedge Fund IT Skills Market

As the proliferation of hedge funds gathers pace, technology jobs done by third-party providers are increasingly being brought in-house either to gain a competitive edge through the use of technology or as a result of the growing size of hedge fund management firms. Traditionally, hedge fund IT was the domain of third-party vendors. But nowadays, the owners of hedge fund firms have realised the benefit of building their own infrastructure teams.

While there is a flurry of activity in the hiring of IT infrastructure staff to fulfil this need, the recruitment of systems developers that can customise off-the-shelf trading systems is also increasing in the IT skills market.

IT professionals that are seeking to break into hedge fund IT have to be aware of the difficulty in achieving this. Hedge funds recruit a limited number of IT staff and hence are very choosy about the calibre of candidate they hire. They are ready to hold out until they achieve a 100 per cent match to the job requirements.

Hedge funds go for talented, experienced individuals typically holding an MSc and PhD in a quantitative subject like statistics or mathematics. They tend to prefer candidates with vast experience in developing front-office trading systems for bulge bracket banks such as Goldman Sachs, Merrill Lynch or Morgan Stanley. These candidates should ideally come from rapid application development (RAD) teams in investment banks. In addition, they should have been responsible for the business-facing aspects of systems development and held prominent positions as opposed to being just another person in a large team of say 20 or more developers.

As for infrastructure and support roles, hedge funds favour IT professionals with strong business knowledge and all-round delivery experience. They should preferably have wide exposure to different technologies. These include familiarity with every version of Windows, knowledge of all firewalls, networking issues and protocols like Cisco, familiarity with virtual networks used in remote working, and the ability to adapt technology to new locations.

Differences between Investment Banking IT and Hedge Fund IT

There are difference between the cultures of investment banking IT and hedge fund IT. Hedge funds are smaller, and they demand a greater level of commitment and wider responsibility, taking on the whole of front to back office. In investment banking there are a lot of separate departments, but in a hedge fund there is less role definition, and IT staff will be expected to be more creative, to come forward with ideas and to have more overall input into decision making.

The following are guidelines to the skills and level of experience required by hedge funds. Please note that the requirements vary from company to company and from country to country and these are just guidelines to standard requirements.

Chief Technology Officer (CTO)

Skills required: Development experience within investment banking or a hedge fund with an understanding of developmental languages as well as architecture principles such as Service Oriented Architecture (SOA), TOGAF and Zachmann. Business knowledge of the hedge fund industry is a must as is product knowledge in a number of asset classes. In general, a very high level of detailed technology proficiency and expertise in the construction and application of financial instruments are a must.

The CTO should ideally be a strategic visionary as these roles require the ability to understand the increasingly strategic nature of IT and how it aligns with business objectives of the firm.

Salary package: As this is an evolving role in most hedge funds, there is not a lot of data on the salaries on offer. Compensation is open, depending on experience.

Development Manager

Skills required: Ideally, experience of managing a team within a sizable team of developers in an investment bank(s). Knowledge of a number of hedge fund strategies is required and experience of development languages such as Java, C++, Microsoft.Net, and VBA and Excel skills. Business knowledge of the hedge fund industry is a must as is product knowledge in a number of asset classes.

The manager should also have outstanding communications skills and ideally proficiency in different languages. This is because the manager has to be able to interface with highly articulate hedge fund managers and also prime brokers and fund administrators.

Salary package: £80K–£150K basic salary up to £300K total compensation.

Project Manager

Skills required: Ideally experience of managing an IT project within an investment bank(s) or hedge fund. Business knowledge of the hedge fund industry is a must as is product knowledge in a number of asset classes. Experience of a number of project management tools such as PRINCE 2 is essential.

The project manager should also have outstanding communications skills and ideally proficiency in different languages for the same reasons as the development manager.

Salary package: £80K–£120K basic salary up to £225K total compensation.

Business Analyst

Skills required: Strong business knowledge of the hedge fund industry is a must as is product knowledge in a number of asset classes, especially derivatives. Knowledge of a wide range of investment strategies as well as intimate understanding of the trading lifecycle. Understanding of electronic trading, especially algorithmic trading, is essential. Strong Excel and VBA skills are also a must have.

In addition, strong data modelling and requirements analysis skills are crucial for this type of role. The ideal business analyst should have experience of a

243

number of the packages on offer from the leading vendors in this field and a deep understanding of the customisation requirements to suit hedge fund strategies.

Knowledge of the operations of the ancillary industries such as prime brokers and fund administrators is essential. A deep understanding of regulatory and tax issues is desirable. Valuation techniques, risk management and accounting methods are also a must.

The ideal business analyst should be able to oversee user testing and implementation of systems and ideally should have vast experience of this in an investment banking or asset management environment.

Salary package: £70K–£150K basic salary up to £200K total compensation.

Developer

Skills required: The skills required for developers in the hedge fund industry vary depending on the size and strategies pursued by the firm. Nevertheless, hands-on experience of development languages such as Java,J2EE, C++,VC++, C#, Microsoft.Net are a must. In some hedge funds, developers without sound experience of quantitative techniques (quants)[83] and an application of mathematics in finance are not considered to be desirable.

A deep understanding of a number of hedge fund strategies is required. The ability to apply the tenets of these strategies to application development techniques is a must. Understanding of coding methodologies such as objected-oriented development, RAD, pairs programming and extreme programming is also essential.

As the developers required are usually all-rounders, they would need systems design experience alongside their programming skills. Hence they would need to have experience of systems design techniques and the ability to use cutting-edge design tools.

Business knowledge of the hedge fund industry is definitely a must have and also product knowledge of a wide range of financial products, especially derivatives.

A technical understanding of the integration of external data feeds, for example from prime brokers and market data providers like Reuters, is essential.

Salary package: £50K–£120K basic salary that can go up to £300K with bonuses added.

Trade Support

Skills required: Strong database development experience (data analysis, stored procedures), and the capacity to deal with traders and all urgent front-, mid- and back-office issues are essential for this type of role.

A detailed understanding of data requirements for "straight-through processing" as well as market data (Reuters/Bloomberg) is required. Good finan-

83 Quants developers use IT programs to build a bridge between traders' daily need for pricing and structuring information and the complex models produced by the front-office quants staff.

cial instrument knowledge is also desirable in order to thoroughly investigate incidents in the trading lifecycle.

Good communication and documentation skills are very advantageous as resolution of incidents should be clearly communicated to a sophisticated business community within the hedge fund and to service providers like prime brokers and fund administrators.

Salary package: £60K–£80K. Data on performance-related bonuses unavailable.

Test Analyst/Manager

Skills required: Good all-round testing experience gained from investment banking. Business knowledge of the hedge fund industry is a must as is product knowledge in a number of asset classes, especially derivatives. Knowledge of a wide range of investment strategies as well as intimate understanding of the trading lifecycle.

A good understanding of data requirements for trade capture as well as market data (Reuters/Bloomberg) is required. Knowledge of different instrument types is also desirable in order to set up test trades to exercise functions in trading systems.

Solid communication and documentation skills are must haves. Experience of a wide range of testing methodologies and tools is also desirable.

Test analysts required by hedge funds must have an appreciation of a wide range of technologies including development languages, databases and operating systems.

Salary package: £50K–£70K. Data on performance-related bonuses unavailable.

Infrastructure Support

Skills required: Hands-on experience in server, desktop and trade floor support as well as overall infrastructure support in an investment banking or hedge fund environment. Good experience in market data (Reuters/Bloomberg), Windows operating systems, UNIX and Active Directory are required. A good knowledge of networking and Voice over IP (VOIP) is also highly advantageous.

Although not a critical requirement, infrastructure support staff have to interact with traders and senior staff of hedge fund management firms given their relatively small size and hence need good communication skills.

Salary package: £50–120K. Data on performance-related bonuses unavailable.

Method of Recruitment

Given the closeness between the hedge fund and investment banking world, recruitment of the right personnel is often through word of mouth. This may apply to the smaller hedge funds but the larger ones tend to go through recruitment agencies who can better match their requirements to the pool of candidates in the job market.

The ideal candidate for a plum job at a hedge fund would be expected to follow the convention of presenting a CV. The CV needs to contain a clear overview of the skills set that relevant to the role that is to be filled as well as to the hedge fund industry. It should highlight the specific industry practice, and be attractive and easy to read.

Candidates attending interviews at hedge funds have to be aware of the culture of hedge funds. The work environment is pressurised like investment banks and as such the interviewer(s) would expect a swift demonstration of strong technical ability and the right attitude. However, unlike the investment banks, hedge funds are usually small in size and the interviewer(s) would be looking out for personal attributes in candidates to ensure that they fit in.

Conclusion

The recruitment trends in the hedge fund IT skill market will be dependent on the sustainability of the stellar rise in the fortunes of hedge funds. Smaller hedge funds will outsource their technology to IT vendors but their back-office operations to specialist providers. Industry experts opine that hedge funds with less than £2bn to £3bn in assets under management will typically continue to outsource their IT. But as the hedge funds get bigger, they tend to be reliant on IT and invest in bespoke or heavily tailored package

List of Useful Websites

Absolute Return	www.absolutereturn.net
Alternative Investment Management Association	www.aima.org
Bahamas Association of Fund Administrators	www.bfsb-bahamas.com
Bloomberg	www.bloomberg.com
Cayman Island Fund Administrators Association	www.cifaa.org.ky
Dun and Bradstreet	www.dnb.com
HFM Week	www.hfmweek.com
Hedge Fund Research	www.hfr.com
Financial Services Authority	www.fsa.gov.uk
Financial Times	www.ft.com
Fitch	www.fitchibca.com
Greenwich Alternative Investments	www.greenwichai.com
Hedge Fund Association	www.thehfa.org
Hedge Fund News	www.hedgefundnews.com
Institutional Investor	www.institutionalinvestor.com
International Swaps and Derivatives Association	www.isda.org
London Stock Exchange	www.londonstockexchange.com
Managed Funds Association	www.mfainfo.org
Moody's Investor Services	www.moodys.com
MorningStar	www.morningstar.co.uk
New York Stock Exchange	www.nyse.com
Reuters	www.reuters.com
Standard and Poor's	www.standardandpoors.com
The Depository Trust and Clearing Association	www.dtcc.com
The Economist	www.economist.com
The Hedge Fund Consistency Index	www.hedgefund-index.com
Thomson	www.thomson.com
Wall Street Journal	www.wsj.com.

Useful Job Boards

Banking Technology Jobs	www.bankingtechnologyjobs.com
Career Center	http://jobs.careerzone.banktechnews.com
Career Center	www.finextra.com/finjobLIST.asp
Computer Weekly	www.computerweekly.com/Jobs
Cv Library	www.cv-library.co.uk
efinancialcareers	www.efinancialcareers.com
IT Job Feed	www.ciquery.com
Job Databases	www.jobdatabases.co.uk
Job Crawler	www.jobcrawler.co.uk
Jobserve	www.jobserve.com
Jobsite	www.jobsite.co.uk
Monster	www.monster.co.uk
Online Job Match	www.onlinejobmatch.co.uk
Planet Recruit	www.planetrecruit.com
The IT Job Board	www.theitjobboard.co.uk
Total Jobs	www.totaljobs.com

Bibliography

Advent Software. (2006). *The Buyside and the Three Phases of Electronic Trading.* Advent Software Inc.

Aite Group LLC. (October 2006). *Trends in OTC Equity Derivatives: Where do we go from here?*

Alford, A. (2006). *Demystifying The Newest Equity Long/Short Strategies: Making the Unconventional Conventional.* Goldman Sachs Asset Management.

Altucher, J. (2004). *Trade Like a Hedge Fund: 20 Successful Uncorrelated Strategies & Techniques to Winning Profits.* John Wiley & Sons Ltd.

Bank, E. and Glantz, M. (2006). *Credit Derivatives.* McGraw-Hill Professional.

Berggren, M. (2006). *Managers Face up to Technological Challenge.* Hedgeweek Special Report.

Biggs, B. (2006). *Hedgehogging.* John Wiley & Sons, Inc.

Brian, S. (November 2007). *Analytics, Data and the Time for High-Performance Computing in Financial Markets.*

Burton, K. (2007). *Hedge Hunters: Hedge Fund Masters on the Rewards, the Risk, and the Reckoning.* Bloomberg Press.

Chaplin, G. (2005). *Credit Derivatives: Risk Management, Trading and Investing.* John Wiley & Sons.

Chen, Y. (2006). *Derivatives Use and Risk Taking: Evidence from the Hedge Fund Industry.* Boston College .pp7-8

Choudhry, M. (2004). *An Introduction to Credit Derivatives.* Butterworth-Heinemann.

Collins, A. (Summer 2007). *130/30 Funds – A New Middle Ground?* Fortis Prime Fund Services.

Connor, G. and Woo, M. (2003). *An Introduction to Hedge Funds.* London School of Economics.pp7

Crockett, A. (April 2007). *The Evolution and Regulation of Hedge Funds.* Banque De France Financial Stability Review – Special Issue on Hedge Funds. pp22.

Das, S. (2005). *Credit Derivatives: CDOs and Structured Credit Products.* John Wiley & Sons (Asia) Pte Ltd.

Dodd, R. (2002). *The Structure of OTC Derivatives Markets.* The Financier Vol.9, Nos 1–4.

Donahoe, B. (First Quarter 2006). *Understanding the Importance of Selecting a Fund Administrator.* Alternative Investment Quarterly.

Donohoe, J. (2006). *New Strategies for Hedge Fund Investing under UCITS III.* Carne Global Financial Services.

Dorsey, A. (2004). *How to Select a Hedge Fund of Fund: Pick the Winners and Avoid the Losers.* Euromoney Institutional Investor PLC.

Drobny, S. (2006). Inside the House of Money: Top Hedge Fund Traders onProfiting in the Global Markets. John Wiley & Sons.

Eurohedge. (2007). *How to Start a European Hedge Fund.* Hedge Fund Intelligence.

Euromoney Staff. (2003). *Evaluating and Implementing Hedge Fund Strategies*. Euromoney Books.

Fraser-Sampson, G. (2007). *Private Equity as an Asset Class*. John Wiley & Sons.

Frievald, J. (2007). *An Agile Framework for Flat, Flexible, Low-Risk Service Deployment*. iWay Software.

Frush, S (2007). *Understanding Hedge Funds*. McGraw-Hill Professional.

Fusaro, C. and Versey, G. (2006). *Energy and Environmental Hedge Funds: The New Investment Paradigm*. John Wiley & Sons Ltd.

FXall. (October 2007). *Algorithmic Trading in the Global FX Market: The Need for Speed, Transparency and Fairness*. FXall White paper.

Gassner, M. S. (February 2007). *Islam and Hedge Funds*. Available from www.islamica-me.com.

Guilbert B. (July 2007). *The New Foundation for Hedge Funds*. Hedge Fund Review.

Haglund, M. (February 2006). *Hedge Fund Trading in Weather Derivatives*. Altevo Research.

Harisson, M. and O'Mahony, N. (December 2006). *Investors See Benefits in Fund of Funds Approach*. Hedgeweek Special Report.

Hedge Fund Manager. (2007). *Opening the Floodgates. Will Global Hedge Fund Business Soon be flowing into Dubai?* Hedge Fund Manager Special Report on Dubai.

Hod, Z. (2006). *Using Straight-Through Processing to Successfully Ride the Equity Derivatives Wave*. IBM Global Business Services.

Horwitz, R. (2004). *Hedge Fund Risk Fundamentals: Solving the Risk Management and Transparency Challenge*. Bloomberg Press.

Hovanesian, M. (19 June 2006). *Where's The Heat on Hedge Funds?* Business Week.

International Financial Services. (April 2007). *Hedge Fund*. City Business Series.

Jaeger, R. (2003). *All about Hedge Funds*. McGraw-Hill Companies Inc.

Jestin, P. (November 2006). *Window to The Future Of Hedge Funds*. Available from www.fundstreet.org/2006/11/window_to_the_f.html.

Jones, M. (2005). *The Role of Technology in Hedge Fund Investing*. Strategic Financial Solutions LLC.

Kalisker, M. (2001). *Mapping a Course to Starting a Hedge Fund*. Bear Stearns Corp.

Kat, H. M. (2003). *10 Things Investors Should Know about Hedge Funds*. Alternative Investment Research Centre Working Paper Series. pp3–4.

Kaufman, P. (2005). *The New Trading Systems and Methods*. John Wiley &Sons Inc.

Keunen, W. (Spring 2007). *Hedge Fund Administration: The New Paradigm – Step Up or Step Out*. Hedge Fund Intelligence.

Kim, K. (2007). *Electronic and Algorithmic Trading Technology: The Complete Guide*. Academic Press.

Kolb, R. W. (2000). *Futures, Options, and Swaps*. Blackwell Publishers Inc.

Kooli, M. (Winter 2005). *Do Hedge Funds Outperform the Market?* Canadian Investment Review.

Laise, E. *The Hedge-Fund 'Clones'*. Available from http://online.wsj.com/
    public/article_print/SB118497668204773569.html.

Laurelli, P. H. (March 2007). *Hedge Fund Industry Asset Flows and Trends*.
    Institutional Investor News. pp16.

Lhabitant, F. (2006). *Handbook of Hedge Funds*. John Wiley and Sons Ltd.

Lo, A. (15 August 2004). *The Adaptive Market Hypothesis: Market Efficiency
    from an Evolutionary Perspective*. pp1.

Lowenstein, R. (2002). *When Genius Failed: The Rise and Fall of Long-Term
    Capital Management*. Fourth Estate.

Maxwell, R. (2006). *Private Equity Funds: A Practical Guide for Investors*. John
    Wiley & Sons Ltd.

McCrary, S. (2002). *How to Create and Manage a Hedge Fund*. John Wiley &
    Sons, Inc.

Nandyal, C. (September 2007). *Order Management Systems: Industry
    Challenges and Trends*. Hexaware Technologies Ltd.

Nicholas, J. (2005). *Investing in Hedge Funds: Strategies for the New
    Marketplace*. Bloomberg Press.

Pole, A. (2007). *Statistical Arbitrage: Algorithmic Trading Insights and
    Techniques*. John Wiley & Sons Ltd.

Prentice, M. O. (August 2006). *Implications of MiFID for Hedge Fund
    Managers*.

Price, M. (July/August 2006). *A Thorny Issue. Hedge Fund Technology*. pp14.

PriceWaterhouseCoopers. (July 2006). *The regulation, taxation and
    distribution of hedge funds in Europe: Changes and Challenges*.

Ramazn, G. (2001). *An Introduction to High-Frequency Finance*. Academic Press.

Sanger, C. and Ward, A. (2003). *Hedge Fund and Taxation – An Overview
    from the UK*. Deloitte & Touche.

Setters, D. (2006). *Hedge Funds and Derivatives: A Maturing Relationship*.
    Special Report Sponsored by ABN AMRO.

Shirreff, D. (2003). *Lessons From the Collapse of Hedge Fund, Long-Term
    Capital Management*.

Stefanini, F. (2006). *Investment Strategies of Hedge Funds*. John Wiley and
    Sons Ltd.

Steward, M. *Industry Dispels 130/30's 'Hedge Fund Lite' Tag*. Available from
    www.pensiongym.com/pensions-news/archive/more.asp?article=1347.

Strachman, D. (2004). *Julian Robertson: A Tiger in the Land of Bulls and
    Bears*. John Wiley & Sons.

Strachman, D. (2005). *Getting Started in Hedge Funds*. John Wiley & Sons Ltd.

Strachman, D. (2007). *The Fundamentals of Hedge Fund Management: How to
    Successfully Launch and Operate a Hedge Fund*. John Wiley and Sons Ltd.

Terhune, H. (2006). *How to Get Your Own Hedge Fund*. Esquire.

The Business. (8 August 2007). *Sub-prime Mortgage Weakness Bet Paying Off
    for the Best Hedge Funds*.

Van Hedge Fund Advisors International, LLC.2005. *Is Worldwide Hedge Fund
    Demand Outstripping Capacity? Hedge Fund Demand and Capacity
    2005–2015*.

251

Index

Index Compiled by Lynette Davidson

Introducing Bizle.biz

Bizle.biz is the first online dedicated to the alignment of IT and business. When fully operational, Bizle will be the reference point for IT students and professionals that want to keep abreast of issues concerning IT and the alignment with the business community. It will also provide answers to on-the-job queries that professionals might have during the course of their everyday tasks.

Bizle.biz will have the following features:

- IT job adverts partitioned into industry sectors to allow both candidates and advertisers to tailor their job requirements;
- Recommended books;
- Industry news;
- Ask support service;
- Glossary of terms;
- Forum;
- Content in different languages.

Other Titles in the Bizle Professional Series

Business Knowledge for IT
in Islamic Finance

Business Knowledge for IT in
in Trading and Exchanges

IT Business Analysis in
Investment Banking

Career Guidebook for IT
in Investment Banking

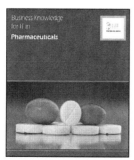

Business Knowledge for IT in
Pharmaceuticals

Business Knowledge for IT in
Private Wealth Management

**These and other exciting titles can be pre-ordered from
Amazon sites worldwide or on www.essvale.com**

Introducing Global Real Estate Investment Series (GREIS)

The Global Real Estate Investment Series by Essvale Corporation Limited is designed to provide invaluable knowledge of the hottest property markets around the world. As real estate is now a bona fide asset class in its own right, private investors as well as investment managers are looking to exploit the undervaluation of emerging property markets in order to create well-diversified portfolios. This does not imply that they have turned their backs on the traditional markets such as the UK and USA, but savvy investors understand the benefits of diversification, especially in the realms of risk management.

These books will reinforce the widely held opinion that building a property portfolio is by far the safest form of investment over the medium to long term, because the fundamental market factors of supply and demand are always going to drive property values over the long term if investors choose to buy in the right market and at the right time.

GREIS books will provide an insight into the burgeoning property markets such as the Middle East and South America as well as India and China. They will provide readers with informtion on the benefits of investing in emerging markets, the pros and cons, the pricing structure, legal and taxation issues and much more.

The books will allow an investor to make an informed choice about their investment options around the world. The various investment strategies discussed will aid the investor in selecting the right approach for entry to and exit from their chosen markets.

This series will cover the fledgling markets in the Middle East and South America as well as india and China. Established markets will also be covered as they deliver low-risk investments that are, as they say, safe as houses.

The maiden edition is due for release in 2008.

CPSIA information can be obtained at www.ICGtesting.com
Printed in the USA
LVOW112039161211

259742LV00002B/129/P

9 780955 412455